ETHNIC-SENSITIVE
SOCIAL WORK
PRACTICE

Second Edition

ETHNIC-SENSITIVE SOCIAL WORK PRACTICE

Second Edition

WYNETTA DEVORE
Syracuse University

ELFRIEDE G. SCHLESINGER
Rutgers—The State University of New Jersey

MERRILL PUBLISHING COMPANY
A Bell & Howell Information Company
Columbus • Toronto • London • Melbourne

Cover Photos: © Clifford Oliver (center and bottom right);
Betty Hurwich Zoss (top right); David Strickler/Strix Pix (top left)

Published by Merrill Publishing Company
A Bell and Howell Information Company
Columbus, Ohio 43216

This book was set in Palatino.

Administrative Editor: Vicki Knight
Production Coordinator: Anne Daly
Cover Designer: Cathy Watterson

Photo credits: All photos copyrighted by individuals or companies listed.
David Antebi, pp. 40, 256; Merrill/Jean Greenwald, p. 98; Clifford Oliver, pp.
148, 220; George Rosinger, p. 80; Gale Zucker, pp. 2, 176, 236.

Other credits: **P. 15.** Extract from *Assimilation in American Life: The Role of Race,
Religion, and National Origin* by Milton M. Gordon. Copyright © 1964 by
Oxford University Press. Reprinted by permission. **P. 272.** Extract from
Medical Sociology, second edition, by David Mechanic. Copyright © 1978 by
The Free Press. Reprinted by permission of Macmillan Publishing Co. **P. 275.**
Extract from "Navajo Indian Medicine: Implications for Healing" by John L.
Coulehan, 1980, *The Journal of Family Practice 10*(1), pp. 55–61. Copyright 1980.
Reprinted by permission.

Library of Congress Catalog Card Number: 86–63267
International Standard Book Number: 0–675-20702–9
Printed in the United States of America

1 2 3 4 5 6 7 8 9—91 90 89 88 87

Preface

In the preface to the first edition of this book, we pointed to an apparent gap in the social work practice literature. It seemed to us that knowledge about the lifestyles and needs of different class and ethnic groups had not been sufficiently integrated into the principles and methods of social work practice. Social work educators' and practitioners' positive response to our book and subsequent publication of other important work on this subject has suggested that there was and remains a need for systematic work on ethnicity and social work practice. This impression has been supported by the publication, in 1984, of the new Curriculum Policy Statement of the Council on Social Work Education that mandates that all undergraduate and graduate programs of professional education pay explicit attention to the lifestyles, needs, and problems of those groups that are especially oppressed in American society.

Therefore, when the time came to update and revise the first edition, we worked in a far different context from the one in which we found ourselves when we first began our work. There was now little doubt that the profession of social work wanted, needed, and used the knowledge and strategies that were and remain the substance of our work.

Other developments have taken place, too, emanating from forces external to the profession but with immediate impact on professional social work practice. These trends, in the incipient stages in the late seventies, had not then begun to capture major public or professional attention.

We refer to the large numbers of new immigrants—especially those of Asian and Hispanic origins—who have become an integral part of the population. Their rich cultures and histories, the varied circumstances under which they migrated, their contributions, and their needs have continuing impact on most regions of this country, especially the Southwest and the East. Some have likened this new wave of immigration and its effects to the vibrant, dynamic period of mass immigration in the late nineteenth and early twentieth centuries. Where appropriate, we have revised our earlier formulations in order to be sensitive to these developments. However, in our view, the basic conceptual formulations presented in the first edition encompass the perspective needed to respond to these population changes, and so our effort to reflect these changes consists mainly of increased attention, by use of example, to the ever-changing mosaic that constitutes the American population.

With these considerations as a backdrop, we made a number of decisions about how to approach the task of revising the first edition. The basic structure of the original work has been retained. Part One focuses on conceptual formulations that need to be understood by the ethnic-sensitive social worker. Part Two illustrates the assumptions and principles of ethnic-sensitive social work practice. Each section and chapter incorporates important new concepts and empirical findings that pertain to our focus.

Explicit changes were made and will be readily apparent in four chapters. Chapter 1 represents a more thorough and well-rounded treatment of the diverse perspectives on the roles of ethnicity and social class in American life. Importantly, the increased attention afforded this subject in the recent social work literature made it possible to present a critical review and assessment of the various definitions and use of such key terms as *minorities, people of color, ethnic groups,* and *ethnic minorities.* We believe this review enriches the work and highlights the important professional use of such terms as *ethclass, ethnic reality,* and *minority groups.* Explicit in Chapter 1, and stressed throughout the book, is our view that all ethnic groups have important histories, special problems, and well-established habits of coping that need to be understood by social workers. Those ethnic groups that are also minority groups and the object of special oppression are of course of particular concern to social workers. The principles of practice enunciated in this text, especially those calling for simultaneous attention to individual and systemic issues, serve to operationalize this element of professional conviction and concern.

Chapter 4 is a much longer chapter and reflects our effort to keep current with ongoing developments in approaches to social work practice and the degree to which these approaches facilitate ethnic-sensitive practice. Constraints of space necessitated limiting our discussion to those new approaches with which most social workers are acquiring familiarity, and those that pay particular attention to the impact of ethnic factors. We decided to present a systematic analysis of the ecological perspective and of two new books focused on cultural and minority practice issues. Each of these books makes an important contribution that warrants analysis and critique, in keeping with the patterns we established in the first edition.

A substantial change was made in Chapter 5. We no longer refer to our work as presenting a model for ethnic-sensitive practice. Instead, we have come to believe that it is more appropriate to refer to the assumptions and principles for ethnic-sensitive practice that can and should be incorporated into any of the rich and diverse approaches to social work practice reviewed here and elsewhere. The reader should also note how Chapter 8, focusing on work with recipients of Aid to Dependent Children, considers the relationship between the increasing emphasis on "Workfare" and ethnic-sensitive work practice.

In addition to the people whose valuable help was most important in the development of the first edition, Vicki Knight, Administrative Editor at Merrill Publishing Company, and Anne Daly deserve our thanks for their patience and encouragement in seeing this edition to completion. And, always of major importance is the contribution made by secretaries and other clerical assistants. Special thanks to Nancy Lewis, Jeanette Indice, and Adrian Humphries of the Syracuse University School of Social Work, and Phyllis Telleri of the School of Social Work at Rutgers, The State University of New Jersey. Thanks also to the reviewers, who provided valuable suggestions: Dr. Patricia Pickford, California State University, Fresno; and Dr. Robert Perry, Bowling Green State University. As was true with the first edition, we look forward to readers' comments, questions, and criticisms.

Wynetta Devore
Elfriede G. Schlesinger

Contents

PART ONE
CONCEPTUAL FORMULATIONS

PART TWO
ETHNIC-SENSITIVE PRACTICE

among socioeconomic status, ethnicity, and illness • The role
of social and community networks • Populations at risk and
ethnic-sensitive practice

PART ONE
CONCEPTUAL FORMULATIONS

Part One develops the conceptual base of ethnic-sensitive practice.

Chapter 1 reviews ethnicity and social class with an emphasis on how forces both internal and external to various groups serve to sustain the role of social class and ethnicity as powerful aspects of social life. The mechanisms by which ethnicity and work impact on dispositions to life's problems are reviewed, and the concept of the ethnic reality is developed.

Chapter 2 surveys prevailing models of life cycle stages and tasks. Our perspective on universal stages of the life cycle and the tasks that accompany each position is presented. Points of stress and coping mechanisms, particularly as these relate to ethnicity and social class, are identified.

Chapter 3 outlines the layers of understanding that call attention to the knowledge, values, skills, and self awareness basic to practice and to the ethnic reality that leads to ethnic sensitive practice.

Chapter 4 examines various approaches to social work practice and assesses the extent to which understanding of ethnic and class factors have been incorporated in the basic assumptions and procedures.

Finally, Chapter 5 presents assumptions and principles for ethnic-sensitive practice. The "Route to the Social Worker" is introduced as a tool for assessment and intervention.

1

CHAPTER
1

The Ethnic Reality

There are many perspectives on how ethnic group membership, social class, minority group status, and culture affect individual and group life. In this chapter we examine and assess a number of these perspectives. In so doing, we are guided by one basic objective: to cull those insights that can serve as the basis for the development of practice principles to guide practitioners in their efforts to respond with sensitivity to the values and dispositions related to ethnic group membership and position in the social stratification system.

A vast body of knowledge identifies how ethnicity and membership in various social class groups shape approaches to the problems of living. When these approaches are examined in the context of American society, a number of themes emerge. One focuses on how ethnic groups and ethnicity are defined. Another emphasizes the sense of cohesion, identity, and solidarity (as well as stress and strife) that derive from association with one's own ethnic group. Another centers on the meaning of social class, the consequences of membership in different class groups, and the inequality of opportunity associated with membership in the lower strata.

Central to these themes are the relationships among ethnic group membership, minority status, social class, and inequality. Those who have been assigned official responsibility "to help" have a particular obligation to be aware of inequality as it derives from ethnic group membership, minority status, and social class. Especially important are sensitivity to and awareness of the strength and coping capacity of those who are the major victims of inequality. Helping professionals often focus on peoples' stress and deprivation while ignoring their important strengths. This book presents some formulations that serve to highlight such understanding.

MAJOR PERSPECTIVES ON THE ROLE OF ETHNICITY IN AMERICAN LIFE

The process by which diverse people who are different in culture, background, language, religion, color, national origin, and socioeconomic status accommodate to each other as they make a life for themselves in the United States has long intrigued both social scientists and the public. Hraba (1979) identifies three major schools of thought that have sought to explain the process and its impact on unique life styles and patterns of habits and thought. He terms these *assimilationism, ethnic conflict theory,* and *ethnic pluralism.* Integral to some of these perspectives are various views on the relative impact of ethnic and social class factors on ingrained patterns of feeling and action. Most important is the body of thought focused on how various types of group memberships constrain or expand opportunities for socioeconomic and psychological well-being.

A major question focuses on similarities and differences in the experiences of white ethnic groups and those groups some now term *people of color,* (e.g., Hopps 1982). Often explicit (and always implicit) are queries about whether the persistent inequities associated with color are of such magnitude as to preclude the usefulness of insights derived from the "white ethnic experience" for contributing to understanding of people of color.

In the next few pages we review briefly some of the major schools of thought that have sought to explain the role of ethnicity in American life. Next we present our view and the rationale for our adherence to a pluralistic perspective. We then elaborate on our formulations, which stress the importance of "ethclass" and the *ethnic reality.*

These concepts highlight the important relationship between ethnic group membership and social class. Gordon (1964) characterized the point at which social class and ethnic group membership intersect as "ethclass." He used this concept to explain the role that social class membership plays in defining the basic conditions of life and to simultaneously account for differences between groups at the same social class level. In this view, these differences are, in large measure, explained by ethnic group membership. We suggest that this intersect of ethnicity and social class generates identifiable dispositions and behaviors. We characterize these dispositions and the behaviors that flow from them as the *ethnic reality* or ethclass in action.

The concept of the ethnic reality, depicted in Figure 1, refers to dispositions on such matters as what are considered to be appropriate child rearing practices or proper ways of caring for the elderly. These dispositions and the behaviors that result from them are deeply embedded, though often subtle.

In beginning this discussion of the major views concerning ethnicity in American life, it is important to note a number of factors that guide these considerations: (1) the growth of civilization has altered and contributed to an increasingly complex basis of self-identification, and (2) the concepts of culture and subculture enhance understanding of the role played by ethnic group membership in shaping responses to the joys and problems of living.

In the past the rules governing family behavior and political life and the values guiding them were intricately intertwined. Group, family, and political life were culturally uniform and took place within a limited and clearly demarcated geographical place. Distinctions between family,

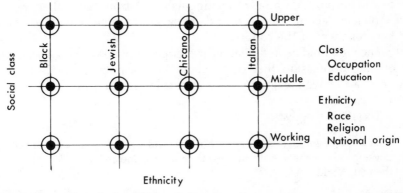

FIGURE 1.   The ethnic reality: ethclass in action.
The "social space" created by the intersect of social class and ethnicity has been called ethclass. The disposition and behaviors that flow from this are termed the ethnic reality or ethclass in action.

Ethnicity and the associated sense of "peoplehood" are represented by the vertical axis and stress the fact that ethnicity is a component of social life at all social class levels. Social class is represented by the horizontal axes.

The circles represent the ethnic reality and suggest that as social class intersects with ethnicity a unique configuration is formed.

social class, ethnic group, work, and place of residence were virtually nonexistent and out of the frame of experience of most people. The development of stable agricultural societies, followed by massive industrialization and urbanization gave rise to diverse bases of identity. Nation, region of birth, residence, occupation, and social class are but a few of the factors that help to shape our sense of who we are, where we belong, and how we should behave.

These factors, together with mass migration, invasion, conquest, and coercive relocation (as in the case of slaves brought to these shores), all contribute to the shape of our present pluralistic society and give rise to the concerns and questions considered here.

Assimilationism

Hraba's succinct analysis suggests that "assimilation is the process by which diverse ethnic and racial groups come to share a common culture and have equal access to the opportunity structure of a society" (Hraba 1979, p.29). In a closely related definition it is proposed that peoples with "diverse ways of thinking, feeling and acting become fused together in a social unity and a common culture" (Hraba 1979, p. 29, citing Vander Zanden, 1972).

Adherents of the view that peoples of disparate backgrounds will fuse and become "culturally indistinguishable" from each other are not in agreement about the nature and character of the newcomers or what is best for them or the country.

Some who hold an assimilationist point of view look at the social and economic oppression that drew many European immigrants to this country and have idealistic visions of creating new types of people in a new society.

Alba (1985) suggests:

This was a vision of America as a pristine world, where a new society could develop free of the social shackles, the political and religious despotisms of the Old World.

This view is also echoed by others.

What is the American, this new man? . . . *He* is an American who leaving behind him all his ancient prejudices and manners, receives new ones from the new mode of life he has embraced, the new government he obeys, and the new rank he holds . . . Here, individuals of all nations are melted into a new race of men, whose labours and posterity will one day cause great changes in the world. (Alba 1985, p. 6, from J. Hector St. John Crevecoeur, *Letters from an American Farmer*, 1782).

The well-known theory of the melting pot, or the view that distinctions between groups would merge into a new whole, is an integral part of this perspective.

Another side of the assimilationist perspective was less idealistic. Rather, it arose out of distrust and fear of the large numbers who immigrated from Europe and Asia. Alba suggests there was a "sense of crisis" engendered. For example, the arrival of many Irish people brought, for the first time, significant numbers of Catholics to this country. Further, many associated the poverty, crowding, and high disease rates that accompanied urbanization with the immigrants. Pervasive distrust of the newcomers was rampant and there was substantial pressure that they become "Americanized."

> The immigrants and their children were expected thereby to throw off the cultures of their homeland as so much old clothing, that would no longer be needed in the benign environment of the New World (Alba 1985, p.5).

History, as well as contemporary developments, suggests that neither the bigotry nor the fervent idealism that generated the notions of what immigrants would and should do were founded on understanding of the social and political dynamics at play. In his foreword to a volume in one of the major series on ethnic groups in American life, Gordon states:

> As the United States, with its racially and ethnically variegated population, moves through the last two decades of the 20th century, the myths of the melting pot and complete assimilation recede farther and farther into the distance . . . (Alba 1985, p. 5).

This is not to suggest that generations of immigrants are left untouched by the American experience, life with and amongst others, or the societal forces that have long pushed toward what has been termed *Anglo-conformity*. Rather, it is proposed that the phenomenon of ethnic identification remains a vital part of American personal, familial, social, and political life. The nature and shape of ethnic and minority experience remain vital and dynamic. How they are "played out" is a continuing matter of inquiry.

Ethnic Conflict Theory

As the newcomers arrived and became part of American life, they became integrally involved in the struggle to work and to attain the ordinary amenities of life. Many immigrants left their homelands hoping to improve upon the meager economic, social, and political opportunities available to them in their own lands. Slaves, and ultimately ex-slaves, were variously involved in the economic life of the country, as it was moving forward towards modernization. Some (e.g., Hraba 1979) suggest that competition and conflict are integral parts of modernization and industrialization. Consequently, competition and conflict among ethnic groups increase. Key concepts of conflict theory are ethnic competition, ethnic conflict, ethnic stratification, and ethnic evolution. The first refers to the efforts of different ethnic groups to attain the same scarce objectives. Ethnic conflict is a form of intergroup rivalry during which groups try to injure each other. This kind of conflict has long been evident. White settlers invaded the territories of American Indians, and Asian Americans who were efficient and productive workers were the object of vilification by unions whose interests they presumably violated. Closely related is the view that there are systems of *ethnic stratification* in which powerful ethnic groups limit access of subordinate groups to wealth, power, and prestige. Systems of ethnic stratification are fluid, and power shifts. The history of the past twenty-five years suggests that there is validity to these concepts.

Those who participated in, and those who read about, the civil rights and Black liberation movement begun in the 1960s know that conflict was engendered, and that an adversary stance was a part of the struggle. As gains were made, other groups took note and generated their own liberation movements, thus generating a new set of conflicts. Present debates about the validity of affirmative action and who the "legitimate" groups are needing such action are further testimony of ongoing conflict.

A current expression of the conflict perspective was advanced by Longres, a social worker (Longres 1982). He suggests that majority and minority groups may be viewed as "interest groups," "self-conscious publics," or numbers of people who recognize themselves as a "we" separate from a "they" who are by definition those not in the group (1982, p.7). Viewed from an interest groups perspective, majority and minority status relates to power, influence, and subordination or domination. Majority groups dominate; minority groups are subordinated. Although majorities and minorities may be distinguishable by matters of ethnicity, religion, or race, these matters do not define majority or minority status. Minority group status arises out of historical circumstances; minority status is not permanent and can shift by the attainment of goals or common factors that bind a group together.

Both minorities and majorities have a legitimate claim to power and have certain rights and obligations. Minorities have fewer rights, more odious obligations, and less control over the circumstances of their lives than do members of majority groups.

Minority status is usually measured by two criteria: socioeconomic well-being, and cultural and social acceptance. Economic, social, and cultural inequality are evidence of minority status. Given these criteria, Longres proposes that five groups can obviously be designated as minorities in contemporary American society: Afro-Americans, American Indians, Native Alaskans, Mexican-Americans, and Puerto Ricans. The interests of majorities and minorities are not consonant.

> It should therefore not be assumed that problems among these groups merely stem from a lack of communication and understanding or even from differences in cultural values . . .
>
> Social workers involved in the delivery of service are caught between the interests minorities have in promoting their communities and the interests the majority has in maintaining its own dominant economic, political, and sociocultural status. Because of this, social services represent one of the arenas in which competition and conflict among groups are played out (Longres, 1982, p. 12).

The majority provides legitimacy and funding for social services, thus making the social work community beholden to them. The history of social work suggests that both conservative elements and liberal or minority interests have been at play.

In Longres's view, social workers who adopt an interest group perspective on majority-minority relations ultimately must "take sides." They may play a mediating role in effecting compromise between groups. However,

> We may either stand in favor of minorities, encouraging their collective self-determination and facilitating their attempts to alter the status of their communities, or we may come down on the side of the majority and aid in the maintenance of its domination. If we choose to work in behalf of minorities, practice and service must be defined to include social reform activities (1982, p.13).

Longres's perspective has considerable validity. Its implementation demands much of ethnic-sensitive social workers. In our view, recognition of the basis of conflict and understanding are required if social workers are to continue "to keep alive the full promise of social work" (1982, p. 13).

Ethnic Pluralism

In contrast with the view expressed by the assimilationists is that of the pluralists, who suggest that ethnic groups and ethnic identity do not disappear as groups adapt to life in a new country. Rather, ethnicity evolves into new forms, responding to the experiences of life in a different society and historical era. Hraba uses the term *ethnic evolution* to refer to these changes.

Two types of pluralism are identified and defined: *cultural* and *structural*. *Cultural pluralism* conveys the sense that there are distinct, identifiable ethnic subcultures that affect how people think, feel, and act. *Structural pluralism* means that ethnic identity comes into play as people interact. It is evident either in restrictions on social interaction or in the use of ethnic identity as a component of free and open exchange. The basic assumptions underlying the views of the ethnic pluralists are summarized by Hraba:

1. Although the relationships between ethnic groups evolve over time, the evolutionary process does not generate the development of a single, monolithic entity.

2. In the evolutionary relations among ethnic groups, the ways in which ethnicity is expressed changes.

3. Ethnicity persists in American society because the nation has tolerance for ethnic pluralism; ethnic groups play a sociopolitical role, and ethnicity serves a social function (Hraba 1979).

This review of key concepts about how ethnic groups interact and adapt to each other suggests that assimilationist and melting pot theories are not consistent with people's experiences. The intensity with which ethnic identity is maintained may vary. Groups who at one point in time were the targets of major oppression and insults often go on to achieve considerable status and power.[1] Our daily experience as social work practitioners, as educators, and as citizens suggests that the strength of feeling and experiences associated with ethnicity remain real facts of social life. Much of ethnic conflict theory conforms to our ongoing experience, as well as to history.

And so it is clear to us that the major elements of ethnic conflict and ethnic pluralist perspectives help to explain much that is often referred to as "intergroup relations." Equally important for the objectives of this book is our view that the body of work thus generated, especially that of the pluralists, helps to describe and analyze the experiences of the various ethnic and minority groups.

Gordon puts it well when he states:

---

[1] Some suggest this can be said for the Irish people, once much maligned.

The stubborn persistence of the racial and ethnic factor as a source of ethnic commonality, and the conflict of ethnic collectivities as interest groups seeking by various means their (frequently previously withheld) fair share of material and status reward make it all the more imperative that the resources of the practitioners of the art and science of understanding human behavior be brought to bear on the problem. Such application should produce both the theoretical knowledge and the practical measures that would help create a state of affairs where the positive potentialities of ethnic pluralism can be effectively realized while the negative results of unlimited ethnic conflict can be minimized and kept within tolerable bounds (from Milton Gordon, foreward to Alba 1985, p.v).

Up to this point we have used many important terms without stopping to define them. Before we can go on to the major point of interest here—more detailed examination of the concepts of ethclass and the ethnic reality and their usefulness for social work practice—the terms *ethnic group*, *minority group*, *ethnicity*, *culture*, and *subculture* must be defined and their meanings assessed.

Ethnic Groups

According to Gordon, the ethnic group is a type of group contained within the national boundaries of America and defined or set off by race, religion, or national origin. In this view religion is a cultural phenomenon. National origin calls attention to the fact that everyone's ancestors, except American Indians, came to the United States from elsewhere (sometimes by force, as in the case of the slaves), usually bringing a set of customs, a language, and a unique history. Race is the result of differential concentrations of gene frequencies responsible for traits confined to physical manifestations, such as skin color or hair form. These have no intrinsic connections with cultural patterns or institutions (Gordon 1964). Many analysts share the view that common to the ethnic group is a shared feeling of peoplehood and a common sense of past and future. This sense of belonging often connotes cohesion, solidarity, and a basis of identity.

A similar definition is offered by Hraba, who suggests that "ethnic groups are self-conscious collectivities of people who, on the basis of a common origin or a separate subculture, maintain a distinction between themselves and outsiders" (Hraba 1979, p.27).

Citing Weber's definition, Alba proposes that an ethnic group is "a human group that entertains a 'subjective belief' in its common descent because of similarities of physical type or of customs or both, or because of memories of colonization and migration" (Alba 1985, p. 17).

Alba summarizes the common themes that run through these definitions of ethnic group. They include a "consciousness of kind" (a sense
of being like others in the group) and a common identity based on a
shared history. The "self-definition in terms of the past . . . makes an
ethnic group different from most other kinds of social groups and
constitutes the *sine qua non* of its existence" (1985, p. 17).

Minority Groups

Perhaps more than most of the terms commonly used in discussions of
this type, the term *minority group* generates considerable emotion and
difference of opinion about its meaning. Even when there is agreement
on definitions, people frequently differ about which groups are properly
designated as having minority status.

Here we review some of the major definitions currently in use. We
also consider why it is so difficult to arrive at a consensus on appropriate
definitions. Following this we present our perspective, which is related
to our interest in using language and concepts that will further effective
practice.

As early as 1965, Shibutani and Kwan offered a useful definition.
They proposed that minority groups are "the underprivileged in a
system of ethnic stratification, and people of low standing—people who
receive unequal treatment and who therefore come to regard themselves
as objects of discrimination" (Shibutani and Kwan 1965). Adams (1975)
suggests there is a tendency to use the term *ethnic groups* when invidious
distinctions are not being made, and to use the term *minority groups*
when invidious distinctions are implied.

These definitions focus on attributes characteristic of minorities:
inequality, discrimination, limited power, limited economic wherewithal, and low status. Minority group members tend to be held in low
esteem by the larger society.

For many years the term *minority group* was used almost interchangeably with the term *ethnic group*. At different points in history, many of
the ethnic groups of eastern European origin could have been characterized as minorities. Gains in education, occupation, and income, and
a more positive societal appraisal of many of these groups changed their
status. Increasingly, the designation *minorities* was used to mean those
groups most affected by racism and poverty: American Blacks, American Indians, many Asians, and many Hispanics.

At the same time the term *minority* came to be used to refer to groups
other than those ethnic groups that were especially oppressed. Women,
the elderly, gay men, lesbians, and the handicapped were among those

who laid claim to the designation. All faced long-standing oppression and vulnerability. Hopps (1983) suggests that the designation of these groups as minorities was a result of governmental resource allocation policies that entitled people of minority status to increased access to opportunities, and remediation of societally triggered inequities. As a consequence she suggests that "it might be more useful for social workers to examine groups within the context of their need for immediate, affirmative actions, rather than to focus on a definition of minority groups per se" (1982, p.3). Because so many groups laid claim to the term *minorities*, the term, in her view, lost meaning. Instead, she proposes abandoning the effort to arrive at a clear definition. She suggests it is *people of color* who

> ". . . face a pervasive kind of oppression and discrimination because of racial stereotypes associated with and indelibly marked by the color of their skin. Although many forms of exclusion and discrimination exist in this country, none is so deeply rooted, persistent and intractable as that based on color" (Hopps, 1982, p. 3).

It is people of color, especially Blacks, American Indians, Native Alaskans, Mexican Americans, and Puerto Ricans who continue to be especially oppressed. Hopps (1982, 1983) and Lum (1986) suggest that color is the most pervasive reason for discrimination. Lum proposes that "the *color factor* has been a barrier that has separated Black, Latino, Asian, and Native Americans from others" (1986, p. 1). He uses both the terms *people of color* and *ethnic minority* interchangeably to refer to all these groups.

Each term captures some, but not all, of the issues and problems that confront various groups. The key component of the definition of the term *minority* reviewed earlier—"the underprivileged in a system of ethnic stratification and people of low standing . . . " (Shibutani & Kwan 1965)—still captures the fundamental realities confronting oppressed ethnic groups. For the most part, these are the *people of color* to whom Hopps refers—Blacks, American Indians, Native Alaskans, Mexican-Americans, and Puerto Ricans. Other *people of color* such as Asian Americans and other Hispanic groups face many kinds of discrimination. Most confront persistent and subtle racism related to their color. This is true even for those Asian Americans whose education and income are equal to those of society's most privileged people (*New York Times,* June 14, 1986).

For the present purposes we will retain the usage adopted in the first edition of this book. That is, we will use the term *minority* to mean "the underprivileged in a system of ethnic stratification." That refers to the groups whom Hopps identifies as people of color. We shall be ever mindful of the difficulties experienced by other ethnic groups—those distinguished by color, by other facial and bodily configurations, and by a common history, language, religion, and sense of identity. Social workers need to be sensitive to the strengths and strife related to these factors. The inequities confronting those who most persistently are victims of oppression and racism are, of course, of special concern.

Culture

"Culture" is a commonly used though not readily defined concept. Dictionary definitions abound with such terms as *explicit and implicit patterns, artifacts, symbols, language,* and the like. What do these really convey? Culture refers to the fact that human groups are distinguishable by the manner in which they guide and structure behavior and the meanings they ascribe to it. Cultures differ in their world view, in their perspectives on the rhythms and patterns of life, and in their concept of the essential nature of the human condition. These perspectives are conveyed in a myriad of symbolic and direct ways via language, socialization practices, abstract forms such as art, and the mundane artifacts used in daily living.

The ideas and values thus conveyed become part of the routine and habitual dispositions to life. Forged out of diverse experience as people attemp to grapple with natural forces and human interaction, culture guides thinking about these forces. For example, those immersed in a culture that views nature as malleable and controllable by people stop to think only about *how* not *whether* to control nature. Members of groups that view natural forces as evil or controlling have a sense that these are to be endured. The basic response patterns, set into the core and substance of group life, involve a variety of injunctions by which every member learns to live. In the view of Kroeber and Kluckhon, culture is the product of action and a major force affecting the nature of subsequent action (Kluckhon 1964). Culture has also been viewed as the "total ways of life" that orient thinking about the universe and the proper nature of human to human and human to God relationships (Valentine 1968). Margaret Mead described culture as a "vehicle for the human emotions of human beings to come into some kind of intelligible order" (*New York Times*, November 19, 1978). This order derives from the social heritage or way of life of a particular society at a particular time. It is a term appropriately applied when human groups share behaviors and norms that differ from those of other groups.

Subculture

What is subculture and how does it differ from culture? As societies become more complex, the tenets for appropriate political, religious, and interpersonal behavior are transmitted by varying groups. There are many types of subcultures or subsocieties. A subculture or a subsociety is a group that may be distinguishable by a common ethnic background, occupation, religion, race, status, or some combination of these characteristics. At the same time the subculture shares certain features with larger social segments or an overriding culture system. For example, the "Protestant ethic" is often viewed as an overriding American cultural theme and one to which all subgroups in the United States are exposed, regardless of the extent of commitment to this ethic by any particular group.

Much that has been presented up to this point suggests that the meanings of ethnic group membership and minority status, and the cultural and behavioral consequences of these memberships are varied. It is important to note that there are diverse and sometimes conflicting perspectives on the origin and importance of these memberships.

Both professional and popular writings provide evidence of an ongoing, dynamic effort to sharpen our understanding of these matters. These efforts take place at an emotional as well as an intellectual level, for the matters at issue are part of the core and substance of our being.

Gordon suggests that in diversified and stratified societies each of these bases of group membership suggest varied and, at times, conflicting bases of identification, guides for behavior, and orientation to the vicissitudes of life.

> . . . the sense of ethnicity has proved to be hardy. As though with a wily cunning of its own, as though there were some essential element in man's nature that demands it—something that compelled him to merge his lonely individual identity in some ancestral group of fellows smaller by far than the whole human race, smaller often than the nation—the sense of ethnic belonging has survived. It has survived in various forms and with various names, but it has not perished, and twentieth century urban man is closer to his stone age ancestors than he knows (Gordon 1964).

THE SENSE OF ETHNICITY

All of these definitions convey in a formal sense what is frequently experienced at a "gut" level by people immersed in various ethnic groups. In assessing the degree to which the sense of ethnicity and peoplehood persist, we examined a variety of materials. These included systematic, quantitative sociological analyses as well as novels, plays, and personal documents intended to express more unique emotional experiences. We also talked with a variety of people—the "schooled" as well as the less educated. When we asked, sometimes half jokingly, "Do you want to be assimilated?" a number of replies were not unlike those of a well-educated Jewish woman who said: "Do you mean giving up my Jewishness and becoming just like everybody else? If that's what you mean I don't want it. I'm part of this country, and I pay my taxes, and I want my children to go to school, but I want to remain different in many important ways."[2]

An older Hungarian woman commented: "You know, when I came to this country I was so happy to be here that I wanted to be a complete American, to do everything the American way. Then I found out that I could not stop being Hungarian; I could not give up the Hungarian ways. I was so economical, so upset about waste that my boss laughed at me. My children are more American but we are still all Hungarian and I like it."[3]

Among the sentiments of young Puerto Ricans presented in *Growing up Puerto Rican* (Cooper 1972) is that of Rosita, a sixteen year old. "Puerto Ricans are special people because they have special food like rice and beans—Puerto Ricans are very special people and they're different from others. Good different. The way they act and the way they treat each other."

The negative characteristics attributed to minority group members by the larger society has been noted. The messages conveyed to members of such groups are often internalized by individuals who in turn degrade themselves and members of their own group. Much of the effort of the liberation movements of the sixties was devoted to reversing a destructive psychological situation in which many Blacks degraded their own physical characteristics and chased "ethereal forms of whiteness." It has been suggested that the phrase "say it loud, black and proud" had serious psychological purpose in that it sought to help young people achieve a positive sense of identity with the group (Jenkins 1969).

Mostwin (1973) reports findings of a study of post–World War II Polish immigrants to the United States, designed to ascertain the association between migration and changes in the immigrant's ethnic identity. Responses to a structured questionnaire suggested that people retain a sense of Polish identity but also come to identify themselves as Americans. The letters that accompanied responses to the structured questionnaires are expressions of the sense of belonging to both groups.

---

[2]Conversation with Ellie Jacob.
[3]Conversation with Margaret Herczag.

"I feel very pro-American in the knowledge that this adopted country has great values and possibilities. I would love to contribute to its greatness, as well as see my children become good citizens—but always aware of their Polish culture and ancestry" (Mostwin 1973).

At a time when many are questioning the degree to which ethnicity retains the power to affect behavior, being, and feeling, e.g., (Alba 1985), evidence of its persistence continuously surfaces. For example, many European ethnic groups are overcoming some of the historical barriers to equal participation in American life, and, accompanying this, their sense of ethnicity may be thought to fade. Yet examples of ethnic resurgence or revival in these groups are readily found. Tricarico (1984) points out that many Italian-Americans who have "made it" in the larger society eagerly read an English language magazine targeted to Italian-Americans (*Attenzione*) as a way of discovering and sustaining their roots. In considering the varying degrees to which American Jews retain a sense of identity with the group Herman points out:

> Some Jews may readily accept their membership and all that goes with it, regarding it as a mark of distinction even if it subjects them to certain difficulties. They know where they stand and their membership in what they regard as a desirable group bolsters their self-esteem. Other Jews may see the membership as a stigma and may develop inferiority feelings about their Jewishness. But they generally cannot escape it. They can only deny it by a formal act of conversion, and even then their Jewish origins will not always be forgotten by their Gentile neighbors (and will also be remembered by Jews in certain situations). In a sense such an individual is trying to reject a part of himself (1977, p. 34).

Implicit in Herman's comments is the notion that ethnic identity, though varied and complex, is not easily torn asunder. This is true for those Americans whose physical characteristics make it possible to "fade into the mainstream." Silberman (1985) documents the continuing sense of identity with the Jewish people experienced by many Jews.

Ethnicity is experienced and persists because there is a sense of comfort and ease when a person attends a wedding or funeral that adheres to familiar rituals and routines; at the same time, the person may experience discomfort when these rituals are carried out in a manner that departs from the tried and true. Ethnicity is expressed in the spontaneous expression of distress by the Jew-turned-atheist who learns that some synagogues hire and fire rabbis in a manner analogous to that used by large corporations in dealing with managers. And it is reinforced by "kielbasa" and "pasta" and "beans and rice" and the joy of eating these foods in the company of others who appreciate them because of what they convey.

A myriad of experiences, persons, and things are feared, loved, hated, and desired by every person. All too often, aspirations, even those of an intense and deeply personal nature, are negatively affected by societal perceptions of what and who one is as this is related to ethnic group membership. And much of what the family transmits— particularly the minority family—is not only that which is valued by the group but also clues concerning the manner in which members of the group are likely to be perceived and received. For those who suffer the particular effects of discrimination—those ethnic groups that are also minority groups, ethnic identity and its transmission serves as a sense of protection from the larger world. This larger world all too often demeans, frequently by vociferous intent, and often out of ignorance. Ethnicity may serve as protection against the message that suggests that if ethnic group identity or related behaviors are abandoned, discrimination will cease. That this message so often proves to be false is exemplified by the fact that Blacks or Hispanics who abandon subtle but characteristic speech patterns and Jews who change their names or have plastic surgery performed to anglicize their features may still experience overt or subtle job discrimination.

Ethnicity is protection from the larger world, which stereotypes the Black scholar who possesses no musical or athletic talent and causes him to cringe when a thoughtless bystander suggests that he would make a good addition to the local jazz band or baseball team; it provides a retreat for the American Indian who feels hurt and at a loss when told by a harried social worker that stopping to help a friend along the way is irresponsible behavior and no excuse for being late for an important appointment.

These and countless other examples highlight the fact that the "world out there" continues to react to people in terms of ascribed images rather than in individual terms. The ethnic group can give solace and put the "ethnic slur" into perspective. It often does so either via humor or by providing a comfortable setting within which to ventilate anger. Much of that comfort is provided by the group and the accompanying sense of ethnicity. The power that such membership exerts over people of color, those whose status is visible and often demeaned, is most critical.

This discussion of the sense of ethnicity suggests that it continues to exert a major and meaningful impact on the important feelings and behaviors social workers need to understand in their work with people. It is important then to understand what factors sustain and which minimize the sense of identity considered here.

MAINTENANCE OF ETHNIC IDENTITY

The interaction of factors both internal and external to the group contribute to the persistence of ethnic identity.

The study of social structure indicates that the groups within which major social relationships take place vary in a number of critical ways. A major distinction, and one of particular importance, is the one between primary and secondary groups. Families, play groups, and informal social networks are examples of primary groups, while secondary groups are found in the work place, political and civic organizations, and large bureaucracies.

Primary Groups

In primary groups, relationships are most often personal, intimate, and all-encompassing. Ideally these are the types of groups in which people can "be themselves," in which their foibles are understood, and they are intrinsically loved and wanted.

The major types of activities performed in primary groups highlight their importance in transmitting the sense of ethnicity. It is these groups that convey values and a sense of belonging, warmth, and cohesion. What is important and striking about the activities confined to or mainly carried out within primary groups is that they involve the core of the personality and important emotional relationships.

How do primary groups such as the family and the peer group convey and sustain this "sense of ancestral and future oriented identification" with the group? It is sustained in subtle reminders conveyed by the way in which children are consoled or admonished, the transmitted clues for appropriate behavior in puberty, and the way in which these are reinforced by the larger society.

The "pull" exerted by family and community and kin as they seek to keep the young within the fold is well known to most youngsters. The almost universal request made of adolescent girls by their parents that their dates pick them up at home reflects a need to protect and a concern for safety and decorum. Yet, the fact that it also contains the question, albeit implicit,—"Is he one of us?"—is not lost. This stage is often preceded by small and subtle actions ranging from looking for the "right" schools, which may really mean looking for neighbors of one's own kind, joining the temple or church "for the children," and sending the children to religious school. It means finding enough money for extras if the extra is a church trip, but lacking sufficient resources to finance the summer at a nonsectarian camp. A three-generational study of Jewish, Italian, and Slavic-American women in the Pittsburgh area finds that ethnic-group-related differences are transmitted in a number of ways (Krause 1978).

Many Italian-American families continue to exert a strong pull on grown offspring to remain within the confines of the family. Many believe that daughters should not leave the family home except in a"wedding gown" or "casket" (Johnson 1985, pp. 185–186). Home is considered "good" and the place where one is safe and protected. Much effort goes into "bringing" the young back home.

Rogler and Cooney (1984) studied the persistence of ethnic identity in two generations of Puerto Ricans who had come to the mainland. Distinguishing them by such factors as age, sex, and age of arrival, the researchers measured adherence to ethnically related values and noted a tendency for these to diminish in the younger generation. Nevertheless, all ages were similar in perceiving themselves as Puerto Ricans in values.

The degree to which these deeply ingrained ethnic dispositions persist into the third and fourth generations of immigrant families is of interest. There is a high degree of intermarriage among Italians. Many have experienced substantial increases in levels of education and occupation. Yet, most Italian adults alive in the late 1970s had some memory of the immigrant experience. At least half had one immigrant parent (Alba 1985). These patterns suggest fluidity as well as stability. The dispositions transmitted by the family are important and not readily "shaken."

The importance of group identity and "marrying one's own kind" is transmitted and conveyed in some extreme responses to "transgression." Where guidelines are clear and parents vehement, there is often pain and turmoil; not infrequently a total rupture in the family relationships ensues. Some Orthodox Jews may go so far as to "sit shive" for a child who has married outside the group.

Despite the increasing rate at which young Jewish people "marry out," "even the most liberal and assimilated Jewish families remain highly sensitive to the issue, which may continue to signify betrayal of the family and the community" (Herz and Rosen 1982).

Sophie suffered the agonies and scorn that sometimes accompany ethnic identity, and societal prejudice when she, a young Italian woman, became pregnant by a Puerto Rican man. When she attempted to introduce her son to his maternal grandmother, this was the mother's reaction:

> They heard the woman from inside the apartment shouting, "Get out, I'll call the police, go away. Go some place with those people who kill my daughter.

The niggers. Go there. My daughter is dead gone finished. No more. I call the police" (Mohr 1974).

When parents are permissive and "democratic" in their views concerning cross-ethnic primary relationships, they often voice their concerns about the possible discomfort of the unknown and unfamiliar in a relationship with someone of a different background. The refrain, "Marriage is difficult enough even if you have a lot in common," is well known.

The family, then, usually kind and protective, sometimes destructive, guides the young into the "right" schools, into playing with the "right" kinds of children, into marriages with the "right" people, and these often are thought to be "our own kind." "Man's most primal needs and emotions declare themselves first within the family. Man learns his greatest fears, loves, hatreds, and hopes within this social unit" (Greeley 1974, p. 174).

Ethnicity and Language

Ethnicity is experienced and persists through language. The extent to which groups share and use a common language varies enormously. For example, among recent immigrant groups, such as the Vietnamese and other southeast Asians, some Puerto Ricans, Mexicans, and other Latin Americans, the native language is the major form of communication in the family and local community. Children, usually more quick to learn English than their elders, become both teachers to and translators for the adults in the family. In other groups, a self-conscious, deliberate bilingualism is sustained as members seek to preserve their own culture even after English has been mastered.

It may be Spanish, Polish, Italian, Hungarian, Yiddish, or a soulful sound "metered without the intention of the speaker to invoke it," as in the language of soul (Brown 1972). A common language provides a psychic bond, a uniqueness that signifies membership in a particular ethnic group, as well as a base for the coordination of activities both social and political. At times it is necessary to cope with the oppression of the mainstream society, which may forbid the use of the native tongue in the public arena. Ethnicity may be heard or felt when young Blacks "play the dozens" or "get their programs together." It is the deliberation of the Spanish "a poco a poco," the joy of the Italian "aldia," or the audacity conveyed by the Yiddish term, "chutzpa." Each of these words and many others retain their ethnic uniqueness in that they are not readily translated into mainstream language, thereby giving the speaker a sense of distinction.

The persistence of ethnicity and the degree to which key elements are retained or modified and diminished is in part explained by the processes involved in acculturation and assimilation.

Acculturation and Assimilation

Gordon's (1964) "multidimensional model of the assimilation process" is an articulate and incisive formulation. In his view, the "core culture" or "core subsociety" is middle-class and white Protestant.

Acculturation and *assimilation* are terms used to describe what happens when groups with different backgrounds and cultures meet. Efforts to describe and understand this process were triggered by the mass migrations of Europeans to the United States, the importation of slaves, and the contacts between the original settlers and American Indians. "Acculturation makes one group's culture the point of reference and focuses upon the events and processes by which that group responds to more or less continuous contact by variously accepting, reformulating or rejecting elements of the other culture or cultures" (Keesing 1964). In Faris's (1964) view, assimilation " . . . denotes the process in which one set of cultural traits is relinquished and a new set acquired, through communication and participation. The change is gradual and may take place in any degree." Gordon (1964) contends that assimilation is a matter of degree and that various types and stages in the assimilation process can be identified.

There is a distinction between "cultural" or "behavioral" assimilation and structural assimilation. In the former some of the major themes or behaviors of the dominant society, particularly its language, have been adopted. When structural assimilation takes place there are extensive primary group relationships between immigrants and members of the core culture, sometimes including intermarriage. Seven types or stages of the assimilation process are identified: (1) cultural, (2) structural, (3) marital, (4) identificational, (5) attitude-receptional, (6) behavioral-receptional, and (7) civic (Gordon 1964).

When the dominant or mainstream society erects barriers to total participation by various groups in significant aspects of social and economic life, only cultural or behavioral assimilation is likely to take place. Many ethnic groups do not seek total structural or marital assimilation. Indeed, many groups value their traditions and differences from others, and actively try to prevent structural assimilation at the same time as they seek social and economic equality. Despite this type of resistance, structural assimilation, as exemplified by intermarriage between members of European ethnic groups, has increased dramatically in the last few decades. How this will impact on the extent of ethnic identity of affected people remains yet to be fully assessed.[4]

The barriers to structural assimilation affecting minorities hardly need further elaboration here.

This discussion has focused on the ethnic component of *ethclass* and has suggested what ethnicity means, how it is experienced, and what factors contribute to its persistence. It is now time to consider another important concept—that of social class.

SOCIAL CLASS

Social Inequality

No discussion of social class can proceed without consideration of the meaning of social inequality and stratification. The nature of inequality has been examined by theorists from Plato to Marx to Weber to contemporary analysts. All have examined the conditions that intensify or minimize various forms of inequality. In contemporary American society inequality is evident in the fact that some have more income, find themselves in more highly valued and rewarded occupations, and have more prestige than others. This in turn affects the extent of individual well-being, specific indicators of health and illness, real and perceived power to achieve desired ends, one's sense of self-respect, and the degree of dignity conferred by others.

Social Class Defined

Although there is agreement concerning the existence of inequality, there is an enormous amount of conceptual confusion surrounding the term *social class*, a term usually used to designate the existence of different strata. Much of the debate revolves around whether there are social classes. Some theorists suggest that the term is a useful representation of reality (Hodges 1964; Eitzen 1985), while others take the position that social classes are nothing more than convenient fragments of the sociological imagination (Wrong 1959). As evidence of the existence of social classes, Eitzen points to the maldistribution of wealth, variation in educational attainment, occupations, and patterns of deference accorded certain groups. Hodges believes that "social classes are the blended product of shared and analogous occupational orientations, educational backgrounds, economic wherewithal, and life experience."

---

[4]Alba suggests that there may be a gradual reduction of distinctiveness. Yet the upward mobility of some white ethnics may legitimize ethnic resurgence.

Gordon suggests that the term *social class* involves the horizonal stratification of a population, related to economic life. It refers to: "differences based on wealth, income, occupation, status, community power, group identification, level of consumption, and family background" (in Duberman 1976). The experience of social work practitioners and the life experience all of us have shared suggest that the latter positions are accurate reflections of reality.

Measurement of Social Class

Considerable effort has been made to identify and measure the nature of the different strata or classes. A brief review and summary of some of the more commonly used and useful social class measures will be helpful. Much that has been written and said about social class in the United States has used these or analogous classification schemes.

Analysts differ concerning the number of classes and the criteria to be used in assigning people to the various strata. Many view the society as divided into three categories—the upper, the middle, and the lower classes. The six-part classification scheme developed by Warner and the five-class categorization developed by Hollingshead are commonly used (Warner 1949; Hollingshead and Redlich 1958). Warner views the population as consisting of:

1. The upper-upper class, composed of old wealthy families
2. The lower-upper class, whose wealth is newly acquired
3. The upper-middle class, comprised of successful professional and business people
4. The lower-middle class, generally comprised of white-collar workers
5. The upper-lower class, comprised of those we tend to think of as blue-collar workers
6. The lower-lower class, including but not limited to the unemployed and recipients of public assistance

Hollingshead's index of social position is based on the assumption that place of residence, occupation of the head of the household, and number of years of education completed are characteristics of class status. Statistical procedures by which realtive weights are assigned to the three factors permit assignment of individuals to one of five strata ranging from Class I, the highest, to Class V, the lowest (1958). This index is commonly used as an indicator of social class position.

Several approaches are used in determining how to place individuals in the social class structure. Some are related to actual inequalities or differences based on criteria such as those suggested by Hollingshead and some are based on subjective perception. In the subjective approach people are asked to place themselves or others on the basis of a number of criteria including perceived power, decision-making authority, and occupation.

Each of these approaches has its limitations and advantages. Centers (1949) suggests that how people rank themselves may be a function of the terminology used (cited in Duberman 1976). When *Fortune* magazine polled a group of Americans and asked whether they considered themselves upper, middle, or lower class, 80% claimed middle-class status. When Centers repeated the study and added a fourth choice—working class—half of the respondents placed themselves in this category. Centers proposed that people did not like the pejorative implications of the term *lower class*. It is interesting that the fact that a substantial number of those who would not be designated as working class by "objective" criteria (white-collar workers) identified themselves as working class. Despite some discrepancy between perceived status and position as it is "objectively" defined, studies designed to assess the relationships between objective factors such as education, income, and the prestige assigned to an occupation point to close relationships. "By obtaining a certain level of education, people qualify for certain occupations and receive a certain income; education is a 'cause' of occupation and income is the 'effect' of that occupation" (Duberman 1976).

The importance of occupation as a determinant of perceived high status is supported in a study in which respondents were asked to rank ninety occupations in relation to the others. Diverse people across the country consistently ranked such occupations as physician, major governmental official, and scientist near the top, teacher, bookkeeper, insurance agent, police officer, and farmer somewhere along the middle, and janitor, sharecropper and garbage collector at or near the bottom (in Duberman 1976).

The extent to which these indicators are applicable to all minority groups has been questioned. Dodson (1981) suggests that the indicators of social class may be different in white and black communities. Hill (1986) reviews efforts to identify and characterize the class structure found among Black Americans. As early as 1899 Du Bois used two schemes, one based on family income and the other on "moral considerations" and life-style. Billingsley (1968) believes that current social class indicators overestimate the number of lower class blacks. Blacks are often underemployed and have more education, training, or skills than their jobs require. The applicability to the Black community of the commonly used classification schemes is frequently questioned.

Social Class Terminology Used Here

We share Centers' view that the term *lower class* has pejorative implications and shall refrain from use of that term except when citing directly from the work of others. The terms *working class* and *under class* will be used to designate members of these groups. For others, the term *middle class* is employed.

Class and Rank

Research on the characteristic types of education and occupation that generate different strata of society makes it clear that the highest ranking is assigned to those who perform the tasks most highly valued by American society. Included are those who manage and own major business enterprises, those who play leadership roles in government and education, those who interpret the law, and those who heal the sick. In some classification schemes Blacks who are in high status occupations are more likely to be considered upper class or middle class than whites in similar positions. This refects the fact that, historically, fewer Blacks have attained the most prestigious occupational niches.

Those who perform menial tasks (or are not employed at all) and those who take rather than give direction at work are held in low esteem. These rankings are a reflection of basic American tenets, emphases on worldliness, on mastery of nature, and on activism. These basic themes, or ways of structuring and ascribing meaning to behaviors, are translated into standards of adequacy and worthiness and are the basis for gratification and security.

This suggests that much of what is subsumed under the term *social class* is essentially about work and money and the values placed on that work by the larger society. These evaluations are internalized and permeate our lives. The condition of work, its security and autonomy, and the range and type of experiences to which that work exposes us seep into the very core and substance of our beings, affecting the way we feel about work and about what we can or cannot buy with the money we earn. If we earn sufficient money to make meaningful choices about the things we buy, this affects our tastes and preferences in furnishings, music, and clothes. It affects our outlook on the larger world, particularly our perceptions of life's opportunities and constraints. And, in the view of many, our perceptions of opportunities and constraints, as these derive from class position, also affect family life, attitudes toward sex, and extent of involvement in the world of politics and voluntary organizations. Our perceptions affect our views of the education our children receive, our marriages and other intimate relationships in which we are involved, and the importance we attach to what is happening in the world beyond our daily existence.

Analysts disagree on the extent to which the class-related nature of behaviors is understood and known to those who engage in them. There are those who stress the importance of class consciousness, particularly among the members of the working class, believing that consciousness will generate confrontation of the system that perpetuates inequalities. There are others who still consider the United States to be a "classless society." However, there is little question that social class differences have a discernible effect (Eitzen 1985).

Nature of Work and Life in the Various Social Classes

The daily work in which people engage is a major feature of life. Work may be characterized as monotonous, repetitive, and devoid of intellectual challenge, or as varied and mentally challenging. Work also varies in regard to the degree of physical exertion required. It differs in the extent of the worker's autonomy and the permitted degree of control of the direction, pacing, and timing. Often, what is done and when is determined by others, by the speed of the assembly line, or by rigid rules to which the worker must adhere if the job is to be retained or the work carried out.

What is the nature of work carried out by the members of the different classes?

The Working Class

At least two segments of the population fall into this group—those in low-paid, semi-skilled, or unskilled occupations, and those like the "Blue Collar Aristocrats," who are unionized and well paid (LeMasters 1975). These include construction workers, truck drivers, carpenters, electricians and others whose work involves many decisions. Automobile workers are well paid and unionized, yet their work tends to be routine, repetitive, and limited in self direction.

For many, the conditions of workaday life tend to produce cultural responses which reflect efforts to cope with adversity. According to Blumberg (1972), many in this class live in a relatively circumscribed world in which work and income limit the opportunities for movement in a variety of social worlds.

Whether the experience is viewed as "narrow" or different from that of the middle class, so often used as a yardstick, becomes a matter of debate. Sennett and Cobb (1972) suggest that for some, particularly urban ethnics, the standards by which they are judged come from a world "in which human capabilities are measured in terms profoundly alien."

Regardless of the language used, a number of motifs become apparent. Binzen (1970), a journalist who looked at the lives of Black and White inner-city workers, concluded that: "They were unimpressed by abstractions. They wanted meat and potatoes basic education. They wanted homework. They wanted prayers and Bible reading. They wanted physical punishment. They wanted all these things because they had never been exposed to any workable alternatives."

Gans' (1962) review of a number of studies of working class life pointed to the tendency of working class people to be concrete and particularistic, to think anecdotally, and to personalize events. There is the general conception that the outside world is not to be trusted. This often extends also to a skepticism about caretakers, a reluctance to visit settlement houses, and a fear of doctors and hospitals. More recent analysis suggests that many in this group lack education and have limited skill (Eitzen 1985). These shortcomings in turn block aspirations to be upwardly mobile.

Nevertheless, some who fall in the upper strata of the working class have considerable autonomy. LeMasters tried to gain some insight into the lives of heavy equipment operators, plumbers, sheet metal workers, electricians, and other skilled construction workers. As a participant observer, he frequented a bar that was a favorite meeting place of white workers in one community. He points out that they are unionized, earn high pay despite modest education, and appreciate the fact that their work is not monotonous. One worker explains: "I see that the auto workers in Detroit want early retirement. I don't blame the poor bastards. I would want to retire at thirty-five if I had to stand in one place and put fenders on all day."

In this group, supervision is loose. For the plumber, a day's work is planned in the morning with the foreman, and there is no further contact with him that day unless there is trouble. A good carpenter would view close supervision as a reflection on his competence. "The men like the freedom to move around the job, also the fact that problems of one kind or another develop almost every day—these 'jams' make them think and reassure them that they are not stupid machines" (LeMaster 1975).

In their attempt to isolate a number of characteristics basic to "those members of the non-agricultural labor force in manual occupations," Miller and Riessman (1972) suggest that this group is subject to internal and external factors that promote instability and insecurity. Related to this is an emphasis on getting by rather than getting ahead. These workers, despite high pay and union protection, are particularly subject to layoff and to the vagaries of the economic situation. Sick leave and disability provision in union contracts do not allay the fear of layoffs or the fear that benefits will be exhausted. The recent retrenchment in the automobile industry and other sectors of manufacturing attest to the fact that these are not groundless fears. This sense of insecurity may account for the reluctance of some steel workers to become foremen, for they fear loss of job seniority should layoffs occur. This same stress on security appears related to the emphasis noted earlier on the "basics" in education. These are broad generalizations, which by their very nature fail to capture the complexity and variation in working class life and stance.

Regardless of these variations, consistencies emerge. There are distinctions in outlook, educational aspirations, consumption patterns, and residential locations. Past analysis, e.g., (LeMasters 1975; Gans 1962) suggest that there is a distinct and independent working class subculture. Eitzen (1985) supports this notion, pointing to the differences between this group and the middle class in matters of education and aspiration.

The Underclass

There are substantial differences between life in the underclass and life in the working class. These differences relate to the way life is lived and to the way in which society perceives people in these two strata.

Eitzen, using the term *lower-lower* class, suggests that this group includes unskilled laborers who have less than an eighth grade education, the chronically unemployed, and the bulk of people who receive public assistance. They are the people "on the other side of the tracks" who by many are viewed as "lazy, shiftless, dependent, and immoral— traits exactly opposite 'good middle-class virtues'" (1985, p. 258).

Those who are employed do menial work. In our society that work provides the least financial remuneration and low status. Garbage men, domestics, factory workers, janitors, and street sweepers all provide essential services; as they describe their work a picture of drudgery, physical exertion, routine, and fatigue emerges (Terkel 1974). Some employers pay little attention to safety codes or the environment. Those in the underclass who work have limited capacity to define the conditions of their work. There is no dignity, only monotony, heavy labor, and a lack of respect.

Most recently, the term *underclass* has come to have another disturbing set of meanings. The public media, (e.g., Lemann 1986) point to the emergence of a Black underclass, concentrated in the ghettos, in which there is " . . . a way of life . . . utterly different from that in the American mainstream" (1986, p. 32). In Lemann's view a number of features are associated with this phenomenon. These include the rise in the number of female-headed families, unemployment, and high crime rates.

Sixty percent of Black babies are now born out of wedlock. Black unemployment is three times as high as white unemployment, and the crime rate has soared. The historical and contemporary bases for these phenomena are subjects of ongoing debate. Some view the phenomena to have an economic base while others ascribe cultural causes. Proposals vary for reducing the numbers who find themselves rooted in a cycle of poverty and despair from which few escape. Some blame the welfare system, that presumably fosters dependency. Consequently, they propose elimination of major features of that system. Others cite unemployment, and the reduced need for unskilled heavy labor. Those with this view suggest that massive increases in opportunities to participate in the labor force will save the next generation from being caught in the problems described (Lemann 1986).

Needless to say, underclass people suffer disproportionately from the problems with which social work aims to assist. Minorities are overrepresented in this group. Understanding of their needs and dispositions is extremely important for effective practice.

Life in the middle class is the subject that concerns us next.

The Middle Class

What is work like for skilled office workers, teachers, dentists, pharmacists, consultants, and factory owners who constitute the broad middle stratum of the population? In the description of their work, Terkel (1974) reveals that many in middle-class positions enjoy the work they do and have a sense of autonomy as they exercise some control over their work. They are positively evaluated by others. Other middle-class occupations are used as guidelines as they assess the prestige and value of their work. Money is a concern, and the lower down the middle-class ladder they go, the more disappointed they are about the discrepancy between their expectations and what they actually do or earn.

As one tries to capture the relationships between the lives of middle-class people, the work they do, and their perceptions of life, a paradox emerges. On the one hand, it is this group that is generally viewed as the "mainstay of America." In the past, middle-class people typified the American virtues—hard work, diligence, thrift, and independence. These characteristics were believed to be essential for those who wanted to climb the prestige ladder. With the decline of small business and growth of large bureaucratic organizations, "the old middle-class ethic is dying out in reality if not in rhetoric" (Blumberg 1972). These changes in the size and type of organizations in which middle-class people work have generated an emphasis on conformity. Much of this has been highlighted in a number of studies of suburban life, the mecca of the middle class.

These are the people who are eager to get ahead themselves and stress the importance of education for their children. Despite differences of opinion about who constitutes the Black middle class, this class status is highly valued by those Blacks who are designated as middle class. They move readily for jobs, are active in voluntary organizations, and rely heavily on the advice of experts on child rearing and health practices. They are aware of the importance of having credentials in order to obtain desired jobs and have homes in "good" communities.

According to many analysts, the current nature of middle-class work fosters a need to be well liked. The work itself may call for personality traits that facilitate interaction with a variety of people. Blumberg (1972) suggests that much of the work involves "manipulation of persons, not objects." This is true of the farmer who suggests that farming is becoming more management and less labor oriented and the copy editor who guides his staff (Terkel 1974).

The media play on the personal insecurities of the middle class. Television commercials suggest that decaffeinated coffee will minimize tensions and antacids will relieve the results of stress. The need to "look right" is emphasized in a thousand ways in the ads for toothpaste and hair spray and deodorant. With few exceptions, it is the life of the middle class that is portrayed in daily soap operas, in the movies, and in mass circulation magazines. The cars, home furnishings, clothing, and jobs portrayed are for the most part those encompassed by the middle-class vision.

The effort to disentangle the impacts of social class and ethnic group membership persists. There are those who believe that social class serves as the major definer of basic life experiences. Others view racial and ethnic distinctions, and their convergence with economic position, as the major determinants of life within the various strata. The effort to keep these components separate derives from the conviction that both social class and ethnicity make somewhat distinct and definable contributions to the way people live and feel and think. At the same time, the total consequences of life in any of the social classes cannot be fully assessed without consideration of the ethnic reality.

ETHCLASS IN ACTION—THE ETHNIC REALITY

At the beginning of this chapter, we suggested that the intersect of ethnicity and social class, what Gordon has termed *ethclass*, generates identifiable dispositions and behaviors. We characterized these dispositions and the behaviors which flow from them as the *ethnic reality* or *ethclass in action*. Earlier, the discussion focused on how ethnicity and social class are experienced and transmitted and that each has a somewhat distinct and separate effect on the lives we lead. Having examined each separately, we now illustrate how social class and ethnic group membership join to generate the ethnic reality.

Each ethnic group has a unique history with respect to oppression and discrimination, and different emphases and values attached to academic pursuits, to family, to the respective roles of men and women, and to the ways in which religious teachings are translated into dictums for daily living.

In the preceding discussion we have pointed out that the extent to which groups continue to be oppressed and experience discrimination is in an ongoing process of transformation. For example, third and fourth-generation Italian-Americans have "almost caught up" to White Anglo-Saxon Protestants in educational attainment (Alba 1985). No groups are exempt from the impact of the women's movement, which has sought to diminish the sex role distinctions so long a part of much ethnically derived behavior. Economic necessity, rather than ideology, propels many women into the work force. This is often a wrenching experience, adding further to the confusion and challenge accompanying the efforts to adapt to a new land. Many recently arrived Southeast Asians find this to be the case (Conference "Enhancing Asian Family Life," New York, April 25, 1986).

In large measure the traditions transmitted by the family, the special inflection of language, and the foods we eat let us know we're among our own, whether "our own" are those in the middle class or in the lower strata. For the latter the ethnic reality may translate into continuing and persistent discrimination in jobs, housing, poor schooling, and negative reception by the work place and by welfare institutions. All too often, those very aspects of heritage that have sustained and are part of a proud tradition do not serve their members well in segments of the society that do not value that heritage.

Many of those who have achieved the material goals so highly regarded in this country are frequently reminded of the oppression that still plagues their kindred and of their identification with the group. Some in the lower strata are isolated, whether that isolation is imposed by the larger society or sustained by language barriers. Many people do not become acculturated in the terms earlier defined. This is a frequent experience of American Indians when they leave their own communities. Retention of valued cultural traits focused on time and on the unity of person and land are at odds with "Anglo" values.

Language barriers, strong adherence to culturally based norms, and low class status often interact to minimize acculturation. Chicano men are usually extremely proud and consider their roles as leaders of and providers for their families crucial. Faced with unemployment and a threat to their position, some leave the family rather than face daily shame.

How the ethnic reality affects the behavior of many in the middle strata is illustrated by the following examples. A Black writer describes a social gathering of well-to-do Blacks:

> We were the blacks who warmed the hearts of enthusiasts for the American way of life. For each of us had more than one academic degree. And since our median family income was $25,000 or more, we had, as a group, shown the most impressive jump in black earning power . . .
>
> But in spite of our good fortune, it could not be said that we were happy, for something always moved among us that was closer to pain than joy. For we had embraced with a vengeance the values of middle class America. And yet all of our travails and sweat had simply led us to a place where we were among the most isolated urban people on earth. Most of us worked for middle-class whites, entertained them in our homes, and made tentative stabs at bonhomie with them. But while we sometimes called them "friends," so great was the pervasiveness of American racism that they would never become "family." We were left, then, in a plural society, with only the fellowship and succor of others like ourselves—black men and women who had paid a great price for their comfort. And the proportion of blacks who were pushing their way closer to the economic shelf on which we found ourselves was growing smaller every year . . . But more bothersome was the fact that every year we watched ourselves grow more and more alienated from the brothers and sisters who had not been able to use their energies and education to jump over the obvious barriers when they came down (Coombs 1978 p. 32).[5]

Brashler (1978) does not share Coombs' view. "Put simply, blacks who've made it, who have it, are saying today that they have more in common than ever before with their white counterparts—and sometimes more in common with them than with their black street brothers."

---

[5]From "The Black Middle Class: Style Without the Substance of Power" by O. Coombs, 1978, *Black Enterprise* (December), p. 32. Copyright 1978, the Earl G. Graves Publishing Co., Inc., 295 Madison Avenue, N.Y. 10017. All rights reserved.

Yet Brashler, too, casts doubt on his own contention when he recounts the reaction of Rachel, 22-year-old Black ad agency receptionist, well dressed and living comfortably. She spots two young Black men on the verge of "pulling a knife" on a man on a train station platform. "Rachel . . . can spot their thing in a second, knows for certain what's in the pockets. Rachel moves, strides quickly for them. She yells, 'Get the hell out. You're just continuing the stereotype.'" She is middle class, as defined by the work she does, by her income and purchasing power, and by the life-style that accompanies her job, but she is also Black. And out of that aspect of her identity she prevents a piece of socially destructive behavior, not only because she intrinsically abhors the act, but because that act furthers a negative image of her people. Her efforts to struggle against that image derive not her class position but from a sense of identity with her Black heritage, a crucial component of her ethnic reality. Current concern about the persistence and growth of the Black underclass is surely of concern to women like her. Lemann (1986) suggests that even the most advantaged Blacks feel isolated from the mainstream.

Members of different ethnic groups with a history of poverty and discrimination move into certain segments of the middle class at varying rates and paces. When the number from a particular group who do make this move is relatively small, those people keenly feel the lack of opportunity to interact with others who have shared a similar experience. The number of minority group university professors and writers in the United States is still small. Given this, those people who have moved into the middle class have limited opportunity to interact with others who share their occupational aspirations, work experience, and their particular traditions and values. There has been much concern about the relative decline in the numbers of young Black people who enter and remain in college. In some universities the number of tenured or other Black faculty is very small. And so, in the view of some, the role models and commonality of experiences that might sustain the students' efforts to stay in school are gone.

Although many third and fourth generation Italians are rapidly "making it" occupationally and educationally, our informal contacts suggest that tensions between the old and the new are still present. One Italian academic reflects the tension between certain ethnic traditions and what he perceives to be class and occupationally related orientations. "These are two things that are totally important to me . . . In ethnic terms, I'm very much an Italian man in terms of my family. But unlike the old notion of the Italian, I'm also a careerist. There's a constant tension between the two" (Stone 1978). Ethnic reality for some

Italian-Americans still manifests itself in the struggle to straddle two worlds. The notion of the "dual perspective" helps to understand some of the strain. Norton (1978) suggests that the individual is always a part of two systems: (1) the system of the dominant society and (2) the smaller system of the client's immediate physical and social environment. The dual perspective "is the conscious and systematic process of perceiving, understanding and comparing simultaneously the values, attitudes, and behavior of the larger societal system with those of the . . . immediate family and community system" (1978, p. 3). Implicit is the notion that there is a strain or tension between the demands and "messages" conveyed by the two systems.

Not all groups experience these same strains. For many Jews, the gap between life in the working class and the move to the middle class was less problematic. "It's very funny . . . If you were Jewish and working class, people said, 'Oh, well, Jews are into books.' But if you're Italian and working class then it's, 'How did it happen?'" (Stone 1978). This perception of smooth transition is not shared by all Jews. The elderly Jewish poor often feel abandoned by young, liberal Jewish intellectuals who put their energies into efforts to raise the status of other minority groups. Some of these same intellectuals feel that their liberal politics are an outgrowth of the Jewish tradition that obliged one to work with the oppressed (Cowan 1974). Their ethnic reality forces them to confront the fact that some of their own continue to be oppressed.

As we have seen, the sense of ethclass as it has been defined is readily articulated. The nature of work and ethnic heritage do indeed result in persistent and discernible differences in the lives of people of the same social class level who have different ethnic backgrounds. The ethnic reality is perceived and experienced differently by various Asian Americans. Firuto (1986) vividly describes how succeeding generations of Japanese-American women adopt a more egalitarian role in the family and society. Some Asian Americans whose members have experienced extraordinary success in many areas of occupation and education worry about being designated as the "model minority" (Conference "Enhancing Asian Family Life," New York, 1986). For when all is said and done, given characteristic physical distinctiveness, the threat of racism is ever present. This distinguishes members of this group from other highly successful ethnic groups. Yet each experiences a different kind of history and sense of oppression. For many Jews the memory of the Holocaust is never far from the surface. Polish intellectuals cringe at the "Polish joke." Even the most assimilated Italian-Americans cannot avoid the fact that many associate organized crime with their ethnic group.

We have suggested that those who do not speak the mainstream language are tied to their own ethnic groups in ways that provide succor at the same time that they encounter society with myriad handicaps. These are often derived from low occupational status, which narrow the range of options and available experiences.

Similar barriers are faced by those with strong commitments to powerful and meaningful cultural values that are not understood or appreciated, and that indeed are maligned, by the larger society. Among these are many underclass Puerto Ricans, Chicanos, and American Indians. Puerto Ricans have relatively low economic and social status when compared to that of other Hispanic groups. Some efforts to understand the basis of this lag point to a number of possible factors. These include the fact that many Puerto Ricans maintain a continuing relationship with Puerto Rico that results in less than a full commitment to life here. Related are damage to the family support structure, and a crisis of identity (*New York Times*, June 5, 1986, B1). A somewhat similar situation pertains to Mexican-Americans (Muller and Espenshade 1985). There is much in the cultures of the various American Indian groups that is different from "Anglo," or western culture. The sense of unity with nature and differences in the perceptions of time can serve to reinforce oppression and minimize communication.

There are others whose position within the mainstream is much more firmly established. They are "behaviorally assimilated" in that they speak the language, are more solidly ensconced in the work place, and have a greater range of experience with and exposure to the larger society's values and goals. However, the work they do is viewed as marginal by much of the society, and as they struggle with the reality of that work—its hazards and insecurities—they are approached by various institutions as "lesser beings." The blue collar workers of varying ethnic backgrounds are in this group, as are those who, though white collar by designation, are constantly struggling. Among these are the Irish, Italian, Polish, Hungarian, many Asian blue collar or white collar workers, and many of the Jewish elderly. They have a proud history and ethnic heritage on which they draw for sustenance as they deal with the work place, their family lives, and the schools.

There are the Black workers who have major ambitions for their children and a persistent experience with negative evaluation by the larger society. They struggle to attain the goods and services and recognition that this society continues to withhold to some degree, at the same time as the barriers are breaking down.

And then there are those who "have made it" when American success goals are used as a yardstick—the Black and Asian academicians and business people, the Italian writers, and the Jewish intellectuals. Their work entails autonomy and relative economic security and yields prestige.

As individual members of these groups send their children to school, become ill, encounter marital difficulties, and generally live their lives, they bring with them a unique ethnic and class tradition, as well as a personal history within that tradition. As they confront "helpers" or "caretakers" they expect, whether or not they articulate that expectation, that these aspects of their being, what we have called the ethnic reality, will be understood, despite the fact that many may be unaware that some of their strengths and tensions are related to this aspect of their lives.

Those charged with the responsibility of educating and helping have the obligation to be sensitive to the ethnic reality. Examination of these phenomena must become part and parcel of human service practice.

SUMMARY

Social class and ethnic group membership exert profound influences on life-style and life chances. The point at which they intersect has been characterized as ethclass. The differences at each intersection are man-ifested in many ways and include basic dispositions on matters such as child rearing, sexuality, and the roles of men and women. These dispositions and the behaviors which flow from them are defined as the ethnic reality or ethclass in action. Ethnicity and the ethnic reality are transmitted by mechanisms both internal and external to various groups. Values are embedded in individual and group life and, like culture, become part of the routine of daily life.

REFERENCES

Adams, Bert N. 1975. *The family: a sociological interpretation.* Chicago: Rand McNally College Publishing Co.

Alba, Richard D. 1985. *Italian-Americans: Into the twilight of ethnicity.* Englewood Cliffs, NJ: Prentice-Hall, Inc.

Billingsley, Andrew. 1968. *Black families in white America.* Englewood Cliffs, NJ: Prentice-Hall, Inc.

Binzen, Peter. 1970. *White town U.S.A.* New York: Vintage Books.

Blumberg, Paul. 1972. *The impact of social class.* New York: Thomas Y. Crowell.

Brashler, William. 1978. The black middle class: making it. *The New York Times Magazine* 34:138–157.

Brown, Claude. 1972. The language of soul. In *Rappin and stylin' out,* edited by Thomas Kochman. Chicago: University of Chicago Press.

Coombs, Orde. 1978. The black middle class: style wihout the substance of power. *Black Enterprise* 9:32.

Cooper, Paulette, ed. 1972. *Growing up Puerto Rican.* New York: New American Library.

Council on Social Work Education. 1965. *Casebook on cultural factors in social casework.* New York: The Council.

Cowan, Paul. 1974. Jews without money: revisited. In *Poor Jews: an American awakening,* edited by Naomi Levine and Marvin Hochbaum. New Brunswick, NJ: Transaction Books.

Dodson, Joalynne. 1981. Conceptualization of Black families. In *Black families,* edited by Harriette P. McAdoo. Beverly Hills: Sage Publications.

Duberman, Lucile. 1976. *Social inequality: class and caste in America.* New York: J. B. Lippincott Co.

Eitzen, Stanley D. 1985. *In conflict and order: understanding society.* 3d Ed. Boston: Allyn and Bacon, Inc.

Faris, Robert E. L. 1964. Assimilation. In *A dictionary of the social sciences,* edited by Julius Gould and William L. Kolb. New York: Free Press of Glencoe.

Furutu, Sharlene, B.C.S. 1986. Multi-generational profiles of Japanese-American women: implications for social work education and practice. Paper presented at the Annual Program Meeting, Council on Social Work Education, Miami, Florida, March.

Gans, Herbert. 1962. *The urban villagers.* New York: The Free Press.

Glazer, Nathan, and Moynihan, Patrick. 1963. *Beyond the melting pot.* Cambridge: Harvard University Press.

Gordon, Milton M. 1964. *Assimilation in American life.* New York: Oxford University Press.

Gordon, Milton M. 1973. *Human nature, class, and ethnicity.* New York: Oxford University Press.

Greeley, Andrew M. 1974. *Ethnicity in the United States.* New York: John Wiley and Sons, Inc.

Herman, Simon N. 1977. *Jewish identity.* Beverly Hills: Sage Publications.

Herz, Fredda M., and Rosen, Elliot J. 1982. Jewish families. In *Ethnicity and Family Therapy,* edited by Monica McGoldrick, John K. Pearce, and Joseph Giordano. New York: The Guilford Press.

Hill, Robert B. 1986. The Black middle class: past, present, and future. In *The state of Black America,* edited by James D. Williams. New York: National Urban League, Inc.

Hodges, Harold M., Jr. 1964. *Social stratification.* Cambridge: Schenkman.

Hollingshead, August B., and Redlich, Fredrick C. 1958. *Social class and mental illness: a community study.* New York: John Wiley and Sons, Inc.

Hopps, June G. 1982. Oppression based on color. *Social Work* 27:3–5.

Hopps, June G. 1983. Minorities: people of color. *1983–84 Supplement to the encyclopedia of social work.* 17th Ed. Silver Spring, MD: National Association of Social Workers.

Hraba, Joseph. 1979. *American ethnicity.* Itasca, IL: F. E. Peacock Publishers, Inc.

Jenkins, Sidney B. 1969. The impact of Black identity crisis on community psychiatry. *Journal of the National Medical Association* 61:422–427.

Johnson, Colleen Leahy. 1985. *Growing up and growing old in Italian-American families.* New Brunswick, NJ: Rutgers University Press.

Keesing, Felix M. 1964. Acculturation. In *A Dictionary of the social sciences.* New York: The Macmillan Co.

Kluchkhon, Clyde. 1964. Culture. In *A Dictionary of the social sciences*. New York: The Macmillan Co.

Krause, Corinne Azen. 1978. *Grandmothers, mothers, and daughters: an oral history study of ethnicity, mental health, and continuity of three generations of Jewish, Italian, and Slavic-American women*. New York: The Institute on Pluralism and Group Identity of the American Jewish Committee.

Lemann, Nicholas. 1986. The origins of the underclass, Part I. *The Atlantic* 257: 31–61, and Part II. *The Atlantic* 258: 54–68.

LeMasters, E. E. 1975. *Blue Collar aristocrats—life-styles at a working class tavern*. Madison: University of Wisconsin Press.

Longres, John F. 1982. Minority groups: an interest-group perspective. *Social Work* 27: 7–14.

Lum, Doman. 1986. *Social work practice and people of color: a process-stage approach*. Monterey, CA: Brooks/Cole Publishing Co.

Miller, S. M. and Riessman, Frank. 1972. The working class subculture: a new view. In *The impact of social class*, edited by Paul Blumberg. New York: Thomas Y. Crowell.

Mohr, Nicholasa. 1974. *Nilda*. New York: Bantam Books.

Mostwin, Danuta. 1973. In search of ethnic identity. *Social Casework* 53: 307–316.

Muller, Thomas, and Espenshade. 1985. *The fourth wave: California's newest immigrants*. Washington, DC: The Urban Institute Press.

Norton, Dolores G. 1978. *The dual perspective*. New York: Council on Social Work Education.

Rogler, Lloyd H., and Cooney, Rosemary S. 1984. *Puerto Rican families in New York City: intergenerational processes*. Maplewood, NJ: Waterfront Press.

Scanzoni, John H. 1971. *The Black family in modern society*. Boston: Allyn and Bacon.

Sennett, Richard, and Cobb, Jonathan. 1972. *The hidden injuries of class*. New York: Alfred E. Knopf.

Shibutani, Tamotsu, and Kwan, Kian M. 1965. *Ethnic stratification*. New York: The Macmillan Co.

Silberman, Charles E. 1985. *A certain people: American Jews and their lives today*. New York: Summit Books.

Sotomayor, Marta. 1971. Mexican-American interaction with social systems. *Social Casework* 52: 316–322.

Stone, Elizabeth. 1978. It's still hard to grow up Italian. *The New York Times Magazine* 42: 87–104.

Terkel, Studs. 1974. *Working people talk about what they do all day and how they feel about what they do*. New York: Pantheon Books.

Tricarico, Donald. 1984. The "new" Italian-American ethnicity. *The Journal of Ethnic Studies* 12: 75–93.

Valentine, Charles A. 1968. *Culture and poverty: critique and counter proposal*. Chicago: University of Chicago Press.

Warner, W. 1949. *Social class in America*. New York: Harper Books.

Wrong, Dennis. 1959. The functional theory of stratification: some neglected considerations. *American Sociological Review* 24: 772–782.

CHAPTER
2

Ethnicity and the Life Cycle

Universal stages and movements of life are governed by major psychophysiological events such as birth, death, adolescence, and senescence (Gadpaille 1975). Universal movements suggest universal tasks. The ethnic reality suggests that these tasks are perceived and carried out in a variety of ways by diverse ethnic groups. The universal task of adolescence is to move toward adult status. Jewish tradition provides the ritual of bar mitzvah for boys and bas mitzvah for girls to signal movement into adulthood. Italians by tradition permit male adolescents freedom to explore the world, seeking their manhood.

The movement to each psychophysiological stage may entail varying degrees of stress if the expected tasks cannot be fulfilled in ways that meet the standards of the individual or the ethnic group. Jewish adolescents may resist the bar mitzvah or bas mitzvah as they struggle to free themselves from parental and group restraint. Grandparents who view the bar mitzvah as a ceremony only for boys and men may decry the contemporary trend to include girls.

VARIOUS CONCEPTIONS ABOUT THE LIFE CYCLE

The universal movement through life's stages has captured the imagination and attention of many scholars, the most noteworthy being Freud, Erikson, and Piaget.

41

Though their emphases varied, all sought to identify those aspects of the life cycle that represent crucial points of change, the kinds of life experiences during each stage that promote health and well-being, and the social or psychological factors that impede growth and learning. All three have described the parts played by family and society. Most have pointed out that comfortable progression from one stage to the next takes place when the psychological, physiological, and social tasks or events associated with the preceding stage have been completed in a satisfactory manner.

Anthropologists have called our attention to the diverse rituals and meanings associated with movement from one life stage to the next. The extent to which these derive from ingrained beliefs concerning the nature of the universe and person-to-person and person-to-God relationships has often been noted (Van Gennep 1960). Little attention has been paid to the dynamic interplay between life cycle stages and ethnicity, particularly as it occurs in a multiethnic society.

The work of Erik Erikson will be used in this chapter as a base from which to identify the universal stages of development. The tasks and needs of each stage and the ethnic dispositions reflected in the responses to the inevitable changes will be examined. Most important, emphasis will be placed on the potential sources of stress or strength as these relate to the juncture of life stage, particular ethnic disposition, and context of the larger American society.

The stages of the life cycle have been identified in a variety of ways. Some, like Erikson, characterize them in relation to the psychosocial tasks entailed (Erikson 1950). Other theories, particularly those derived from Freudian thought, emphasize the progression through various periods of psychosexual development.

The characterization presented here is descriptive of the stages of life which are in large measure determined by physical growth, change, and ultimate decline. Much activity is guided by and responsive to the physical changes accompanying childhood, adolescence, adulthood, and old age. For example, it is not possible for children to engage in activities beyond the range of those congruent with their physical and cognitive development. It is because of their physically-based helplessness that children everywhere require protection, as they are unable to obtain their own food and such protective shelter and clothing as the elements require. Similarly, menarche and menopause set the boundaries for the childbearing period, and aging inevitably signals some decline in physical faculties. Within these broad limits there is, of course, enormous variability.

In our American society adulthood is a complex stage lasting for several years. The idealization of the nuclear family, the glorification of youth, and the high value placed on autonomy all serve to give a different stamp to the varying periods of adulthood. The early period of childbearing and rearing may be one of excitement and challenge. As children become adolescents and adults there are shifting role expectations. Parental activity once cherished by the child—protecting, nurturing—may be seen as interference. For these and other reasons we divide adulthood into several periods. The first of these is emerging adulthood, a time for mate selection and perhaps marriage, as well as for decisions concerning occupation, which will ultimately determine one's social class. This is followed by adulthood, the middle stage, which requires skills in relationships with mates, nurturing of children to provide them with a sense of ethnic pride and identity, and, most particularly, skills in developing and maintaining a standard of living satisfactory to one's self and family. In the final stage, later adulthood, one is confronted by the physiological changes that signal aging. Children once requiring nurture begin to claim their freedom. Aging parents require more commitment and, upon their death, there is the struggle to grapple with the loss.

Erikson, Freud, and others postulate that each stage of life involves the mastery of a series of psychosexual, psychological, and social tasks. According to Erikson, if a sense of trust is not developed in infancy the ability to relate positively to peers, teachers, and others is impaired. The child denied autonomy may in later years lack the sense of adventure that adds much to the fullness of adulthood.

Freud's delineation of psychosexual stages focuses on stages of development that begin with the gratifications of impulses at the initial oral stage; this gratification continues into the anal stage, when the child becomes able to control the anal sphincter muscles. The phallic stage provides the pleasure of self-stimulation. At each of these pregenital stages the response of adults in the environment will influence the child's ability to respond appropriately at the genital stage and beyond.

Our perspective incorporates these theories and others, with an emphasis on how the tasks are interpreted and defined by various ethnic groups. What message do Slavic children receive from their mothers at the anal stage? Is that message different from the message of an American Indian mother? Focusing then on crucial periods of life as these are bounded by physical growth and change, we identify the following universal stages of the life cycle and accompanying tasks.

I. Entry
   TASKS: Surviving
           Establishing trust

II. Childhood
   TASKS: Developing physical skills
           Acquiring language
           Acquiring cognitive skills
           Acquiring moral judgment
           Acquiring awareness of self
           Acquiring awareness of sex role arrangement
           Moving out of home into peer group, into school

III. Adolescence
   TASKS: Coping with physical aspects of puberty
           Coping with psychological aspects of puberty
           Coping with sexual awareness/feelings
           Developing relationships with peers of both sexes
           Seeking to achieve increasing independence from parents
           Developing skills required for independent living

IV. Emerging adulthood
   TASKS: Deciding about:
                   Relationships, getting married
                   Occupation, career
                   Sexual behavior
           Developing standards of moral/ethical behavior
           Locating and identifying with congenial social group
           Developing competence in political/economic area

V. Adulthood
   TASKS: Relating to:
                   Same sex peers
                   Heterosexual peers
                   Spouse/Companion
           Establishing:
                   An occupation or career
                   A home
           Bearing and nurturing children
           Developing and maintaining a standard of living
           Transmitting sense of peoplehood and the ethnic reality

VI. Later adulthood
   TASKS: Adapting to:
                   Physiological changes
                   Emancipation of children
           Maintaining relationships with aging parents
           Coping with loss of aging parents

VII. Old age
  TASKS: Combating failing health
            Coping with diminishing work role
            Passing on wisdom, the ethnic reality

The perceptions of people and how they move within these stages are subject to enormous variability. Whether children are viewed as small replicas of adults or as emerging human beings, are coddled and pampered or treated matter-of-factly, is often a matter of cultural and class perception. The view of adolescence as the period of preparation for the tasks of adulthood as opposed to one that sees adolescence as the beginning of adulthood is a matter of historical and group perspective.

The discussion that follows develops each stage in greater detail with particular emphasis upon the ethnic reality.

ENTRY

In all societies and at all times the task at birth is to survive the trauma of birth. The neonate is imperfect. Indeed, it may be a disappointment to its parents in regard to sex. Its physical appearance reminds one of an aging being rather than a new arrival. Hair, skin, eyes, and skull formation give little indication of what its appearance will be as the newborn grows. Preferring its former home, the infant sleeps about twenty hours a day (Lidz 1976).

Having accomplished birth, the infant must rely on those in the surroundings to supply the basic survival needs, which are experienced as the discomforts of thirst and hunger. These discomforts are vague, diffused, and relieved by others. The process of becoming "hooked on being human"[1] has begun, for the centrality of other beings is conveyed by the fact that relief from discomfort comes only through them. At the same time, the manner in which infants are touched, fondled, and fed says much to them about the emotions of adults: Is the infant wanted or merely tolerated? Was the arrival a joy, a disaster, or an event to be neither celebrated nor negated?

The successful experiencing of trust will depend upon the manner in which early needs are met by individuals and the group into which the child has been cast. If adults have insufficient food and lack emotional support needed to cope with the dependent new being, comfort and warmth may be difficult for the child to obtain.

Social class position determines the ability of a parent to supply the concrete needs for nurturance. A prosperous Polish merchant whose

---

[1]Phrase used by Professor Bredemeier, Rutgers University, course on "Sociological Theory," circa 1964.

shop provides specialty food items in an affluent suburb has ample ability to provide for his infant son. His income is more than sufficient to enable the child to develop in the environment, by virtue of the abundance of goods available through his father's middle-class status. The Polish clerk who checks out and bags groceries in the large supermarket chain is faceless to the many harried shoppers. His job provides a meager income that must be stretched to provide his infant son with the bare necessities. Yet each child has the potential of receiving nurture that comes from the soothing sounds of caretakers, the stroking of skin, or the embrace that dispels discomfort (Winch 1971).

When the media blare out news of the abandonment or killing of a newborn, the inability of the involved individuals to nurture, to welcome, and to guide is highlighted. The fact that such events are newsworthy points to the fact that most groups and individuals celebrate new life and expect new parents to preserve it.

At the celebration of baptism the Chicano child becomes a member of the church. At the same time, "campadres" of the parents present themselves as caretakers, assuming responsibility with the parents for continuity in the faith as well as in the group. The giving of gifts celebrates entry and rituals symbolize its importance. Hispanic and European female infants are "marked" by the ceremony of ear piercing. This act identifies them as female, one of the group, and in need of protection. The "marking" of a Jewish male infant through circumcision is a "sign of union," a permanent mark that incorporates him into the social group. At the time of celebration parents are informed of the community expectations for their son. The parents in turn publicly reaffirm their commitment to meet these expectations. There are the themes of joy and pride on the birth of the child (Eilberg 1984). The gifts given on each of these occasions will follow ethnic tradition. They spell acceptance and ethnic continuity.

The preparation for birth and manner of entry into the group derives in large measure from the ethnic reality. The manner of birth relates to a group's beliefs about the nature of the social order, their economic security, and the esteem held for children. Early on, then, the child's life course and sources of strength, weakness, and struggle are evident in the nature of the preparation for and management of the event of birth.

The activities of women during pregnancy are often designed to protect the child from real or perceived danger while in the womb in the belief that adverse behavior may mark the fetus in some way. In some instances these beliefs and the surrounding rituals are powerful, serve a psychologically reassuring function, and in no way put mother or unborn child at risk. For example, some Black women avoid eating strawberries while pregnant, fearing that the child may be born with a strawberry-shaped birthmark on the abdomen. Other women are careful about certain aspects of posture, believing that if they fold their arms around their abdomens or cross their legs they may cause the umbilical cord to wrap around the baby's neck and cause it to choke.

Other ingrained beliefs and fears may lead to action that puts mother and baby at risk. There are Navajo women who believe that both mother and child are vulnerable to the influences of witchcraft and, therefore, keep the news of the pregnancy from even the husband until it is observable (Brownlee 1978). Wariness of witchcraft may keep the mother from seeking prenatal care, thus risking preventable problems. The Black woman who rubs her abdomen with dirty dishwater to ensure an easy delivery or others who insert cobwebs and soot mixed with sugar into the vaginal tract to prevent hemorrhage are placing themselves and their unborn children at risk.

There are genetic factors linked to ethnic group membership over which parents have little control. Tay-Sachs disease and sickle cell anemia plague some Jewish and Black families. Although found most often in Black families, sickle cell disease also occurs in other groups, including southern Italians and Sicilians, northern Greeks, and central and southern Indians. The disease is a severe blood disorder in which red blood cells become abnormal in shape, "sickled cells," and cannot carry oxygen normally. The disease is usually severe, debilitating, and often fatal in early childhood (Schild and Black 1984). The Jewish infant affected with Tay-Sachs appears normal at birth. At about six months of age a progressive mental and physical decline begins that leads to death in early childhood. Carriers of both diseases, the parents, are usually healthy and show no signs of the disease, yet their children are at risk due to their ethnic heritage.

For children the major task at entry is to learn to survive in an alien world. The trust that comes from warmth and comfort may be difficult to attain for those who are in ethnic minority groups at lower income levels. Social class and ethnicity in these instances deny parents access to the various resources which would guarantee the child a joyful entry.

CHILDHOOD

Childhood is the beginning of the life cycle. Each child is a "new recruit" into the ethnic reality, where the universally assigned tasks will be perceived and carried out in specific ways common to each ethnic group

(Koller and Ritchie 1978). The achievement of these tasks may be termed "socialization," for through this process the child becomes an accepted member of the group, the family, the neighborhood, and the larger society. Parents, primarily mothers, are assigned the role of culture bearers and respond to the assignment in various ways that influence the child's development at this early stage.

West Indian mothers, like Italian mothers, assume a major responsibility for nurture in child rearing. Discipline, however, is important, with spankings a primary form of punishment. These may be accompanied by scolding or "tongue lashing." Respect for elders is required. They are the people whose life experiences guarantee that they know what is best for children (Brice 1982). Fathers are not without influence and, with the mothers, they carry responsibility for continuation of the cultural ethos.

There are differences among ethnic groups in relation to the degree and direction in the amount of control that is appropriate in child rearing. A Cherokee father reflects, "I have been given a child, a life to direct. I will remain in the background and give direction. To yell at the child places the child in an embarrassing position. I am not an authority."[2] In such an instance the behavior of children is not required to be submissive to the adult.

There are other American Indian parents who are more anxious about their children than the Cherokee father. Abraham, Christopherson, and Kuehl (1984) suggest that the Navajo Indian mothers and fathers whom they studied tended to worry that their children could not care for themselves or that something might happen to them. This concern and tending toward protectiveness may well stem from the pervasiveness of the Navajo belief in the power of the supernatural to work evil upon them. Children's universal tendencies toward exploration, testing the world, and searching for autonomy render them vulnerable and, therefore, in greater need of parental protection.

For some Italian parents child rearing also demands continual vigilance, given their belief in the fallibility of human nature, particularly evident in children. Many feel there is a potential for evil; parents must prevent its expression in neglect of family, disrespect, or sexual misbehavior by females. Children, male and female, must be taught to conform to family expectations (Johnson 1985).

The role of the Italian father, so clearly defined in the past, has begun to change. Still holding an elevated position regarding the degree of power to make decisions in family matters, he is less likely to have the

---

[2]Conversation with Ronald Lewis, D.S.W.

degree of power suggested by Gambino (1974). There is a dilution of his authority as he participates more in the child rearing activity of the home. Yet there is an expectation that he *should* be the authority figure as the mother assumes responsibility for the emotional well-being of the family (Johnson 1985).

The authority vested in the Chinese father serves to provide an emotional distance between him and his children, leaving child rearing responsibilities to the mother, who decides what is best for their children. Obedience is expected and received (Kitano 1980).

The imposition of parental authority and the contrasting practices of noninterference, protectiveness, and vigilance are examples of ethnic dispositions to which children must learn to respond in appropriate ways; however, the adaptations may entail varying levels of stress.

Stress may become evident in the developmental experience of the Slavic child whose parents' emotional involvement vacillates between the closeness of hugs (which tend to bind and incorporate, suggesting that the child has no will of his own) and the abruptness of being pushed away as the child seeks a separate autonomous existence. The ambivalence is compounded by the need to "be strong." A Slavic mother comments, "You teach children to be strong. . . . Johnnie never had a cold for me. . . . Teach a child to be strong—let life take its course" (Stein 1976, p. 43). While this may be viewed as acceptable within the ethnic reality, the child may be at some disadvantage when coming in contact with those outside of the group who are prepared to respond differently to the needs of children in distress. A visit to the dentist requires strength; no medication for pain is permitted, even though modern dentistry has the ability to reduce pain for almost all patients. Parents may well prohibit the use of anesthetics as they prepare their children for adult responsibility. For some children this may indeed pose a conflict between two worlds; others may internalize this ethnic reality and view the stoic approach to pain as valuable in their search for autonomy.

Japanese mothers assume young children to be independent by nature with a need to be drawn into dependence. Infants are indulged as they mature; persuasion and reasoning are used to assure compliance to the mother's edict. By school age, children know what is expected. Because of their mothers' sacrifice in their behalf they must succeed. Their failure would be their mothers' failure as well. Tension may be seen in Japanese-American families, influenced by the mainstream American society; they are less grateful for parental sacrifices (Nishimoto 1986). The stress of these children may be similar to the stress felt by Slavic children whose parents attempt to hold them.

Almost all families expect that children will assume household tasks related to their ages and abilities. This may be clearly seen in the childhood of Mexican-American youngsters who gain status as family members as they carry out errands, care for younger siblings, and share in the family work for the good of all. The reward from parents is an environment of permissiveness, indulgence, perhaps even spoiling, but less ambivalent than that of the Slovak child, who is responsible for cleanliness of the household and picking up after play without similar rewards. Work, even for children, is seen as an indication of the capacity for good; laziness suggests work of the devil, gaining no rewards.

Sex Roles

Sex-specific experiences and assignments begin early in childhood. The clarity and specificity vary among ethnic groups. Mexican-American and Italian males are taught early that they are men and that this role entails the obligation to protect female siblings, even if they are older (Krause 1978a; Murillo 1976). Girls, in turn, derive some of their female role expectations by virtue of this assured protection. This is reinforced by their learning household and child rearing skills (Gambino 1974). They are expected to care for both male and female younger siblings, clean house, and prepare food, while their older brothers take on those "outside" chores that are carried out by men in this world. Thus, both are prepared for adulthood (Gambino 1974; Krause 1978b). More specific sex-related experiences take place later as childhood merges into adolescence.

Language usually begins to develop between the ages of two and four. If ethnic group membership has provided a multilingual environment, children may become multilingual very comfortably and easily (Gadpaille 1975). But bilingual children often find that their schools reject the language that makes them a "real" people. Mexican-American children in some cases have been forbidden to speak Spanish in the classroom and on the playground. This practice can limit the institution's ability to test and further the development of cognitive skills.

The conflict around language in the school system is most evident in the experiences of Hispanic groups. However, adult first-generation Jews, Slovaks, and Italians may still recall the slur cast on their native languages during their early years in this country. The persistence of Ukrainian, Hungarian, and Greek schools to which children are sent by their parents after regular school hours attests to the ties to the native language and suggests that the positive aspect of bilingualism as a factor in child development bears serious attention.

Indeed, we would go further and suggest that bilingualism is more likely to be viewed as problematic when the language of minority groups is involved. The value of learning a second, more "prestigious," language is evident in the practice of some upper-class families who hire French nannies in order to expose children to a second language early in their lives.

Although the school plays an important part in the experience of childhood, much of life takes place in the home, in the neighborhood, and with extended family. In instances in which roles are clearly assigned and economic circumstances not too harsh, child rearing and tending needs are provided for within the natural ebb and flow of family and community life. In times of change, trauma, or dislocation, tried and true patterns break down and institutional forces come into play.

The ready integration of a Black child into an extended family with a cohesive kinship network provides the child and parents solace and comfort, material support, advice about child rearing, and personnel for child care (Stack 1975).

Child care may be provided by any number of persons in the family or community. This is essential for those families in which the parent or parents are employed. Those with limited means may turn to older siblings or neighborhood children. More competent help is found in more mature persons, grandmothers, or elderly neighborhood women. Ladner (1971) describes these women as good supervisors who feed the children regularly, require that they take naps, and often teach them games, depending upon the caretakers' physical abilities. The mother pays a nominal fee; sometimes there is no fee. Children in their care have the benefit of nurture from two generations.

Parents who go outside of the immediate network for child care may precipitate family emotional crises and pay the price in guilt, as do some Slovaks who move outside family boundaries. "Taking care of our own" and "doing things for ourselves" serve to sustain cohesive family systems. At the same time, the failure to use community resources may deprive children of stimulation, developmental challenges and peer group interaction.

Children have much to do and much to learn. Their socialization is an ongoing process. The positive and negative images developed in childhood, the skills learned, and attitudes internalized are subject to modification based on subsequent life experiences. However, children who have been loved, taught, and given a chance to "test their mettle" without being subjected to extensive familial or societally induced trauma are likely to be successful and integrated human beings, ready for transition to a crucial and perhaps intrinsically dramatic stage, adolescence.

ADOLESCENCE

The move to adolescence or puberty is both physiologically and socially determined. Although it can never readily be said that childhood has ended, there are events that are indicative of impending manhood and womanhood. The onset of menstrual flow, development of pubic hair, and breast growth in girls are in large measure public and visible, as are the growth of facial hair and the voice changes in boys.

The ethnic response to these physiological and anatomical events is diverse. In some societies these events signal the time for assumption of the rights and obligations associated with adult life. In others, they appear to be treated as unwelcome events, for they portend the emergence of sexual capability and sexual arousal in a social milieu never quite prepared to deal comfortably with these realities. Whichever the case, adolescence is a time of continued growth and serious preparation for the responsibilities of adult life. Social puberty is of great concern in our considerations of the ethnic reality, for children move from the asexual world of childhood into a more sexual world in which girls become "ladies" and boys become "men." The expectation for a "lady" may be expressed in this manner: "When I was eleven years old my father came home with a . . . manicure set for me. He told me to keep my nails nice, to sit on the porch, and not to play in the street anymore because it was time for me to be a lady" (Krause 1978a).

Such is the experience of many adolescent females. Although they are given directives to be ladies, much other information necessary for advancing adulthood is often withheld, particularly that which pertains to sexual matters.

As the Puerto Rican female child learns the female role through imitation of her mother she receives much affirmation from the entire family. Gradually she takes on more female responsibility in caring for young siblings, the babies, but there is no talk of sex. She gains knowledge of sex from friends with similarly meager experience and from overheard conversations of adults.

This practice is not limited to the Puerto Rican experience. Talk of sex is taboo among Irish and Italian people as well (Biddle 1976; Krause 1978a). Daughters know little of sexual functioning. The limited information that is given is at best mysterious. The education of our children in matters related to sex and sexuality is an issue that transcends the ethnic reality and in many communities becomes a source of much tension.

The course from asexual childhood to sexual adolescence is universally traumatic. But the ethnic reality imposes greater stress for some. As suggested earlier, the messages adolescents receive may vary and are often unclear. In some urban Black communities there are two messages, one for adolescent males and one for females. The latter message often suggests that the experience of motherhood, despite social immaturity, is essential to becoming a woman (Ladner 1971; Aschenbrenner 1975). Manhood, on the other hand, must be attained before one can be an effective father, in spite of social fatherhood (Aschenbrenner 1975). These conflicting directives have the potential for generating tension in male-female relationships as emerging adulthood approaches.

Black urban mothers may give at least three different sexual messages to their daughters. The first is one of fear and anger. Sexual information is withheld. When questions about men or other sexual concerns are posed, they are pushed aside. Freedom is restricted, and girls must be home before dark. Although girls are warned about the dangers of socializing with boys, the dangers are seldom specified.

Ambivalence is characteristic of the second message. Appearing to support youth, love, and a rich sex life, mothers push their daughters into adulthood. At the same time, they object to behavior that suggests sexual activity, such as time spent at a boy's home when his parents are away.

In the third instance mothers are diligent about presenting daughters with the facts of life. Considerable freedom is allowed with a warning to be aware of girls who are "not nice" (Aschenbrenner 1975).

No matter what the message, the mothers in Aschenbrenner's study had little control over whether or not their daughters became pregnant. There were other social and environmental forces, such as peers, that were probably more important. The reader is reminded here of the power of peer relationships at this stage of the life cycle.

The course from asexual childhood to sexual adolescence is traumatic to some extent for everyone. But the ethnic reality imposes greater stress for some, and, as suggested earlier, the messages adolescents receive are often unclear.

Puerto Ricans have special concerns about girls; brothers as well as fathers have an obligation to protect them. Boys are granted a great deal of freedom, as is the custom in many ethnic groups. They are expected to have sexual experiences before marriage, and at times are even encouraged. These traditional patterns of sexual behavior are changing as families begin to grant girls more freedom. On the other hand, in the light of changing sexual mores and realistic fears of crime and drug addiction parents may become extremely strict and overprotective (Garcia-Preto 1982).

In the informal social groups known as *Palomillas* adolescent boys have the opportunity to gain knowledge and share experiences with other males. Machismo (maleness) is demonstrated and developed, and each boy earns a reputation based upon skill, knowledge, and experience. This "rite of passage" accomplished, the adolescent may move to manhood with prestige in family and community (Murillo 1976).

As sexual boundaries are set, boys may be damaged by straying from traditionalized definition. For example, a boy's straying from the "pure" masculine image into more aesthetic pursuits may cause considerable strain in his relationship with his father.

The young Puerto Rican girl may be startled by the onset of menstruation, but within her family and community she is now "senorita" and her activities are more closely observed by the adults (Padillo 1958). Her brothers, much like their Italian peers, gain greater freedom at this stage of their development, moving into the larger society. But girls are defined by and limited to the traditional functions of the maternal role. However, strict definition of roles may have adverse effects, leading many girls to feel like second-class citizens (Gadpaille 1975).

Adolescents must develop skills for independent living to prepare for emerging adulthood. These skills are taught in educational systems and training programs. All parents are not equally eager for their children to be influenced by these institutions for fear of their influence on family life. An old Sicilian proverb advises, "Don't make your children better than yourself." Some immigrant Italian fathers were of the opinion that too much school made children lazy and opened their minds for unhealthy dreams (Rolle 1980). Jerre Langeone (1978) writes that it was his mother's belief that too much reading would drive a person crazy.

The climate has changed for third- and fourth-generation Italian adolescents. When money is available parents encourage college education for sons and daughters. If resources are scarce a son's education takes precedence over a daughter's. The college selected for either is likely to be near home, a local community or a small Catholic college. The message parents transmit is that a college education is the best way to get ahead today (Johnson 1985).

Another task of adolescence is to move away from the family of origin into the larger society. This is among the most stressful episodes in the life cycle. While the freedom given to male Italians or Mexican-Americans described here is a signal, there is no specific ceremony, no point in time, at which manhood is announced. For the Jewish adolescent, particularly the male, bar mitzvah is a visible moment of transition. The ritual reaches through centuries from the past and holds religious and social significance in the present. It is the proclamation of religious maturity at age thirteen. The expectation is that one becomes bar mitzvah, "a man of duty," responsible for his religious activity for the rest of his life. This rite of passage permits the adult privileges of reading the Torah in public and being counted in the "minyan" required for conducting the sabbath service (Birnbaum 1975). Both transmit the feeling of emerging adulthood. And yet, in the reality of contemporary American society, there is a lack of fit between the Jewish rituals that signal adulthood and the responsibilities and rights assigned to a thirteen-year-old boy.

The situation is even more complex for the Jewish female. While tradition provides a ritual for the male, there is no traditional ceremony for the girl as she enters puberty. Contemporary communities have established the bas mitzvah. This "coming of age rite" provides the opportunity for parents and friends to recognize the developing young woman at a gathering of the clan, highlighted by festivities and gift giving designed to transmit the message, "You are one of us!" (Rosenzweig 1977).

Eilberg (1984), in her consideration of Erikson's perspective on development and Jewish rituals, suggests that the bar mitzvah ritual propels a youth immediately into adulthood. He is not encouraged to rebel or to enter into the turmoil of a search for a separate identity. Adulthood comes immediately as he affirms the value system of the community and of his father. But, the new status may not "take hold" for some time.

A young Jewish man of twenty recalls his bar mitzvah, stating that he realized that real adulthood does not suddenly appear as a result of having taken part in the ritual.[3] Rather, the event proclaims his potential for development into a "man of duty." A dimension not to be ignored is the conflict of "being Jewish." It is difficult to separate clearly the aspects of adolescence and Jewishness, but it is evident that for some a struggle emerges, possibly derived from a societal anti-Semitic attitude. In a hostile world surrounded by hostile persons, religion may become a scapegoat for universal feelings of hostility common among the young. Self-hatred is a phenomenon that cannot be ignored, for it may well continue into later stages of development (Kiel 1967).

The universal tasks of adolescence may be traumatic for some members of any ethnic group. Clashes between adolescents and those in the older generation may be intensified by cultural conflicts, as the young depart from ethnic and cultural traditions. Some ethnic traditions may intensify adolescent turmoil. Nevertheless, a review of several

---

[3]Conversation with Larry Schrager.

studies of adolescent behavior reveals that "turmoil and conflict are not necessarily the hallmark of adolescent development" (King 1972). Adolescents may not suffer from great identity crises or from poor relationships with parents, siblings, and peers. While many have questions and doubts about themselves, most have the competence to handle stress because of their high level of self-esteem. Where ethnically based guidelines and values are clear-cut, these serve to reinforce competence and minimize trauma.

The sense of peoplehood—ethnicity—has provided many Japanese families with the strength to overcome the various onslaughts of their American experience, which included internment at the height of World War II. The emphasis upon ethnic identity has served as a force to develop social conformity. Rewards for good behavior, as well as punishment by shame or guilt for misdeeds, provide elements of social control reinforced by senses of dependency, duty, and responsibility, (Kitano 1974a).

The point midway between childhood and adulthood may be variously defined, yet events occur that change children's bodies, their voices, and their perspectives, suggesting that childhood is waning and a new, more responsible person is developing.

EMERGING ADULTHOOD

Adolescence with or without trauma centers about the search for self within the context of family and community, both having intimate connections to the ethnic reality. As adolescents emerge into adulthood, they direct their energy into wider areas. There is increasing potential for intimacy, emotional commitment, and giving to others. It is the time during which wives and husbands are wooed and won, past relationships deepen or vanish, and emancipation from parents continues (Valliant 1972). It is a time of decision making. Perhaps the question, "Who am I?" arises. Decisions center around mate selection and marriage, employment or career opportunities, ethical behavior, identifying with congenial peers, and participation in the larger political arena.

Mate Selection

While freedom to select one's own marriage partner is the American ideal, parents make decisions to locate their families in certain neighborhoods and to provide recreation for the purpose of having children associate with certain other families, "like us." These decisions may bear fruit as their children approach adulthood. Italian parents may withhold permission for a daughter to date until they know "who he is" and "who his family is." An Italian male is more acceptable and more likely to continue the ethnic tradition (Krause 1978a).

Although Italian males have a great deal of freedom, as previously discussed, there is an expectation of behavior toward women that is respectful and moral. In reviewing his experiences as a young man within the family, an Italian adult recalls the disappointment felt by his father when he realized his son was returning home much after midnight, and suspected that his son was keeping his intended wife, an Italian young woman, out too late. His father's concern was with caring for and respecting the young woman. He was much more comfortable when he learned that the young woman had been home at a respectable hour and that his son had then met and socialized with a group of men until the late hour. The father's regard for women included not only those in his family but those who would become family members.[4]

The mate selection process is often fraught with conflict caused by ethnic group expectations. A majority of young people are urged by their families to seek partners from within their own ethnic groups. However, the young increasingly do not respond to the parental mandate. They find mates outside of the ethnic group. In order to control such behavior states have issued statutes prohibiting interracial marriages between whites and Blacks, Japanese, Chinese, Mongolian, Indian, or Malaysian. These statutes have been overturned by the United States Supreme Court (June 1967). While they may be viewed as racist in nature, they were clear messages about marriage to "people like us" (Cretser and Leon 1982).

In an examination of Chinese interracial marriage, Kitano and Yeung (1982) present a typology of Chinese families and the attitudes of emerging adults toward intermarriage. The traditional immigrant family could be expected to have a low rate of intermarriage due to traditional roles still held by parents and children, language, values, and life-style. A young man's response to questions about intermarriage reflects the position of this type family. "When I ask for a bowl of won ton noodles, she [a wife from another culture] might propose something else. My only choice is a Chinese girl who speaks Cantonese."

The bicultural family, second or third generation from the traditional family, has been exposed to Chinese and American cultures. They are comfortable with acquaintances from either group. The young are not deliberate in seeking a mate from their own group. Selection is based more on opportunity, housing location, and choice of schools. They may

---

[4]Conversation with Frank Becallo, MSW.

have no negative attitudes toward persons who out marry but may not consider doing so themselves.

The modern Chinese-American family, more cosmopolitan and middle-class, may be viewed as more American than Chinese. A higher rate of intermarriage may be expected from this group that speak, think, and write more "American." The reminder of Chinese heritage is in their physical features. A young woman explains, "I would not exclude the idea of eventually marrying a Chinese man but I prefer going out with someone more attractive . . . in public places I would feel more comfortable with someone who is more Americanized than me. The more American [he is] the more I feel accepted." In the latter instance, social class has bearing on the decision to out marry. The higher the social class, the more likelihood of out marriage. Kitano and Yeung (1982) suggest that for the Chinese-American there are correlations among upward mobility, increasing acceptance, and interracial marriage.

Murguia and Cazares (1982) see the same trends in Chicano inter-marriage. They predict an overall slow increase in the rate of Chicano intermarriage as increasing numbers move into the middle class. Porterfield (1982) concludes that, while Black awareness will have some negative effect on the rate of Black-white intermarriage, if there is a decrease, it will be slight and for a short period of time.

Several observations have been made about marrying out among young Jewish adults (Schneider 1984). There is a greater likelihood of marriage to non-Jews if early Jewish experience is limited, with no intensive Jewish education, no experiences in Jewish summer camps, youth movements, or trips to Israel. When Jewish women marry out their husbands are likely to be of equal or similar education, economic level, and social class. Jewish women choose a Black partner more frequently than do Jewish men, who tend to marry non-Jewish women of lower socioeconomic status. As with intermarriage in other ethnic groups, there are social class tendencies.

Intermarriage among the many ethnic groups in America continues. As it increases, there has been a change in societal attitudes with a more general acceptance. Despite this tolerance, ethnic intramarriage remains the statistical norm for the American population (Cretser and Leon 1982). The majority of emerging adults select mates who are "one of us."

The Emerging Woman

Ethnic dispositions relating to the role of woman as caretaker are questioned as women reevaluate that role. This reevaluation, however, may place them at risk of diluting or losing many of the characteristics that made them "feminine" and initially attractive to their ethnic male counterparts. Murillo (1976) cites the example of a Chicano male graduate student greatly concerned about his decision to marry a young Chicano woman. He wishes her to maintain the old ways, which require her to be devoted to her husband and children, serve their needs, support her husband's actions and decisions, and take care of the home. She opposes this and conflict arises. As emerging adults, both are in the process of preparing for a career, but for the Chicano woman this is a relatively new adventure, the more familiar career being that of wife/ mother.

For young Jewish women there is less of a problem. A plan to work continues a tradition established long ago by grandmothers and mothers whose diverse occupations were important to the survival of the family. Jewish tradition more easily accepts employment of women, which brings money into the home. In the present, however, the emerging Jewish woman has a choice. The Jewish value placed on education is traditional, but in the past higher education was more reserved for men. Women now attend college in equal numbers with men, but may experience conflict as they make a career choice. "As a young Jewish woman I am achievement-oriented, committed to individual achievement, accomplishment, and career, but I am equally committed to marriage. What then of my children? If I am to be a responsible mother then I must remain at home with my young children." Such is the ethnic dilemma also shared by young Italian and Slavic women (Krause 1978a).

Young Asian women, Chinese and Japanese, often find that they are more accepted than Asian men into mainstream society. As some gain education and skills in communications they have even held news anchorwomen positions. Through these positions they are in the public eye daily. Asian men, on the other hand, still maintain the servant image (Kitano and Yeung 1982). Chinese and Japanese parents antici- pate that their children will acquire as much education as possible. In order to accomplish this, families will make great sacrifices. Education will endow the family with pride and become a means to the upward mobility anxiously sought (Kitano 1980).

But entry into the work force is often difficult for ethnic minorities. Of particular note are those American Indians who have attended Bureau of Indian Affairs (BIA) boarding schools. Led to believe that they have the competence that comes with a high school diploma, young adults discover that, in fact, their level of achievement is comparable to seventh or eighth grade in public schools. This limitation denies them opportunities needed for self-esteem and movement to adult responsibilities. One response to denied access to the mainstream has been suicide. In many American Indian tribes suicides peak in the twenties or early thirties, the emerging adult years. Unemployment, stress of accultura- tion, involvement with alcohol, "on and off" reservation living have all been suggested as factors related to the high suicide rate (McIntosh and Santos 1981). Byler (1978) adds a consideration of the influence of childhood experiences off the reservation. He describes the social characteristics of an Indian most inclined toward suicide: "He has lived with a number of ineffective or inappropriate parental substitutes because of family disruption. . . . He has spent time in boarding schools and moved from one to another" (1978, p.9). Efforts to "make Indian children white" through education may destroy them before they have a chance at adult status.

Howze (1979) has observed the emerging Black male adult in a poor urban setting and discovered a high suicide rate to be "a primary means of coping with problems." Among those problems is the inability to achieve an important accomplishment in their value system, a good job. Jobs bring status and place an individual and his family in a partic- ular social class. The better the job, the higher the status. Young adults with no job or hopes for a job that will supply the wherewithal to assume adult responsibility seek what appear to us to be irrational solutions.

More recently Chunn (1981) has added another dimension to obser- vations about suicide among young Black males. As Blacks have entered mainstream America, they have adopted middle-class values and, in that transition, have abandoned the traditional support systems such as the nuclear and extended family, the church, and the Black community. The loss has been costly for the young who continue to need such foundations. In desperation they end their lives.

Emancipation through self-support and/or marriage, a reasonable expectation for the emerging adult, may be elusive for those who are members of extended families in which their incomes are essential to the survival of the group. This is vividly expressed by a young woman: "Me and Otis could be married, but they ruined all that. . . . Magnolia knows that it be money getting away from her. I couldn't spend time with her and the kids and giving her the money I do now. I'd have my husband to look after" (Stack 1975, p. 114). Ruby, the narrator, describes the pressures exerted to keep her within the group; this young Black woman is entrapped by the kinship network that has so much potential for ethnic cohesion. She is anxious to move on to full adulthood but constrained by her ethnic reality.

Sexuality

Seldom do ethnic groups prepare their young for adult sexual encounters. Sexuality, a primary aspect of adulthood, remains hidden from male and female children. Information about menstruation, sexual intercourse, conception, and childbirth is often withheld or is related in vague terms by adults. Lack of preparation for menarche leaves many young women startled by the event. Krause reports that a significant number of women in her study of Jewish, Italian, and Slavic women, were totally unprepared for menstruation and so were frightened, distressed, surprised, or believed themselves to be injured. Most unprepared were Italian women, who are beset by strong taboos against discussion or exchange of information about anatomy and physiology (Krause 1978a). Although we expect menarche to occur during adolescence, lack of earlier information about it influences behavior or responses in early adulthood. Preparation for parenthood and marriage is lacking in most ethnic groups. There are few guidelines provided for new parents, and so, like their parents, young adults stumble into adulthood "ready or not" (Hill 1974).

In the Puerto Rican life cycle it is clear that, "ready or not," a child moves directly into adulthood by virtue of physically mothering or fathering a child. This circumstance confers adult status, and one is expected to assume adult roles and behavior, which may mean dropping out of school to take on employment (Hidalgo 1974).

Political Competence

We have suggested that, in order to have the competence to move to adulthood all young persons need to accomplish several universal tasks. There are those ethnic characteristics that give them assistance and support in mate selection, career choice, development of ethical behavior, and finding of congenial friends. At the same time, there are those ethnic forces that deter movement, as well as mainstream forces that deter accomplishment. Some of these forces also deny competence for political involvement; thus many, particularly those of minority status, are accused of noninvolvement.

It is the young nonregistered, nonvoting Hispanics that reduce overall Hispanic voting and, thus, the impact of the total Hispanic vote. Their general feelings of apathy and alienation in relation to a variety of political incidents keep them from the polls (Tostado 1985). However, young Puerto Ricans who are able to take on a variety of tasks within their communities do emerge. Because of these experiences they are able to hold responsible leadership positions (Westfried 1981). In 1983 many young Black adults were enthusiastic campaigners for Chicago's first Black mayor, Harold Washington (Clark 1984).

While some emerging adults still stand on the sidelines, others are challenging the mainstream through greater political participation. They intend to move confidently into adulthood ready for the tasks of *generativity*.

ADULTHOOD

Generativity, an aspect of adulthood suggested by Erikson, is primarily concerned with establishing and guiding the next generation; it is a time of productivity and creativity (Erikson 1950). It is the longest stage in the life cycle, during which individuals assume responsibility for the care of others, primarily through the role of parent, but also in varying career and political experiences.

Children move from entry to adolescence and emerge into adulthood under the supervision of adults. Imparting a sense of ethnicity is a task that is accomplished, for the most part, unconsciously. But in this process children receive a sense of belonging to a special group that has special food, a language of its own, exciting holidays, and celebrations with family and friends; usually there is devotion to a particular religion. For Thomas Napierkowski, recollections of an ethnic childhood include a father aware of discrimination against Polish-Americans, who remained proud of his Polish-American identity and openly contemptuous of the "cowardice" of Poles who anglicized their last names. As an adult Thomas Napierkowski has the Polish heritage transmitted by his father. He feels a conscious need to help his children to grow up to be Polish-Americans. This means that he is their protector when their names are garbled, when they are called "Polack," or are victims of the insensitive Polish joke, an experience that brings a tightness to his chest (Napierkowski 1976). To be the bearer of ethnicity is not always a pleasant task. The Polish experience is paralleled by that of Italians, who recoil from the term "dago" or "wop," Puerto Ricas from "spick," Asians from "Chink" or "Jap," or Blacks from the viciousness of "nigger." As one assumes the role of adult protector and feels increasing pride in this achievement, one may realize that the ethnic heritage held so dearly is viewed by others as a joke.

Other adult Polish-Americans speak of a childhood in which aspects of Polish heritage were set aside in order to become American, for example, the Polish language was not spoken and English was used daily. To speak Polish would be to call attention to the fact of Polish descent, which may serve as a barrier to upward mobility (Wrobel 1973).

The purpose of this conscious denial of ethnicity is to protect children from the experiences of discrimination. Adults, in their own ways, function as protectors of their young from the hidden injuries of ethnicity.

Color, the banner of ethnicity for Blacks, identifies them immediately. Parents again become the protectors as well as the bearers of ethnicity. In moving their children toward an ethnic awareness they enable them to understand that their black skin is not just wrapping paper around them but a part of them, that their hair, though kinky, is not "bad," and that they are Yourba's children (Harrison-Ross 1973). An extreme example of parental failure may be seen in Pecola Breedlove, a central figure in Toni Morrison's novel, *The Bluest Eye* (1972). Pecola wishes for "blue eyes, prettier than the sky, prettier than Alice-and-Jerry-storybook eyes." Such a wish cannot be fulfilled. Unprotected by her parents, she becomes unable to cope with life. Most Black parents understand and do protect their young, knowing that they will not acquire blue eyes. With their parents, children will not suffer from the effects of racism that calls their skin color, hair texture, and lack of blue eyes into question. Such racism is manifested in harassment from the mainstream society.

In addition to protection, there are the tasks of nurture of the young through the provision of basic needs of food, clothing, and shelter. These are provided through the income received from activity in the work place. The job or jobs and the level of income will determine the social class of the family.

Middle-aged, middle-class Blacks have spent time in adolescence and emerging adulthood investing in an education that has moved them to this social class. Both men and women have made this investment, despite institutional racism. As adults they marry and together gain a social status that gives them the ability to provide their children with opportunities they missed in childhood. These may include music lessons, recreational activities, and perhaps private schools.

The vigor with which these parents have taken on the tasks of generativity has presented them with a dilemma. They have discovered that with integrated neighborhoods and schools, they must strive to guide their children into a strong ethnic awareness. While they provide the better life they must help their children to "establish a Black identity and pride while they are learning white mainstream cultural values . . ." (Morgan 1985, p. 32).

Work for many ethnic adults is an absorbing experience. Middle-class Blacks manifest the Puritan orientation toward work and success; this striving leaves many with little time for recreation and other community experiences. The regard for work is shared by Slavic-Americans, who live to work and who believe that, if one cannot work, one is useless. "Work is the capacity for good, not to work lets in bad. Work is God's work, laziness is the devil's work" (Stein 1976). Slavic-Americans have labored at almost any employment to be found, but primarily in blue collar occupations. When both husband and wife work, this joint effort yields a comfortable existence. Efforts to move into the professional ranks may be viewed as more problematic.

It is important to note that ethnicity may discourage certain types of employment. Although such employment is not ruled out, the Italian-American woman rarely works as a domestic. Employment in the homes of others is seen as a usurpation of the family loyalty. And so such employment has been left to Irish, German, Black, Hispanic, English, Scandinavian, and French women (Gambino 1974). The primary responsibilities for Italian women are to nurture the children and maintain a home that is immaculately clean (a symbol of a sound family) and attuned to the needs of her husband. Italian women married to Italian men are less likely to work outside the home than women in other ethnic groups. However, the differences in numbers who hold paying jobs are not significant, suggesting a change in adult role assignments. Socioeconomic status and the ethnic reality will influence the decision to enter the work force, working class women being more likely to work when their children are older (Johnson 1985).

The consequences of failure to respond wholeheartedly to the nurturer role may be seen in the story of one of our Italian undergraduate students. An exceptional student in her thirties, she was proud of her Italian heritage and during her senior year was deeply involved in preparations for her teenage daughter's wedding. However, one year after graduation she appeared at a college function fifteen pounds lighter, with a new hairstyle and a special radiance. In that year she had found employment and had separated from her husband. She explained the tremendous energy that it took for her to be the good Italian wife/mother. She added the role of student quite successfully, but lost favor in the community. Her children, like many others, disapprove of her new life-style and her rejection of their father. But it is her feeling that part of their discomfort is with her rejection of the Italian way of life she, as bearer of ethnicity, had taught them. As culture-bearer she played the woman's role of nurturer, supportive wife, and mother. The comments of family and others implied that she was expected to continue to assume the assigned domestic responsibilities rather than enter higher education, a pursuit properly left to men. Status was lost when she shifted her interest, resisting the responsibility that is the focus of Italian-American life, the family. Her written conclusions show considerable insight into aspects of ethnic disposition and move her well along into an understanding of herself (Sirey and Valerio 1982).

This Italian woman chose to be a single parent, a position of risk. But for many Black women the choice has not been a conscious one. Many Black women assume this head of family status by virtue of being widowed or separated from their husbands involuntarily, often by the husband's incarceration. Emasculation of the Black male by institutional racism has made him less available instrumentally and expressively to his family. The low-income Black woman, unlike the middle-class Black woman described earlier, is aware that the woman may become the primary support for her children. This is a role she often does not cherish, but wishes for a more viable family unit (Painter 1977). Generativity, caring for the next generation, is acted out alone, but not without difficulty. Greater energy is needed to accomplish the universal tasks.

Admittedly there is usually a lack of preparation for marriage and parenthood. We have indicated such in the discussion of emerging adulthood. Individuals take on these roles without adequate credentials, although subtle ethnic messages as to how to behave are conveyed. The Puerto Rican male pushed into adulthood by circumstance of fatherhood knows the meaning of machismo, a desirable combination of courage and fearlessness. As macho he is the head of his family, responsible for their protection and well-being, defender of their honor. His word is his contract (Abad, Ramos, and Boyce 1974). His wife knows that she will be protected and carries out her parental duties, being particular about teaching her children respecto, an esteem for individuals based on personal attributes rather than class.

Consider another Hispanic group, Mexican-Americans, whose adult responsibility includes the bearing of children. If they are denied this potential for fulfillment, there is the risk of personal disaster for Mexican-American women. Such is the experience of a group of low-income women who, apparently without consent, have been sterilized, denying them the opportunity to continue to bear children. Their feminine identity is denied and their social identity jeopardized. They have become cut off from social networks of godparents, friends, and relatives. They suffer insomnia, depression, and social isolation. Adulthood for them is incomplete; they have not been protected by machismo, which found itself powerless against the mainstream force (Ainsworth 1979).

Jewish men, like Hispanic men, are expected to protect their women. Adults are expected to marry. Marriage is "mitzvah" (duty); besides procreation, it provides companionship and fulfillment. The Biblical directive, "Be fruitful and multiply," and "It is not good for man to be alone; I will make him a helpmate," legitimize the expectation, but the vow of the groom makes public his intention: "Be my wife in accordance with the law of Moses and Israel. I will work for you, I will honor you, support and maintain you as it becomes Jewish husbands who work for their wives, honoring and supporting them faithfully" (Birnbaum 1975).

The traditional marriage contract is seen by some as an act of acquisition by the man. The woman's role is a passive and dependent one. The ceremony contains unilateral action on the part of the groom, with the bride's role limited to her silently indicating her consent. In order to circumvent such inequities many couples write their own contracts that eliminate some of the inequities for women under Jewish marriage law (Schneider 1984).

Biblical directive again dictates appropriate behavior for the Jewish housewife. On each sabbath eve the religious Jewish man is expected to remind his wife of these expectations: "she is trusted by her husband, obeyed by her servants, admired by the community, kind to the poor and needy; she cares well for her household and is not idle. And in return her children rise up and call her blessed and her husband praises her" (Proverbs 31:10-31). This passage also gives affirmation to the Jewish tradition of work for adult women; indeed, the work allows for creativity, a characteristic of the adult phase of life. The directive includes selecting a field and planting a vineyard, making linen garments and selling them to a merchant, taking produce to the market for sale, and making her own clothes. Schneider adds that nothing is said about doing the laundry, raising the children, or participating in any volunteer organizations except in being kind to the poor (1984).

Jewish women have a varied history in America in relation to work. One of their significant contributions of generativity was in the organization of the International Ladies Garment Workers Union following the tragic 1911 Triangle shirtwaist fire in which many working Jewish women lost their lives.

Each ethnic group benefits if there is a tradition that gives support to behavior that is experienced and observed in the present. Ancient Asian tradition of filial piety provides a framework for parent-child relations in Chinese and Japanese families. The directive is for reciprocal obligations from parent to child and child to parent in day-to-day family interactions as well as in major family decisions (Kitano 1976).

In Jewish and Asian families men traditionally hold positions as protectors, heads of household. On many occasions Black men seeking the role of protector are denied this role. Often the media and literature present Black men as unable to fulfill the position of husband/father;

they say little about what Black men may really be like, alluding only to toughness and ignoring tenderness (Hannerz 1969).

Applying the term "boy" to all Black males regardless of age, suggests a childlike, helpless state of dependency. Examples of the results of such treatment may be found in the work of Liebow (1967), Hannerz (1969), and Billingsley (1968). Ethnicity is denied affirmation; so, when the Black male attempts to take his place as head of the household, he is rebuffed. The children's public school teachers talk only to the mother. Teachers do not expect the father to show interest in the education of his children. The assumption is that he is incompetent by virtue of heritage.

Another more positive view of the Black male may be seen in the television character of Cliff Huxtable. Dr. Huxtable is a soft-spoken, sensitive obstetrician, the father of five children. Along with his barrister wife Claire, he becomes a role model for American parents, certainly a new position for the Black male. Bill Cosby, the producer and star of the television series, suggests that the message presented is that the Huxtable family is human with the same wants and needs everyone has (Gold 1985; Johnson 1986). These model parents continually struggle with the tasks of generativity and are for the most part successful. In this instance the media redefines the earlier view of the Black male adult as "boy," inadequate and incompetent.

Child Rearing

The intricate day-to-day tasks of child care require much concentration, for the outcome will influence the future. Given the privilege of motherhood, the Slovak-American mother's ethnically inspired behavior may deny her children early autonomy by binding them to her, letting them know that they have no minds of their own, no wills of their own, no separate existence apart from her. They are expected to be strong, resist adversity and fight worry, and begin to understand the importance of work by picking up after their play (Stein 1976).

A contrasting practice permits the American Indian child more freedom. An Indian child may have innumerable adult family members who assume responsibility for care. Parents do not see themselves as figures of authority, but as guides or role models. This style, however, has placed Native American children in jeopardy, for the mainstream interpretation has been that these children are "running wild" without the care of their parents. Permissiveness, allowing for individual development, is a different way of discipline accepted by the American Indian community that can be very effective. American Indians adults are amazed when parents they regarded as excellent caregivers are considered to be unfit, thereby losing custody of their children, and seeing them placed in the foster care of BIA schools. Slavic-American and Native American children may then suffer in different ways from the behaviors of their parents who follow ethnic tradition. Unfortunately, the American Indian children are in greater jeopardy, for, once they are removed from their families, their experiences in BIA schools often prevent the learning of skills necessary in later stages of development. They have no parental or community models. Their social growth and development are hampered (Byler 1978).

Friends

For the adult peer friendships round out one's existence and provide confidantes and associates for recreation. The initial source for these friendships is the extended family, and then members of the same ethnic group, which often means the same religious affiliation.

The hierarchy of friendship for the Italian begins with those who are *sangu du me sangu* (blood of my blood) and adds *compari* and *comare* (godparents), who are intimate friends. Few Italians limit their friendships to other Italians. Increasing intermarriage makes this difficult. Respondents in Johnson's (1985) examination of Italian-American families found the creation of "Little Italies" distasteful. Childhood experiences in insular communities had limited their exposure to other American values. As a result, 60% of those interviewed reported a mixed friendship group. This group and other Italians have close friendships with family, neighborhood friends, friends from childhood, and persons who in earlier times were viewed as *strameri* (strangers) (Gambino 1974).

Compadrazo and *compadres* are terms that identify those Mexican-American adults who hold the same status as *compari* or *comare* to Italian-Americans. They are godparents and most cherished friends, reliable in times of stress imposed by various insensitive institutions. In times of joy they are available for the celebration, for they are family. While the Mexican-American adult male has freedom of movement in the larger society, the woman is expected to remain close to the home, and so her friendship group contains her daughters, even after they have gained maturity, and other female relatives, such as cousins and nieces. The women comfort each other and often become confidantes (Murillo 1976).

In the Polish experience, friends outside of the immediate family may be found in the neighborhood, but they still are not as close as family (Wrobel 1973).

As ethnic adults attempt to build friendships with others like them, they form ethnic communities, ethnic islands; sometimes these are labeled "ghetto" or "barrio" in the negative sense of the words. These may be communities of rejected people who, despite the barrenness of their existence, find a sense of belonging and cohesion that is characteristic of ethnic communities. It is here that the adults find friends and a church. Howell (1973) and LeMasters (1975) suggest that in such a Polish neighborhood a homeowner may work in a local factory, while his wife remains home to care for the children. On Wednesday evenings he bowls in an all-male league but on most evenings he stops by the local tavern to drink with the other men. On Tuesday his wife occasionally plays bingo and on Sunday she goes to church (he goes only on special occasions). Their neighbors are their best friends, but they maintain relatively close relationships with their parents, siblings, and extended family and are wary of outsiders. This pattern is found again and again within the ethnic groups with which we are concerned. Blacks have long maintained kinship networks that have provided emotional as well as financial resources. Stack (1975), in her study of kinship networks, has established their presence for low-income families, while Willie and McAdoo (1974; 1981) have done the same for middle-income families.

An analysis of Krause's (1978a) data indicates that Italian and Slavic families in Pittsburgh often live within a reasonable proximity, some at the same address, others in the same neighborhood, and still others in different neighborhoods with similar zip codes. Jewish women tend to live a greater distance from each other. Those Slavic and Italian women remaining in the city visited as frequently as daily, while Jewish women were more likely to visit weekly. In each instance, adults provide each other support across generations, a sense of family, and ethnic continuity.

Outside the family circle, the adult task of relating to peers is achieved in the ethnic neighborhood where the sense of peoplehood pervades the environment and ethnic reality is surely in action. The daily or weekly contact among the grandmothers, mothers, and daughters studied by Krause gives evidence of a major adult task, that of maintaining generational ties. The adult stands between the young and the aged, sometimes bombarded by demands from both. The response to the older generation may also be guided by ethnic tradition. This tradition is broad, covering all ethnic groups.

LATER ADULTHOOD

To recognize that one is in later adulthood is to realize that time is in constant motion and with this movement come physiological and emotional changes. The climacteric tells women very clearly that their childbearing years are ended. What then will be the life for women whose ethnic assignment was to bear children and care for them? Time has moved the children into adulthood and independence, but in many instances the ethnic dispositions encourage a closeness in geographical distance. It is not unlikely that Italian, Polish, or Black grown children and their families remain in the neighborhood. Those who move from the city to the suburbs are seen as being far away (Gans 1962). The telephone provides the possibility, daily or weekly, for communication.

The expectation for care of aging parents manifests itself in various ways. To the middle-aged Italian responsibility for aging parents is unwritten law, a tie that can't be broken. The motives for caring range from duty and repayment to love (Johnson 1985). The tradition of filial piety in Chinese families directs that children, youth and adults, respect and care for aging parents (Yu 1984).

It is difficult to measure the depth of relationships, but McAdoo (1979) attempts to determine the sense of pressure felt by Black adults as they share their resources with their parents and other family members. Stating generally that they feel no sense of obligation because "this is what is done in families," 45% feel pressure to share ranging from "a little" (16%), to "some" (21%), to "a great deal" (8%). The sense of ethnicity remains strong. Most ethnic older Americans expect some measure of regard from the younger generations. The passage of time, technology, and life-style changes have all contributed to the need for older family members to adapt to a world which, although it holds them in regard, does not respond in the old ways.

OLD AGE

Many elderly persons in our society arrived in this country early in their youth from societies that were primarily agrarian. The Chicano and the Chinese, though different in so many ways, shared their agrarian experience and similar patterns of family life. The extended family had need for each family member. In the Chicano family mature men and women were the workers; the aged provided knowledge, based on their experience, and cared for the very young. They were useful members of the family (Maldonado 1975). Similarly, Chinese families were self-contained units in which the elderly had no fear of unemployment. Even before physical decline, they retired, living on the fruits of their children's labors. Their advice was sought on important matters. The young held them in high regard and infants grew up in their grandparents' arms.

Old age is a proud station in life. This has been the pattern of life for generations, but change has come to cause tensions not anticipated. Technology has caused families to move to urban centers where employment provides greater opportunities for the young. The extended family changes in form as an urban life-style evolves. The result for the aging Chicanos and Chinese is a world unknown to their grandparents.

Settled in Chinatowns or barrios, the elderly watch the young move into more heterogeneous communities in the city or the suburbs. The respect and regard for them remain, but the extended family under one roof is less common than in Mexico or China or earlier periods in America. In the city, their children do not need their knowledge, skills, and experience.

Cheng, in a 1978 study of the elder Chinese in San Diego County, California, describes characteristics of "Chinese-ness" among older Chinese that enable them to maintain their sense of peoplehood in a changing society. Among these characteristics are:

Expectation of children supporting and helping them in their old age

"Clanishness"—living in neighborhoods with Chinese neighbors and belonging to Chinese associations

Celebration of family happenings with family and friends, especially birthdays

Identification of themselves as Chinese or Chinese in America, regardless of the dialect they speak

These ethnic dispositions and others provide the framework around which daily life may be constructed with some assurance of success and comfort, even after the activities of youth and early adulthood, including work, are less available. These characteristics have sustained many throughout their lives.

In chapter one the importance of work in relation to ethnicity and social class was discussed. As old age approaches, work performed with ease in earlier years becomes a burden. Limitations are obvious. There are those who, recognizing this, would not accept employment if it were appropriate and available. The lack of work may be humiliating for others. Earlier we have noted the Slavic-American drive for work, which is perceived as good. When the Slavic male approaches retirement age, a change in his behavior may be noticed. Rather than admit to aging, which implies incapacity, inactivity, weakness, and dependency, he may attempt to work even more vigorously. This invariably fails. Retirement follows and with it, for many, depression, apathy, despair, and assumed uselessness. Time formerly used at labor is used in wandering aimlessly around the home and neighborhood. Once a respected figure, he now becomes dependent, aimless, perpetually in slow motion; his wife and children respond by becoming bossy (Stein 1976).

Stein poses the possibility that in some instances long-hidden conflicts surface in regard to the retired male's loss of authority, power, and respect, even though there is evidence of the apparent universal respect and deference for the aging.

The last vestiges of power and authority which came with work diminish after retirement and the fruits of that labor become the center of power struggles. Land, houses, property—the last symbols of power, authority, and prestige—represent independence; at the same time, declining age suggests that some authority or power should be assigned to the young. But the Slavic disposition suggests that to be taken care of is dependence. Good intentions on the part of their children are not seen as worthy of trust and so, rather than retiring peacefully like some American Indians, the Slavic elderly have great potential for tension and stress (Stein 1976).

The authority that wanes for the Slavic elderly maintains itself in the life of the Native American. An Iroquois woman describes the position of older women in her tribe:

> The clan is the basic structure of the Iroquois family and of most other Native American families. The clan mother is the oldest woman in that family group. Her authority reigns over every aspect of that family's daily life even to the nominations of the chiefs. The men vote, the women give the symbols of office to the new chief (Haile 1976).

With a definite role to perform, elderly women have no time for retirement. As Curley describes his grandmother, a Navajo, a picture similar to the early life of the Chicano and Chinese evolves, but with different results. Mr. Curley's grandmother never worked outside of the home. Her education was received from her grandmother, who taught her to behold and revere the land. She learned of the balance and order in creation and of the relationships between mountains, rivers, trees, and wind. Her work at home was to open the gate for the sheep and goats to forage for food. It is now her turn as grandmother to teach these things to her grandchildren. The world is somehow different; the gate will be opened by the grandchildren while she continues to pray at dawn. This will be taught to her grandchildren, along with knowledge of the morning as the time in which good things exist: good health, increased wealth, and wisdom. This is not a job from which one retires; it is what must be done. The new role is teaching her grandchildren the lessons of her grandmother. Like her Iroquois sister she is in the position of wielding wisdom and knowledge, sought after when the order and balance of the world seem to be undone. Retirement age, rather than excluding her from the family clan, incorporates her more completely into the role of teacher, a process that is inevitable and definite (Curley 1978).

The role of the grandmother is clear in these American Indian families. Seldom does one hear mention of loneliness, yet in other groups this is an important issue. Much of this loneliness could be removed by relationships with grandchildren in the manner of the American Indian. This is illustrated in Krause's (1978) sample of Italian grandmothers.

Grandchildren provide the opportunity to tell the family history; such exchanges seem to be initiated by grandchild or grandparent. Seldom do parents appear to encourage the telling of the story. Studies indicate that it is often the third generation that attempts to revive family history (Robertson 1977).

Grandparenting provides other opportunities and resources. These range from giving child care and financial support to serving as role models or playing a modulating influence in family strife (Robertson 1977). But grandchildren cannot be expected to assume major responsibility for giving later life its vitality; other sources must be explored.

Kinship ties among all generations would seem to be a resource, particularly if all are in the same household. Such is not always the case. Given the reality of the oppressive results of institutional racism, many elderly Blacks reside with children, grandchildren, and great-grandchildren without receiving emotional support. The arrangement is necessary, but economic difficulties add stress to the situation. There are also many older Black people living alone. The results of a San Diego County study (Stanford 1978) and the work of Faulkner, Heisel, and Simms (1975) and Jackson (1978) all support these findings.

Along with other ethnic groups, Blacks prefer to live in the vicinity of family members. Contact may be limited in certain urban areas due to fear of the environment. The threat of violence is a reality in many urban centers. This may reinforce loneliness and isolation from family and friends even when there is a need, desire, and physical health to get out (Faulkner, Heisel, and Simms 1975). In areas of less danger, recreational activities that are enjoyed include church activities, family picnics, card playing, and getting together to talk.

Religion plays an important part in the life of many elderly Black persons. Church attendance has provided spiritual involvement for some and a basis of social life for others (Stanford 1978). Others have found positions of status in the church that are self-affirming and provide for respect and honor in the community. The Black church is among the very few Black institutions in our society that is independent of control by the mainstream society. It is entirely controlled and supported by the Black community, with elder Blacks often holding important administrative positions.

We have stressed the importance of kinship and neighborhood ties as positive aspects of this stage of the life cycle. However, it is important that we consider the possible negative aspects of these relationships. In 1978 Cohler and Lieberman reported on a study of the assumption that close ties with family and friends fostered personal adjustment and reduced the impact of otherwise stressful events. The study included Irish, Italians, and Polish Americans who were middle-aged and older. The presence of an extensive network was actually stressful for Italian and Polish women. Socialized to be caretakers in earlier life stages, they cared for their children and various other kin. As children grew and became more independent of parents, women seemed to show an increasing involvement in themselves, moving away from the caretaker roles. This was particularly evident in the Italian and Polish women, less evident in the Irish women. The presence and demands of an extensive social network appeared to have an adverse impact on mental health.

As role expectations and personalities change over the years, distress may be evoked by the demands of caring for others. The ethnic community is not a positive environment for all aging persons, particularly those women who seek release from earlier caretaking roles demanded by their ethnic reality.

Ethnicity indeed has its strengths and weaknesses. It has power to hold a people together, yet there is the potential for stress when the demands are excessive. Most aged people have the universal tasks of combating failing health and diminishing capacity and confronting the ultimate reality of death. Health problems that become critical may necessitate unacceptable actions.

The nursing home has become a viable alternative for many. For others it is not a reasonable solution. Many Slavic families find nursing care homes repulsive (Stein 1976). This is also true for many Chicanos (Sotomayor 1977). Some other ethnic minority groups, such as Blacks, Asians, Hispanics, and Native Americans may hold strong ethnic prescriptions against institutional placements and dismiss the nursing home as a plan for care. This "cultural aversion" is seen as a reason for limited use of nursing homes by ethnic groups. Morrison (1983) suggests that accepting this hypothesis for limited use avoids an assessment of the excessive costs for these families in financial and psychosocial terms.

Continuity is a fundamental necessity for human life, collectively and individually. Our elderly people offer us continuity in the social, cultural, historical, and spiritual aspects of our lives (Myerhoff 1978b). Their death places the responsibility for that continuity upon those at earlier stages of life. We know little of ethnic dispositions in relation to death. Black, Japanese, and Mexican-American residents of Los Angeles were studied by Kalish and Reynolds (1976) to cast some light on how these ethnic groups feel about death, dying, and grieving. A study of funeral customs of Black Americans (Devore 1979) examines similarities in African and American rituals and Negro spirituals such as "Soon I will be done with the trouble of dis world" or "Swing low sweet chariot, coming for to carry me home," and gives a Black perspective in which death for many is a release from the oppression of the mainstream society.

Native Americans view death as part of life and are able to visualize themselves as performers in the "Dance of Death." No matter what the tribal burial custom may be—in sleeping, sitting, or fetal position—life is to be lived to the fullest and death accepted as a natural conclusion (Dial 1978).

Death does not always wait for the last stage of the life cycle, but if one is able to survive, the pervasive reality is that death will be at the end of this stage. It may be faced with integrity or despair, with an acceptance of decline that recognizes the affirmation of the past, or with submission to forces that seem designed to make life unbearable.

SUMMARY

The stages of the life cycle are acted out in as many variations as there are groups of people. The stage of development will not only give us clues as to the universal tasks that need to be achieved, but an indication of the ethnic dispositions that are imposed upon those tasks. Life cycle stage, universal task, and ethnic disposition are all items of data, along with social class, that are essential for our practice.

REFERENCES

Abad, Vincente; Ramos, Juan; and Boyce, Elizabeth. 1974. A model for delivery of mental health services to Spanish-speaking minorities. *American Journal of Orthopsychiatry* 44:584–595.

Abraham, Kathy; Christopherson, Victor A.; and Kuehl, Robert O. 1984. Navajo and Anglo childrearing behaviors. *Journal of Comparative Family Studies* 15:380–388.

Ainsworth, Diane. 1979. Cultural cross fires. *Human Behavior*, March.

Aschenbrenner, Joyce. 1975. *Lifelines—Black families in Chicago.* Prospect Heights, ILL: Waveland Press, Inc.

Biddle, Ellen Horgan. 1981. The American Catholic family. In *Ethnic families in America: patterns and variations*, edited by Charles H. Mindel and Robert W. Habenstein. New York: Elsevier Scientific Publishing Co.

Billingsley, Andrew. 1968. *Black families in white America.* Englewood Cliffs, NJ: Prentice-Hall, Inc.

Birnbaum, Phillip. 1975. *A book of Jewish concepts. Rev. ed.* New York: Hebrew Publishing Co.

Brice, Janet. 1982. West Indian families. In *Ethnicity and family therapy*, edited by Monica McGoldrick, John K. Pearce, and Joseph Giordano. New York: The Guilford Press.

Brownlee, Ann Templeton. 1978. *Community, culture and care: a cross-cultural guide for health workers.* St. Louis: The C. V. Mosby Co.

Byler, William. 1978. The destruction of American Indian families. In *The destruction of American Indian families*, edited by Steven Unger. New York: Association on American Indian Affairs.

Cheng, Eva. 1978. *The elder Chinese.* San Diego: Center on Aging, San Diego State University.

Chunn, Jay. Suicide taking its toll on Blacks. *Crisis 1981* 88:401.

Clark, Joseph. 1984. The American Blacks; a passion for politics. *Dissent* 31:261–263.

Cohler, Bertram J., and Lieberman, Morton A. 1978. *Social relations and mental health among three European ethnic groups.* Chicago: University of Chicago Press.

Cretser, Gary A., and Leon, Joseph J. 1982. Intermarriage in the United States: an overview of theory and research. *Marriage and Family Review* 5:3–15.

Curley, Larry. 1978. Retirement—an Indian perspective. In *Retirement: concepts and realities*, edited by E. Percil Stanford. San Diego: Center on Aging, San Diego State University.

Devore, Wynetta. 1979. *The funeral practices of Black Americans.* Union, NJ: Kean College of New Jersey.

Dial, Adolph L. 1978. Death and life of Native Americans. *The Indian Historian* 11:32–37.

Eilberg, Amy. 1984. Views of human development in Jewish rituals: a comparison with Eriksonian Theory. *Smith College Studies in Social Work* 55:1–23.

Erikson, Erik. 1950. *Childhood and society.* 2d ed. New York: W. W. Norton & Co.

Faulkner, Audrey Olsen; Heisel, Marsel A.; and Simms, Peacolia. 1975. Life strength and life stresses—explorations in the measurement of the mental health of the Black aged. *American Journal of Orthopsychiatry* 45:102–110.

Gadpaille, Warren J. 1975. In *The cycles of sex*, edited by Lucy Freeman. New York: Charles Scribner's Sons.

Gambino, Richard. 1974. *Blood of my blood, the dilemma of the Italian-Americans.* Garden City, NY: Anchor Books/Doubleday and Co., Inc.

Gans, Herbert. 1962. *The urban villagers: group and class in the life of Italian-Americans.* New York: The Free Press.

Gold, Todd. 1985. Bill Cosby: the doctor is in. *The Saturday Evening Post* 257:42–45.

Haile, Elizabeth. 1976. The Native American untold story. In *Untold stories*. New York: United Presbyterian Church, Third World Women Liaison.

Hannerz, Ulf. 1969. *Soulside—inquiries into ghetto culture and community*. New York: Columbia University Press.

Huang, Lucy J. 1981. The Chinese-American family. In *Ethnic families in America: patterns and variations*, edited by Charles H. Mindel and Robert W. Habenstein. New York: Elsevier Scientific Publishing Co.

Harrison-Ross, Phyllis, M.D.; and Wyden, Barbara. 1973. *The Black child—a parents' guide*. New York: Peter W. Wyden, Inc.

Hidalgo, Hilda. 1974. The Puerto Rican. In *Ethnic differences influencing the delivery of rehabilitation services*. Washington, DC: National Rehabilitation Association.

Hill, Reuben. 1974. Modern systems theory and the family. In *Sourcebook in marriage and the family*. 4th ed., edited by Marvin B. Sussman. Boston: Houghton-Mifflin Co.

Howell, Joseph T. 1973. *Hard living on Clay Street—portraits of blue collar families*. Garden City, NY: Anchor Books.

Howze, Beverly. 1979. Black suicides—final acts of alienation. *Human Behavior*, February.

Jackson, Jacquelyn, and Walls, Bertram E. 1978. Myths and realities about aged Blacks. In *Readings in gerontology*. 2d ed., edited by Mollie Brown. St. Louis: The C. V. Mosby Co.

Johnson, Colleen Leahy. 1985. *Growing up and growing old in Italian-American Families*. New Brunswick, NY: Rutgers University Press.

Johnson, Robert E. 1986. TV's top mom and pop. *Ebony* 41:29–34.

Kalish, Richard A., and Reynolds, David. 1976. *Death and ethnicity*. Los Angeles: University of Southern California Press.

King, Stanley H. 1972. Coping and growth in adolescence. *Seminars in Psychiatry* 4:355–366.

Kitano, Harry H. L. 1974a. *Race relations*. Englewood Cliffs, NJ: Prentice-Hall, Inc.

Kitano, Harry H. L. 1974b. *Japanese-Americans*. 2d ed. Englewood Cliffs, NJ: Prentice-Hall, Inc.

Kitano, Harry H. L., and Yeung, Wai-Tsang. 1982. Chinese interracial marriage. *Marriage and Family Review* 5:35–48.

Koller, Marvin R., and Ritchie, Oscar W. 1978. *Socialization of childhood*. 2d ed. Englewood Cliffs, NJ: Prentice-Hall, Inc.

Krause, Corinne Azen. 1978a. *Grandmothers, mothers, and daughters: an oral history study of ethnicity, mental health, and continuity of three generations of Jewish, Italian, and Slavic-American women*. New York: The Institute of Pluralism and Group Identity of the American Jewish Committee.

Krause, Corinne Azen. 1978b. "Grandmothers, mothers and daughters: especially those who are Jewish." Paper presented at the Meeting on the Role of Women, American Jewish Committee.

Ladner, Joyce. 1971. *Tomorrow's tomorrow: the Black woman*. New York: Anchor Books/Doubleday and Company, Inc.

LeMasters, E. E. 1975. *Blue collar aristocrats*. Madison: University of Wisconsin Press.

Lidz, Theodore. 1976. *The person. Rev. ed. New York: Basic Books, Inc.*

Liebow, Elliot. 1967. *Tally's corner*. Boston: Little, Brown, and Co.

Maldonado, David, Jr. 1975. The Chinese aged. *Social Work* 20:213–216.

McAdoo, Harriet Pipes. 1979. Black kinship. *Psychology Today* 12:155–169.

McAdoo, Harriet Pipes. 1981. Patterns of upward mobility in Black families. In *Black families,* edited by Harriett Pipes McAdoo. Beverly Hills: Sage Publications.

McIntosh, John L., and Santos, John F. 1980–81. Suicide among Native Americans: a compilation of findings. *Omega* 11:303–316.

Mangeone, Jerre. 1983. *An ethnic at large—a memoir of America in the thirties and forties.* Philadelphia: University of Pennsylvania Press.

Merian, Lewis. 1956. The effects of boarding schools on Indian family life. In *The destruction of American Indian families,* edited by Steven Unger. New York: Association of American Indian Affairs.

Morgan, Thomas. 1985. The world ahead. *The New York Times Magazine* 135:33–35, 90–99.

Morrison, Barbara Jones. 1983. Sociological dimensions: nursing homes and the minority aged. In *Gerontological social work practice in long-term care,* edited by George Getzel. New York: The Haworth Press.

Morrison, Toni. 1972. *The bluest eye.* New York: Pocket Books, Holt, Rinehart and Winston, Inc.

Murguia, Edward, and Cazares, Ralph. 1982. Intermarriage of Mexican-Americans. *Marriage and Family Review* 5:91–100.

Murillo, Nathan. 1976. The Mexican-American family. In *Hispanic culture and health care—fact, fiction, folklore,* edited by Richard Aguigo Martinez. St. Louis: The C. V. Mosby Co.

Myerhoff, Barbara J. 1978a. A symbol perfected in death: continuity and ritual and the life and death of an elderly Jew. In *Life career—aging: cultural variations on growing old,* edited by Barbara J. Myerhoff and Andrei Simic. Beverly Hills: Sage Publications.

Myerhoff, Barbara. 1978b. *Number our days.* New York: Simon and Schuster.

Napierkowski, Thomas. 1976. Stepchild of America: growing up Polish. In *Growing up Slavic in America,* edited by Michael Novac. Bayville, NY: EMPAC.

Nishimoto, Cyril. 1986. "The Japanese family." Paper presented at *Enhancing Asian Family Life Conference.* New York: Manhattan Community College.

Padillo, Elena. 1958. *Up from Puerto Rico.* New York: Columbia University Press.

Painter, Diann Holland. 1977. Black women and the family. In *Women into wives—the legal and economic impact of marriage,* edited by Jane Roberts Chapman and Margaret Gates. Beverly Hills: Sage Press.

Porterfield, Ernest. 1982. Black American intermarriage. *Marriage and Family Review* 5:17–34.

Robertson, Joan F. 1977. Grandmotherhood—a study of role conceptions. *Journal of Marriage and the Family* 39:165–176.

Rolle, Andrew. 1980. *The Italian-American's troubled roots.* New York: The Free Press.

Rosenzweig, Efraim M. 1977. *We Jews: invitation to a dialogue.* New York: Hawthorn Books, Inc.

Schild, Sylvia, and Black, Rita Beck. 1984. *Social work and genetics: a guide for practice.* New York: The Haworth Press.

Schneider, Susan Weidman. 1984. *Jewish and female—choices and changes in our lives.* New York: Simon and Schuster.

Sirey, Aileen Riotto, and Valerio, Anne Marie. 1982. Italian-American women: women in transition. *Ethnic Groups* 4:177–189.

Sotomayor, Marta. 1977. Language, culture, and ethnicity in developing self-concept. *Social Casework* 58:195–203.

Stack, Carol B. 1975. *All our kin—strategies for survival in a Black community.* New York: Harper Colophon Books, Harper and Row.

Stanford, E. Percil. 1978. *The elder Black.* San Diego: Center on Aging, San Diego State University.

Stein, Howard F. 1976. A dialectical model of health and illness—attitudes and behavior among Slovak-Americans. *International Journal of Mental Health* 5:31–45.

Talbot, Toby, 1974. *The world of the child—clinical and cultural studies from birth to adolescence.* New York: Jason Aronson.

Valliant, George E., and McArthur, Charles C. 1981. Natural history of male psychological health, X: work as a predictor of positive mental health. *American Journal of Psychiatry* 138:1433–1440.

Van Gennep, Arnold. 1960. *The rites of passage.* London: Routledge and Kegan Paul.

Westfried, Alex Huxley. 1981. *Ethnic leadership in a New England community.* Cambridge, MA: Schenkman Publishing Company, Inc.

Willie, Charles V. 1974. The Black family and social class. *American Journal of Orthopsychiatry* 44:50–60.

Winch, Robert F. 1971. *The modern family.* 3d ed. New York: Holt, Rinehart, and Winston.

Wrobel, Paul. 1973. Becoming a Polish-American: a personal point of view. In *White ethnics: their life in working class America,* edited by Joseph A. Ryan. Englewood Cliffs, NJ: Prentice-Hall, Inc.

Yu, Lucy C. 1984. Acculturation and stress within Chinese-American families. *Journal of Comparative Family Studies* 15:77–94.

CHAPTER
3

The Layers of Understanding

A Mother's Struggle

The past six years have been a lonely, unrelieved ordeal for Mrs. Verna Davis. At age thirty-five she has four children: Lillian, 17; Harold, 13; Richard, 10; and Jimmy, 6. Soon after Jimmy was born her husband Charles deserted the family. Mrs. Davis's younger sister Louise moved into the home for the next two years and looked after the children while Mrs. Davis went to work as a domestic. Louise married and moved into a home of her own, causing Mrs. Davis to quit her job and apply for public assistance. In another year, however, Lillian was able to take on some responsibility for her younger brothers. This enabled Mrs. Davis to work nights cleaning in an office building.

One night last summer while preparing dinner before leaving for her job, Mrs. Davis suffered third degree burns on her hands and arms when grease in a skillet burst into flames. Since then the family has been managing on public assistance, for Mrs. Davis cannot yet use her right hand. It was concern for Lillian that brought Mrs. Davis to the family service center. Lillian, formerly a good student, began to cut classes last spring and lost interest in her studies.

When Mrs. Davis meets with the social worker at the Family Service Center she brings not only the problem of Lillian's truancy, but her particular perspective on that problem and on the many others that have plagued her for the past six years. Her view of these is influenced by her personality, life cycle stage, family of origin, views about work and education, and response to illness as well as to economic stress. Previous experiences with social service agencies, primarily public welfare agencies, have shaped her expectations of the client role. The social worker brings a professional perspective that recognizes Mrs. Davis's hope for insights into Lillian's difficulties and knowledge of resources to help the family attain a greater sense of well-being. The professional perspective consists of six components which we term the *layers of understanding*. These layers are comprised of the knowledge, values, and skills that are important to all approaches to practice.

They are:

1. Social work values
2. A basic knowledge of human behavior
3. Knowledge and skill in social welfare polices and services
4. Self-awareness, including insights into one's own ethnicity and an understanding of how that may influence professional practice
5. Understanding of the impact of the ethnic reality upon the daily lives of clients
6. Adaptation and modification of skills and techniques in response to the ethnic reality

Most of these have been and continue to be considered basic ingredients of professional practice. Indeed, several are incorporated into the Statement on the Purpose of Social Work and the Code of Ethics.[1] They are reviewed here in order to highlight their basic thrust and to suggest additional dimensions required for ethnic-sensitive practice. The situation of Mrs. Davis and her family illustrates how and why these "layers" must be incorporated into ethnic-sensitive practice.

LAYER 1: SOCIAL WORK VALUES

The foundation values of social work continue to be scrutinized. This is as it should be. For social work as a profession is, first and foremost, committed to people, to their well-being, and to the enhancement of the quality of their lives. Levy (1973) comments: "The social work profession is well advised to tolerate difference and diversity about some things but not about its ideology. That is too critical a unifying force and one which is essential for its character and role as a profession in society."

---

[1]*Social Work* Vol. 26, January, 1981.

Of all the varied statements about social work's value base, the one developed by Levy is particularly relevant to ethnic-sensitive practice. His basic formulations involve (1) values related to conceptions of people, (2) values related to preferred outcomes for people, and (3) values related to preferred instrumentalities for dealing with people.

The first focuses on orientations about people and the relationships between people and their environments, the second on the quality of life and beliefs about social provision and policy designed to enhance the quality of life, and the third on views about how people ought to be treated.

In respect to the first set of values, Mrs. Davis is viewed as a person of intrinsic value with the capacity to grow and develop the skills necessary for coping with the present family situation as well as problems that may present themselves in the future.

These values recognize that individuals such as Mrs. Davis have a responsibility not only to themselves and their families but to the larger society as well. At present, her participation in the larger community may be marginal due to stress, yet the potential remains. Of particular importance in this value is the recognition of the uniqueness of each individual. We will see how the ethnic reality and other characteristics make Mrs. Davis "special" in her own right.

The second set of values involves familiar areas of self-realization, self-actualization, and equality of opportunity. Mrs. Davis's social worker and other members of the profession must continually affirm individual and group struggles for growth and development. It is our contention that the ethnic reality sometimes enhances the struggle but, at other times, presents impediments.

The final category focuses on the importance of treating people in a way that maximizes their opportunities for self-direction. Stereotyping and prejudgment of Mrs. Davis as a hopelessly incompetent single parent limits her possibility for self-direction. Incompetent persons need guidance to take charge of their lives. If the social worker incorporates this value Mrs. Davis can be assured of practice that encourages her participation in the helping process.

LAYER 2: BASIC KNOWLEDGE OF HUMAN BEHAVIOR

The curriculum policy statement of the Council on Social Work Education declares that: "Students need knowledge of individuals as they develop over the life span and have memberships in families, groups, and organizations; of the relationships among biological, social, psychological, and cultural systems as they affect and are affected by human behavior"[2]. This mandate provides a guide for the consideration of this second layer.

Life Cycle Position

An awareness of the significance of varying behaviors that occur from the time of entry to old age enhances the social worker's opportunity for success. Attention must be focused on the fact that Mrs. Davis is approaching middle age and probably has all the apprehensions that accompany movement to that stage of life. Her four children range from childhood to adolescence; each is attempting to complete the associated developmental tasks. At the moment Lillian appears to have the greatest problem. Knowledge of family interaction suggests that her brothers may be affected by her behavior in ways yet to be expressed. Because she has had total responsibility for the rearing of four children, Mrs. Davis has used a variety of coping mechanisms that have included seeking help from her family, obtaining tedious employment, and resorting to public assistance.

When Charles Davis abandoned his wife and children he placed Verna in the position of a single parent. Without his assistance she must now fulfill tasks usually assigned to two parents. In addition to the ordinary tasks of supplying instrumental resources she must establish a new family structure, assigning new roles among the children so that family living may continue in a reasonable fashion. Hopes for a family future must be set aside, to be reassessed at a later time. The new single parent status may have elicited a variety of responses ranging from anger to relief. Attuned to this fact, a worker will also consider the possibility that Charles's departure may have engendered a variety of responses from the children, related to their stages in the life cycle. This includes Jimmy, who, from the time of his birth, has had but one parent. His experience is unlike that of his siblings, who knew the presence of both mother and father in the early years. They had to adapt to a single parent family.

Without warning, grease and fire combined to cause serious injury to Mrs. Davis and deprive her of the ability to support herself and her children. She is able, however, to continue to assume other expressive responsibilities assigned to her. But, out of concern for teenaged Lillian, who appears to be floundering, she contacts the social service agency.

[2]Curriculum policy for masters degree and baccalaureate degree programs in social work education, adopted by the Board of Directing, Council on Social Work Education, May, 1982, effective July 11, 1984.

The pressures on Lillian seem to be denying her the joys of carefree adolescence.

Social Role

Knowledge of the concept of *social role* adds even greater vitality to understanding of the Davis family (Strean 1979). In most families, members are assigned roles related to age, usually to sex, and to other positions in the family. Particular behaviors are assigned to each of these roles and, when the different roles are not complementary, problems may be anticipated. Individuals are often expected to fulfill roles for which they have few skills or are assigned more roles than they desire or can manage. This appears to be the case in the Davis family. Although the social worker enters at the time of Lillian's difficulty, the data collection process will no doubt reveal problems in others' role performances that relate to Charles Davis's leaving. When he abdicated the father role he left it for his wife to perform in addition to her own mother/nurturer role, which may already have taxed her at that point because of the care of her newborn child. Accepting the single parent role, Mrs. Davis entered the work force. Some of the mother roles were assigned to her sister. After Louise's marriage Mrs. Davis was forced to look to other resources. In a short time young Lillian was required to assume a mother/nurturer role. Her past life experience may not have provided her with sufficient skills for this role, which she may prefer not to hold, wishing rather to concentrate on the roles of daughter, sibling, and teenager. The burden of numerous roles may have been the inadvertent cause of the kitchen accident. In any event, it thrust Mrs. Davis into the sick role. In this adverse position she is unable to carry out any of her responsibilities effectively and adds another role, that of welfare client.

The sick role must be played out in a particular way in our society (Parsons 1958). Though no blame is placed upon Mrs. Davis, the welfare system and her family will expect her to "get well soon," by using the appropriate health care providers, and return to her regularly assigned tasks as soon as possible. Unfortunately, if her progress is slower than seems necessary she may become suspect. Extended dependency in the sick and welfare client roles threatens the family system, which up to this time had maintained a satisfactory equilibrium.

Personality Theory

Mrs. Davis's success or failure is in large measure dependent upon her personality and the characteristics she has developed to enable her to adjust to her life situation. The social worker who meets Mrs. Davis finds a warm, good-humored woman who is less confident about her ability to cope than before the trouble with Lillian began. In order to help her cope with the problem she brings, the worker must know something of her past reactions to trauma and loss. Her history suggests a high degree of emotional stability, the ability to assume responsibility, and a capacity for trust and friendliness. Though distressed by the turn of events, she has no evidence of pathological depression or withdrawal. She wants help so that all will be well with her eldest child. It is her hope that the social worker will be able to help her to return her family to a more comfortable state.

Social Systems Theory

The incorporation of social systems theory into the practice of social work has provided a means by which we may gain a clearer perspective of the reciprocal influences among individuals, families, groups, and the environment. Hartman (1979) has an ecological focus as she reminds us that all living things are dependent on each other for survival and that it is the unforeseen that often disrupts relationships. The worker with this view is aware of the physical environment as well as the impact of social, economic, and political forces. Understanding the concept of the family as a social system gives greater insight into the Davis family (Hartman and Laird 1983). The members are seen as interdependent, with the behavior of each affecting the behavior of others. Lillian's truancy causes discomfort not only for her mother but for her brothers, who may have new roles to perform or who may suffer ridicule because Lillian is in trouble.

As a boundary-maintaining unit the family has struggled to support itself financially; the boundary has been partially open to allow transactions with the welfare, health, and educational systems. The family has shown itself to be successful at equilibrium seeking and adaptation. Each stressful event has required new behaviors, which have been acquired and used successfully up to this point. Desertion, illness, and truancy all impose stress and have the potential for crisis. But, crisis has been averted so far. Mrs. Davis, as head of the family, has performed the traditional tasks of providing food, clothing, shelter, and socialization and maintaining order and family morale.

LAYER 3: KNOWLEDGE AND SKILL IN AGENCY POLICY AND SERVICES

Mrs. Davis's meeting with the social worker has been preceded by her request for services. This was handled by the receptionist, who gave her a date for an appointment. It was at this initial meeting that "intake" occurred and decisions were made about the ability of the agency to assist. The function of this family service center is to provide services for those who are concerned primarily with interpersonal relationships. It is a people-changing agency. Had Mrs. Davis been seeking vocational rehabilitation or supplementary monetary assistance, she would have been referred to other agencies that have defined such services as their function. Having determined that services can be provided, the receptionist has assigned Mrs. Davis another worker so that the services may begin. The organizational aspects of the agency have immediately begun to influence Mrs. Davis's experience. The worker, too, is influenced by structure, goals, and functions. Recognizing this, a worker must become aware of the ways in which the organization may constrain as well as facilitate effective practice. The worker may deem a visit to Mrs. Davis's home essential, while agency policy may discourage visits into the housing project where Mrs. Davis lives. In order to provide the services needed, the worker must recognize and use those organizational resources that facilitate practice. These may include funds for transportation to enable Mrs. Davis and Lillian to visit the agency without using their meager public assistance income for the trip.

Unwittingly, Mrs. Davis has entered a complex social service bureaucracy. It is made up of a variety of units, subunits, and individuals whose tasks are assigned in relation to their positions in the agency hierarchy. Johnson (1986) describes the distinctive qualities of a social service agency with goals of caring for people rather than producing a product. In the caring process, goals are set for changes in knowledge, beliefs, attitudes, and skills. It is difficult, however, to measure the outcome of the helping process, the work of the agency.

The major component of the agency is a core of professional persons who function with a degree of autonomy and commitment to the client. This may at times conflict with the classic, efficient functioning of organizations. Mrs. Davis may expect a professional social worker to assist in ways that will bring about some significant change in her life. The social worker hopes to find supports within the system to aid in the process.

The agency provides a supervisor who will assist in decision making regarding services to Mrs. Davis. Perhaps a consultant may be available to advise in areas in which social worker and supervisor need greater insights and supports. The structure demands a director and a lay board, since this is a voluntary agency. Although Mrs. Davis may be unaware of the structure and its influence, the worker must be aware of the structure as well as the organization's interdependence with other agencies. Mrs. Davis already has a relationship with the public welfare agency. During the course of the helping process, contact with the public school would seem to be a reasonable expectation, as well as other agencies that might supply various outlets for Richard, Harold, and Jimmy. At some point vocational rehabilitation service may be considered for Mrs. Davis as her hand heals.

Knowledge of policy and services available in this family service center helps the social worker to carry out professional responsibility in ways that enhance Mrs. Davis's chances to return equilibrium to her family.

LAYER 4: SELF-AWARENESS,INCLUDING INSIGHTS INTO ONE'S OWN ETHNICITY AND AN UNDERSTANDING OF HOW THAT MAY INFLUENCE PROFESSIONAL PRACTICE

The 1958 working definition of social work practice proposed that workers have knowledge of themselves "which enables them to be aware of and to take responsibility for their own emotions and attitudes as they affect professional function."[3] Time has not changed the need for such awareness.

Self-awareness is essential because the disciplined and aware self remains one of the profession's major tools and must be developed into a fine instrument. The beginning of the honing process is the heightening of self-awareness, the ability to look at and recognize oneself, not always nice, sometimes judgmental, prejudiced, and noncaring. Self-awareness is the ability to recognize when the judgmental noncaring self interferes with the ability to reach out, to explore, to help others mobilize their coping capacities. Self-awareness involves the capacity to recognize that the client's foibles and strengths may trigger the worker's tendencies for empathy or destructiveness. And, it refers to the ability to make use of this type of understanding to attempt holding in check those narcissistic or destructive impulses that impede service delivery.

Although it is considered essential for practice, educators acknowledge difficulty in "teaching" self-awareness. Hamilton (1954) identified self-awareness in social work practice as attendant learning; when pursued as an object in itself it becomes more elusive. It must be "caught." How, then, how does one catch it?

In an attempt to teach self-awareness Eveline Schulman (1983) presents procedures for self-understanding. An exercise entitled "Getting at the who of you" poses three questions.

---

[3]*Social work* Vol. 3, April, 1958.

1. Who am I?
2. Who do others think I am?
3. Who would I like to be?

The exercise that follows has been designed to enable students to begin to consider these questions. The actual process involves a lifetime, and the answers change continually during a professional career. Answering these questions taps students' abilities to recognize with some accuracy their perceptions of themselves, the perceptions of others about them, and their dreams of what they might be.

The initial question, "Who am I?" must move from a superficial one that would identify the various roles assumed, to a level at which it is expanded to "Who am I in relation to my feelings about myself and others?" This subjective question has the ability to bring hidden feelings to the surface. Answering these questions is part of "catching" self-awareness. It grows from within and has been described as a process midway between knowing and feeling. One may be aware of something without being able to describe it (Grossbard 1954).

Crucial to this process is social workers' awareness of their own ethnicity and the ability to recognize how it affects their practice. "Who am I in the ethnic sense?" may be added to the original question, followed by: "What does that mean to me?" and "How does it shape my perceptions of persons who are my clients?"

The childhood experience of a social worker in an ethnic setting points out how such experiences will influence practitioners who have begun to answer the "Who am I?" questions.

> I am the younger of two daughters born to middle-class first-generation Jewish parents. I was born and raised in an apartment house in Brooklyn, New York, where I remained until I was married at twenty years of age. The neighborhood in which I lived consisted predominantly of Jewish and Italian families. Traditions were followed and young children growing up fulfilled their parents' expectations. This was a very protected environment in one sense in that, until high school, I did not have contact with people other than those of Jewish or Italian ancestry. However, Brooklyn was then a relatively safe place to live, and, at an early age, I traveled by bus or train to pursue different interests.
>
> Reflecting back, I think of both my parents as dominant figures in my growing up. My father was a laborer, believing in the old work ethic, working long hours each day. However, when he came home life centered around him. My mother and father raised my sister and me on love, understanding, and consideration for others, allowing me flexibility to discover my own self.
>
> My parents were simple people. Religious ritual played a minimal part in their life. They did not even go to synagogue on the High Holy Days, though

my mother fasted on Yom Kippur, the Day of Atonement, and fussed because my sister, father, friends, and I insisted on eating.

But, the family was most concerned about their fellow Jews in Europe, and the fate of Israel was eagerly followed on radio and television.

There was no question that I identified myself as a Jew. When I dated non-Jewish boys, my mother could not help but show her concern on her face.

Thinking back on this, I realize that, without much verbalization, my parents conveyed a strong sense of family, derived strength—and some pain—from their identity as Jews. I realize now that when I see Jewish clients who are in marital distress, or Jewish parents treating children with lack of consideration, my "gut reaction" is negative and judgmental.

Without ever having been told in so many words, I realize that I grew up with the sense that that's not how Jews are supposed to be. And somehow, in realizing that "my own people" don't always shape up to ideals, I also begin to realize who I am in relation to other kinds of people. For I recognize that just as I approached "my own" from a dim, somewhat unarticulated perception of what "they were supposed to be," I was viewing others in the same vein.

"Textbook learning" about Blacks, or Chicanos, or Orientals was not sufficient to overcome the effects of media or other experiences. I began to both "think and feel through" my reactions.

When workers begin to "think and feel through" the impact of their own ethnicity on their perceptions of themselves and others, there is more involved than the particular ethnic identity. What emerges is a total perception of "appropriate" family life roles.

The Jewish practitioner from a lower-middle-class, intact Jewish family in which children "fulfilled their parents' expectations" must be aware of a possible tendency to be judgmental toward Lillian (the daughter in the family described earlier) who is truant and begins to bring pain and turmoil to the family. "Who am I in the ethnic sense?" becomes more complex in an era when more and more people of different groups intermarry.

Dual Ethnic Background

Earlier discussion (in chapter two) has considered the increase in intermarriage between racial and ethnic groups. Persons who may share the same religious backgrounds but different ethnic histories, as well as those with totally different religious heritage, marry and establish new families. The social worker who has a partner of another ethnic background or is the child of such a marriage has more ethnic influences to consider. The answer to "Who am I in the ethnic sense?" becomes more complex. The following account by a social worker is illustrative:

My father is Irish Catholic and my mother German Lutheran. I identified with the Irish ethos to some degree because, first, my father was the dominant member of the family, and secondly, my religion was Catholic (our parish church staffed by Irish clergy). There was little contact with my mother's family because disapproval of her marriage kept them at a distance. External social pressures tended to force my identification with paternal ethnicity, as my name was Irish. Though of course I realized I shared an Irish heritage, I don't remember ever having a feeling of a shared future with the Irish as a group.

I in turn married a man whose background was overwhelmingly Italian, in spite of a French great-grandmother. My children have no ethnic identification that I can perceive. St. Patrick's Day is just another day; Columbus Day is a school holiday.

When workers of dual heritage begin to "think and feel through" the impact of ethnicity on their perceptions of themselves they may return to an earlier question: "Who am I?" The pervasive influence of an Irish Catholic heritage did not, in this particular instance, carry with it the sense of peoplehood with a shared future. In the background there is the lost German Lutheran heritage, the loss imposed by the rejection of a daughter who would not marry within the ethnic tradition.

Workers who have little sense of ethnic identification must realize that for many others ethnicity is a force that shapes movement through the life cycle, and determines appropriate marriage partners, language, certain dietary selections, and many subtleties of daily life.

Mrs. Davis's social worker must consider the "Who am I?" questions as work proceeds, as well as "Who am I in the ethnic sense?" and "Does that influence my practice in any significant way?

A heightened self-awareness and a greater awareness of ethnicity as it influences the personal and professional life form this fourth layer of understanding.

LAYER 5: THE IMPACT OF THE ETHNIC REALITY UPON THE DAILY LIFE OF THE CLIENT

At the beginning of this chapter Verna Davis and her family were introduced. We did not identify their ethnic group membership, although their social class was evident from their present circumstances. If this family is now identified as Black we can measure the impact of the ethnic reality upon them and move closer to a consideration of ethnic-sensitive practice.

It must always be recognized that ethnicity is but one of the many pieces of identifying information necessary for assessment in any approach to practice. We know Mrs. Davis's age, sex, marital status, employment status, and names and ages of her children; we know that Lillian, the eldest, presents the immediate problem. This additional ethnic data enables the worker to establish the Davis's ethclass and the dispositions that may surround that juncture.

Mrs. Davis's former employment in janitorial work and present welfare status place her firmly in a lower-income position. Her ethclass, low income-Black, has no power. Its occupants work at unskilled, low paid employment, are unemployed, or receive public assistance. They are often the victims of institutional racism.

This is a difficult position for Mrs. Davis. During the early years of their marriage Charles Davis worked diligently for his family. He understood his adult tasks and tried to fulfill them. His perspectives on manhood were much like those of the Black men in Cazenave's study in which employed letter carrier fathers felt that to be a man was to be responsible. The most salient masculine identity was that of economic provider. Guide and teacher, authority, companion, and protector were other salient roles. As they found success in each of these roles they were proud that they had the resources to achieve them (1979). While the subjects of Cazenave's study succeeded, Charles Davis failed. Unable to be the provider he hoped to be, he withdrew. In his absence, without the resources he had provided, the family declined in social class position.

Responding to the emergency, Mrs. Davis's sister moved into the household and remained there for the next two years. Such a response to the stress of kin may be considered to be an ethnic disposition; it is expected that a family member will respond. So, an attenuated extended family is formed consisting of Verna Davis, now a single parent, her sister Louise, and four children.

Billingsley (1968) suggests that this is but one of the many variations in Black family structures that place emphasis upon the responsibility of kin, particularly as the family strives for economic independence. Stack's (1975) study of kinship ties in the Flats of Jackson Harbor and Aschenbrenner's (1975) study of Black families in Chicago both highlight the sense of responsibility for kin even beyond the usually expected blood ties. This is not to say that such supports are not available in other ethnic groups, but that they may be more prominent as an ethnic reality for working-class or lower-income Black families (McAdoo 1978). Louise was not "taking from" Verna; she was giving her services, allowing her sister to move more successfully into the role of single parent.

The husband's departure puts Mrs. Davis in a position of leading the family. Though some would then characterize her as a matriarch, this is a deceptive and inaccurate description. Matriarchy implies power and control. She has limited power and limited resources. The position may be defined more precisely as matrifocal. The leadership role has been thrust upon her, not acquired through lineage. It is a de facto status (Hannerz 1969), limited in power because of her ethclass position.

Her powerlessness is reflected in her inability to provide an atmosphere in which Lillian may have a carefree adolescence, a respite before adulthood. Neither is she able to protect her sons Harold, Richard, and Jimmy from the potential insults of racism. All of her children are oppressed, and it is her task to provide them with as many viable coping techniques as possible to help them develop a maturity and creativity that will strengthen them, enabling them to work their way through environmental situations with dexterity (Ladner 1972).

In this ethclass environment children are more responsible for their own protection. Black children at the middle and upper-class levels may expect and receive greater protection from their parents. This is not the case with Mrs. Davis's children. Her strengths are used up in the daily drudgery to supply the basic needs for her family. The social worker must assess institutional resources in relation to their responses to the Davis children and their peers and must also be aware that the children's responses to their ethnic reality involve the development of sophisticated coping mechanisms that are not always accepted or understood by the larger society.

Lillian is unable to cope with the many roles given her: supervisor of siblings, student, perhaps even mother's confidante. She would rather be an adolescent struggling with the tasks that will give her adult status when accomplished. Responsibility has come too soon. Truancy may be a response to this interruption in her life cycle development. She is not necessarily a rebellious, acting-out, phobic child determined to defy the school and her parent. Rather, an ethnic-sensitive worker recognizes the impact of working or lower-income class status and ethnicity. These work together to produce for Lillian a situation of sufficient discomfort that she avoids school, where she has had earlier success.

The impact of the ethnic reality upon the daily lives of clients is evident at all phases of the life cycle and in any environment in which they may find themselves. The following family experience focuses upon individuals in the adult years of their lives. Poor health has caused a parent to be placed in a nursing home. This often generates trauma, despite the protection and care that are available. Difficulties are related to and compounded by the ethnic reality and life cycle positions.

A Mother's Distress

Bella Meyer spent her adult life working with her husband David in their small variety store and caring for their two children, Rose and Mark. The children left home as emerging adults to establish their own households and families. David died when he and Bella were both age sixty. Soon after, Bella's health failed and she became a resident of Ashbrook Manor, a nonsectarian nursing home. Mrs. Meyer is Jewish.

After a year in the home she is unhappy. A hearing impairment causes her great despair. She is unpleasant to the other residents and prefers to be alone. The nurses on her unit have nearly turned against her because of her attitude.

Her daughter, Rose Niemann, is employed as a clerk-typist in a local insurance company. She visits her mother regularly but stays only a few minutes because she is on her lunch hour. Mark, a shoe salesman, seldom visits. Both of the children make contributions to their mother's care.

Rose's and Mark's children visit their grandmother only on holidays.

The impact of the ethnic reality upon Mrs. Meyer's life may be overlooked in a nonsectarian setting that has no commitment to her Jewishness. The primary purpose of the nursing home is to provide care for aging persons with failing health. In this setting she is denied the traditional aspects of Jewish family life.

The food, although healthful, lacks what Mrs. Meyer calls "tahm" (character). Food has been an important part of her life. She had previously been able to express love and sociability to her family and to her friends by preparing and serving food. Here, like all patients, she is cut off from daily family life and the tasks of a caregiver. For a Jewish woman this may well be devastating.

Reverence for the Jewish aging may be seen in an extensive network of charities and residential and nursing settings. This adheres to historical expectations that children will have a caring regard and respect for the elderly, including their parents (Linden 1967). Mark and Rose, Mrs. Meyer's children, do care and have not totally abandoned her, but they are involved in small, nuclear family units that cannot readily lend themselves to the incorporation of a frail, disgruntled, elderly grandmother. Mrs. Meyer feels alienated and rejected; the nonsectarian nursing home, devoid of "Yiddishkeit," intensifies her already profound sense of isolation and alienation.

The ancient belief that, as a Jew, she is one of the "chosen people" has at times given her a sense of comfort, of having been favored by God. But God and tradition have failed her. When she refers to her heritage in her communication with others, they don't understand and may interpret her behavior as snobbery. Nursing staff and other residents are unaware of the tradition or its significance in Mrs. Meyer's life (Linden 1967).

Aging and poor health engulf Mrs. Meyer in the despair of old age. The productivity of her earlier years, in which she carried out a historical tradition of laboring women, is no longer possible. Her daughter Rose is able to carry out tradition through her employment and uses some of her resources to aid in the support of her mother. At middle age, she is torn between her regard for her aging mother and the needs of her own family. This is the struggle of many women, but for Rose there is the ethnic disposition which places particular emphasis upon both relationships. She is constant in her attention to her mother, although she limits visits to "looking in" during her lunch hour. On the other hand, her brother Mark is less attentive. He may well be considered to be neglectful except for his regular financial contribution. This behavior can be considered from the perspective of the intense mother-son interactions found in some Jewish families. There are indications that overprotective and affectionate mothers may withhold love for the purpose of discipline. The resultant stress felt by sons may, as the mother grows older, be observed in behavior similar to Mark's (Linden 1967). He contributes regularly to her support but refuses close contact, much to Mrs. Meyer's despair. Although filial duty is accomplished by contributing to her support, his absence suggests rejection. She does not enjoy the attention and peace that she feels she should expect from a reverent son; neither do her grandchildren bring her joy.

The social worker who observes Bella Meyer finds an ailing elderly woman who complains of poor hearing to the extent that the staff avoids contact with her. With a grasp of the layers of understanding the worker is able to expand upon this initial observation and see more of Mrs. Meyer, who is a unique older Jewish woman in failing health. She has been removed from the Jewish community that has given her support and a sense of well-being, and placed in a nursing home that does not respond to her ethnic needs in any way. Her age denies her the satisfaction of work, and her children and grandchildren do not respond to her in ways she feels are appropriate in Jewish families. This information, added to knowledge about the administrative structure and policy of the nursing home, enables the social worker to seek alternatives in health care to more positively respond to Mrs. Meyer's ethnic needs as well as those of other Jewish residents.

As the social worker seeks alternatives to enhance Mrs. Meyer's life at Ashbrook Manor, there must be an awareness that one's own ethnicity may influence perspectives on the lives of others. The Meyer family cannot respond in ways that are completely familiar to the Irish, Italian, or Black social worker and must not be viewed from that perspective.

Verna Davis and Bella Meyer both have problems that may well be alleviated through social work intervention. When their social workers and others have gained a professional perspective, including the layers of understanding presented here, they may be expected to become more effective in the practice, more aware of themselves and others.

SUMMARY

This chapter has identified the layers of understanding for social work practice. These are:

1. Social work values
2. A basic knowledge of human behavior
3. Knowledge and skill in social welfare policy and services
4. An insight into one's own ethnicity and how that may influence one's perspective
5. Understanding of the impact of the ethnic reality upon daily lives of clients

These are the first five of six layers that lead to ethnic-sensitive practice. The final layer is comprised of those skills already available to the profession. They must be reviewed, reconsidered, adapted, and modified in relation to the ethnic reality. Chapter six addresses this sixth layer of understanding:

6. The adaptation and modification of skills and techniques in response to the ethnic reality

REFERENCES

Aschenbrenner, Joyce. 1975. *Lifelines—Black families in Chicago.* Prospect Heights, IL: Waveland Press, Inc.

Billingsley, Andrew. 1968. *Black families in white America.* Englewood Cliffs, NJ: Prentice-Hall, Inc.

Cazenave, Noel A. 1979. Middle-income fathers: an analysis of the provider role. *Family Coordinator* 28:583–593.

Grossbard, Hyman. 1954. Methodology for developing self-awareness. *Social Casework* 35:380–386.

Hamilton, Gordon. 1954. Self-awareness in professional education. *Social Casework.* 35:371–379.

Hannerz, Ulf. *Soulside—inquiries in ghetto culture and community.* New York: Columbia University Press.

Hartman, Ann. 1979. *Finding families—an ecological approach to family assessment in adoption*. Beverly Hills: Sage Publications.

Hartman, Ann, and Laird, Joan. 1983. *Family-centered social work practice*. New York: The Free Press.

Johnson, Louise. 1986. *Social work practice a generalist approach*. 2d Ed. Boston: Allyn and Bacon, Inc.

Ladner, Joyce A. 1972. *Tomorrow's tomorrow—the Black woman*. New York: Anchor Books, Doubleday and Co.

Levy, Charles S. 1973. The value base for social work. *Journal of Education for Social Work* 9:34–42.

Linden, Maurice E. 1967. Emotion problems in aging. In *The psychodynamics of American Jewish life: an anthology*. New York: Twanye Publishers, Inc.

McAdoo, Harriet. 1978. The impact of upward mobility on kin-help patterns and the reciprocal obligations in Black families. *Journal of Marriage and the Family*. 40:761–778.

Parsons, Talcott. 1958. Definitions of health and illness in the light of American values and social structure. In *Patients, physicians, and illness: a sourcebook in behavioral science and health*. 2d ed., edited by E. Gartley Jaco. New York: The Free Press.

Schulman, Eveline D. 1983. *Intervention in human services*. 2d ed. St. Louis: The C. V. Mosby Co.

Stack, Carol. 1975. *All our kin—strategies for survival in a Black community*. New York: Harper and Row, Harper Publishers, Colophon Books.

Strean, Herbert. 1979. Role theory. In *Social work treatment: interlocking theoretical approaches*, edited by Francis J. Turner. New York: The Free Press.

CHAPTER
4

Approaches to Social Work Practice and the Ethnic Reality

In the preceding chapters we have described our perspectives on ethnicity, social class, and the life cycle, and have presented conceptual formulations intended to develop an image of how these factors affect perceptions of problems in living. These are important dimensions of human functioning that have received insufficient attention in the social work practice literature.

In this chapter major focus is on reviewing a number of prevailing approaches to social work practice and assessing the extent to which each pays attention to the ethnic reality. In making this assessment, we are sensitive to the fact that there are divergent theoretical formulations about how human beings are shaped and how these theories relate to the problem-solving activities social work undertakes.

A strong social reform stance has long been taken by many social workers. For some adherents to this perspective, the major sources of individual and social dysfunction are to be found in social structural inequity. Those committed to this view of the human condition explain behavior in sociological and structural terms; they advocate intervention strategies designed to effect social and environmental change. According to some analysts, major understanding of human functioning can be found in psychologically based explanations of human behavior. These analysts have influenced the selection of helping strategies.

Another group has sought to understand how the interplay of social and psychological forces impinge on and shape the individual; both bodies of thought are drawn upon in the effort to heighten understanding and generate appropriate helping strategies.

Some analysts believe that these various perspectives on human behavior have come to dictate the purpose of the social worker's practice and deflect attention from work designed to develop a social work frame of reference derived from a clear notion of the function and purpose of the profession (Pincus and Minahan 1973). This kind of thinking has generated a number of efforts to distinguish between social work practice principles and strategies on the one hand, and the diverse theoretical orientations that can aid in understanding the problems with which social workers deal (Fischer 1978; Pincus and Minahan 1973).

These divergent points of view have bearing on our assessment of prevailing approaches, as do the varying definitions of terms such as *theory, assumptions, models, practice theory, strategies, principles,* and *skills.*

We begin by reviewing the common usage of these terms; following this, we summarize a number of major points of view about how theory, concepts, and knowledge of human behavior affect the practice of social work. We then turn our attention to a number of practice models and examine them in light of our perspective on the ethnic reality. We conclude by presenting the point of view about the relationship between theory and practice that guides our work.

ASSUMPTIONS, THEORIES, AND MODELS

Assumptions and Theories

These terms are often used interchangeably. In some respects this is justified. At least one dictionary defines an assumption as "something taken for granted," and indicates that it is a term synonymous with theory and hypothesis. Theory has been defined as "a plausible or scientifically acceptable general principle or body of principles offered to explain phenomena" (*Webster's 9th Collegiate Dictionary* 1984). The status of the explanation is conjectural. Turner proposes that "theory builds a series of propositions about reality; that is, it provides us with models of reality and helps us to understand what is possible and how we can attain it" (1986, p. 2). Key terms are *concepts, facts, hypotheses* and *principles.* Concepts are symbols used to characterize the phenomena of interest, and the labels by which we communicate with each other within a discipline. Abstractions from experience, they aid in clear and effective communication between the members of a discipline. Facts can be verified; they relate to observations of concepts. Hypotheses are conjectural statements about the relationship between variables. Principles emerge out of hypothesis testing and theory development. Principles are dependable, predictive statements about some aspect of reality.

These abstract definitions and distinctions assume importance because they all focus on systematic delineation of concepts used in behavioral and social science inquiry and the relationships between them. Essentially, these definitions suggest that when we speak of a relationship between social class and ethnic group membership and the way people feel about marriage, child rearing, or work, we have some evidence—based on systematic inquiry—that these relationships exist. Similarly, when it is proposed that there is a connection between childhood experiences with loving or hostile relationships and adult personality patterns, persistent, systematic observation supports the existence of this relationship. A crucial component of the definition of theory presented is the term *conjectural*. This highlights the fact that the assertions made are ever open to revision and calls our attention to the need for continuing and persistent study.

Also important is the term *proposition* and the way it is used here: "something affirmed." This indicates that the relationships under scrutiny have been sufficiently investigated and supported by scientific inquiry so that little doubt remains concerning the truth of the assertions. Few of the theories used in the social and behavioral sciences can be said to have been, in Turner's term, "empirically verified." This is true of psychological or sociological theories. But, this state of affairs does not negate the major importance of such bodies of theory as psychoanalytic theory, behaviorist theory, or theories about social class, ethnicity, and the life cycle; these form the foundation of much of our work and thinking. That they are not to be viewed as immutable fact alerts practitioners to the ever-present need to look for new relationships and to approach problems with a fresh and open stance.

Models

In contrast to a theory, which looks at a class of interrelated facts and seeks to explain the logical relationships between them, a model is a visual or metaphoric image of an area of interest. Often likened to a model of a ship or plane, it describes or presents an image of the phenomena of interest; a theory, by contrast, seeks to explain the relationships between them. This can be illustrated by referring to the material presented in chapter one. A number of prevailing definitions of social class and ethnic group were reviewed and the intersect between the two defined as *ethclass*. A description of how social class and ethnic group interact can be translated into an image of how people function at this intersect. Like most models, this kind of description begins to explain the relationship between social class and ethnic group membership, suggesting that the two are inextricably linked in a manner that generates ethclass. No claim has been made that persistent scientific investigation proves these relationships are indisputable facts.

Much of the knowledge used by social work derives from varying models that seek to explain human behavior. The perspective on ethnicity, social class, and the life cycle presented here can be characterized as a model describing important components about our clients and their world. Like all models, it has potential for moving beyond description to explaining major areas of thought, feeling, and experience.

PREVAILING VIEWS ON THE RELATIONSHIP BETWEEN UNDERSTANDING OF HUMAN BEHAVIOR AND INTERVENTIVE PROCEDURES

This section focuses on the relationships between theories, models, and the helping activities social work undertakes.

Ideally, interventive procedures are derived from the various theories of personality and social systems (Siporin 1975). For example, the life cyle model identifies points of transition and suggests potential areas and types of stress to which members of different ethnic groups may be especially vulnerable. This perspective aids the social worker in identifying behaviors that are indicative of stress or smooth transition. Stress may be revealed in parent-child conflict triggered by disagreement over ethclass versus mainstream standards. For example, an Italian adolescent girl may refuse to adhere to the strict supervision of dating her family seeks to impose. Identification of the trouble and its source can generate social worker activity designed to aid both parent and child in understanding and coping with the difficulty. Joint interviewing of parents and child by a worker familiar with the culture might be directed toward identifying possible points of compromise. A good *theory* would aid in predicting whether this approach would reduce the stress.

Turner (1986) reviews the current state of thinking about the relationship between theory and practice in social work. Some decry the lack of a strong theoretical base. Others are skeptical of theory as if it were somehow antithetical to social work's basic commitment to take account of unique individual experience. In Turner's view we "have not made full use of what we already have" (1986, p. 5). Some operate from an impressionistic base rather than one solidly based on theory. Considering "what can theory do for us," Turner proposes that:

For the clinician seeking to offer responsible, effective intervention, the most essential and important contribution of theory is its ability to predict outcomes, or, in other words, its ability to explain. Theory helps us to recognize patterns and relationships that aid in bringing order to the reality with which we are confronted, to 'compare, evaluate, and relate data.' The practitioner who consciously formulates a treatment plan based on an assessment of a situation is involved in either a theory building or theory testing activity; that is, a treatment plan aimed at achieving a particular goal presumes a situation is understood to the extent that specific alterations of the situation can be made with predictable outcomes (1986, p. 11).

Sound theory should help us: (1) to recognize the similarities and differences in the changing elements of daily practice, (2) to enhance the concept of client self-determination by focusing on the resemblance of clients to each other, as well as to their uniqueness, and (3) to test concepts as practice seems either to support or refute them.

In his earlier work, Turner held firm to the conviction that explanation and description of our clients and their world should lead logically to identification of problematic behavior and to guidelines for helping (Turner 1974). Later he entertains the possibility that a theory of intervention could be developed that is different from the theories of personality, learning, and behavior so familiar to most social workers (Turner 1986).

The view that causal knowledge may not provide an adequate base for practice is held by a number of analysts. Fischer (1978) and Reid (1978) are among those who have presented this perspective.

Fischer makes a distinction between causal/developmental knowledge and intervention knowledge. The former answers the question *why* and aids in understanding and "diagnosing;" the latter answers the question *what* and deals with theories, principles, and procedures for induced change (Fischer 1978). There is increasing doubt about the assumption that understanding the causes of or history of problems provides clues about what is sustaining the problem, or guidelines for intervention. This view is not shared by all. Middleman and Goldberg (1974) contend that understanding of the causes of a problem goes a long way toward defining it and projecting solutions.

Practice Theory

Fischer views practice theory as consisting of two elements: (1) systematic interpretation of those principles that help understand the phenomena of interest, and (2) clear delineation of principles for inducing change (1978). Siporin (1975) suggests that two levels of practice theory can be identified. The first focuses on how social work affects personality and social systems. Included here is *assessment theory*, focused on how judgments are made about what the problem is, how it is defined, and how change objectives are selected. *Intervention theory* is focused on how changes are to be effected, that is, on interventive procedures. The second level of practice theory identified by Siporin centers on the various theoretical orientations to helping. These tend to derive from a body of foundation knowledge, in the form of personality and social theories. Each has a distinctive set of assessment and intervention theories as well as practice principles, strategies, and procedures. In this second level of practice theory it is clearly demonstrated how the view of the human condition assumed by the theory guides problem definition and intervention.

Both Fischer and Siporin advocate an eclectic stance. Fischer emphasizes an approach to selection of theories and strategies of intervention based on practice principles and procedures that have been tested and found effective and that are congruent with basic social work values. He explicitly rejects the search for integration based on divergent theories or causal knowledge. Siporin proposes a fluid, eclectic stance, suggesting integration of diverse schools of thought and doctrines.

PREVAILING APPROACHES TO SOCIAL WORK PRACTICE

Considerable work remains to be done in clarifying the relationship between what is known and believed about human behavior and about the causes of problems and how social work uses that knowledge.

A number of distinct, though inevitably overlapping, approaches to social work practice can be identified. For the most part these approaches are based on a body of assumptions and theories about and descriptions of the human condition. The related practice procedures represent an attempt to translate the understanding of how people function into principles for problem resolution.

There are any number of ways to categorize and characterize the various social work practice models. In Turner's most recent analysis (1986) he arrives at a classification system in which the thought systems or practice models are distinguished from each other by which element of the "psychosocial reality" they emphasize. Over twenty are identified. Their distinguishing foci are: (1) person as psychological being, (2) person as thinker, (3) person as learner, (4) person as contemplator, (4) person as communicator, (5) person as doer, (6) person as biological entity, (7) person as individual, (8) person as family member, (9) person as group member, (10) person in relation to society, and (11) person in relation to the universe.

We have identified six major approaches for review: (1) the psycho-social approach (as per Turner, person in relation to society), (2) the problem-solving approaches (as per Turner, person as doer), (3) the social provision and structural approaches, (4) the systems approach (these, in Turner's view, focus on person in society), (5) the ecological approach (as per Turner, person in relation to the universe), and (6) the approaches focused on cultural awareness and minority issues. There are, of course, other important approaches to practice, as implied by Turner and others. Our emphasis is on a number of those commonly used and known to social workers. More recent, though perhaps less widely known efforts to incorporate understanding of culture and minority status into practice, are of special interest here.

In reviewing and assessing the first five approaches, we summarize the assumptions on which they are based and the related interventive procedures. Particular attention is paid to matters concerning the ethnic reality.

We pose a series of questions designed to determine whether attention has been paid to the special needs and life-styles of various ethnic and minority groups.

1. Does the approach give recognition to the part played by mem-bership in varying groups in shaping people's lives?
2. Is the approach based on narrow "culture-bound" perspectives of human behavior, or is it sufficiently fluid and broad-based as to generate interpretations of behavior that are consonant with world views and outlooks that differ from those most prevalent in mainstream America?
3. Have interventive procedures been proposed that guide practitio-ners in their use of knowledge concerning the different world views of various groups?

In reviewing and assessing the culturally sensitive approaches we also summarize the assumptions and related interventive procedures. Our questions are directed toward determining (1) the congruence of these approaches with other prevailing approaches to social work practice, and (2) the degree to which the concepts and strategies presented guide practitioners in their work with the ever-varied and increasing numbers of ethnic groups found in the United States.

THE PSYCHOSOCIAL APPROACH

In some respects, it is inappropriate to speak of a distinct psychosocial approach to social work practice. In many ways, the term *psychosocial* and the view inherent in the term, that people are both psychological and sociological beings, is synonymous with social work's perspective. Indeed, Turner (1974) suggests that it is a term fully the "prerogative of our profession." And yet *psychosocial therapy* has come to be associated with a particular view of the human condition and approaches to practice, the total meanings of which are not uniformly shared. As a result, the configuration of ideas and treatment approaches termed psychosocial practice can be viewed as separate and apart from the more general view, shared by most social workers, that many of the issues with which they deal can be understood in psychosocial terms.

The psychosocial approach has a long and honorable history; much attention has and continues to be focused on efforts to refine, reformulate, and specify the basic assumptions, interventive strategies, and techniques that continue to evolve.

Assumptions

Part and parcel of the view that people are psychosocial beings is the assumption that we are in large measure governed by unique past histories and the internal dynamic generated by those histories. This view of human beings translates into a perspective on practice emphasizing the need to maintain a dual focus on people as psychological and sociological beings, that is, on intrapersonal, interpersonal, and intersystemic beings (Turner 1974).

Richmond (1917) emphasizes this dual perspective in her definition of social casework as "those processes which develop a personality through adjustments consciously effected, individual by individual, between men and their social environment."

A number of pervasive themes emerge. These include a belief that all people have both the capacity and responsibility to participate in shaping their own destinies. People are social beings who reach their potential in the course of relationships with family, friends, small groups, and the community. Belief in the capacity to choose and to make decisions from among alternatives is related to the belief that each of us is unique and unpredictable and that all have the capacity to "rise up above and beyond . . . history" (Turner 1974). This does not negate the importance of genetic endowment, personal history, and the environment in shaping actions.

The view that the past has major bearing on behavior in the present is stressed in the psychosocial approach. Considerable importance is attached to nonconscious phenomena that influence but do not determine behavior. Psychoanalytic insights into human behavior are vital. These include the Freudian view that all individuals throughout life are characterized by libidinal and aggressive drives that make a continuing demand on the environment (Hollis 1972). At the same time the personality includes a set of adaptive qualities termed the *ego*.

The psychosocial approach is also heavily influenced by sociological conceptions. The family, the social group, and the community affect social functioning in major ways. Increasingly, the influence of socio-economic status, ethnicity, and the family are stressed (Turner 1978).

Hollis (1972) proposes that breakdown in social adjustment can be traced to three interacting sources: (1) infantile needs and drives left over from childhood that cause the individual to make inappropriate demands on the adult world, (2) a current life situation that exerts excessive pressures, and (3) faulty ego and superego functioning.

Problems stemming from persisting infantile needs and drives generate a variety of pathologies and disturbances in capacity to assume adult responsibilities. Or, disturbances may be generated by environmental pressures, such as economic deprivation, racial and ethnic discrimination, inadequate education, and inadequate housing. Family conflict or loss occasioned by illness, death, or separation are also viewed as current life pressures. Faulty ego functioning is manifested in distorted perceptions of factors operating both internal and external to the individual. Breakdown is often triggered by disturbance in more than one of these areas, as they tend to interact in affecting functioning.

Turner (1978) suggests that the goal of psychosocial therapy is to help people to achieve optimal psychosocial functioning in keeping with their potential and value system. These goals may be accomplished through the development of human relationships, available material and service resources, and human resources in the environment. Involvement with a psychosocial therapist may effect change in cognitive, emotive, behavioral, or material areas so that there is relief from suffering.

In summary, the psychosocial approach stresses the interplay of individual and environment, the effect of past and present, the effect of nonconscious factors on the personality, and the impact of present environmental as well as psychologically induced sources of stress and coping capacity. There is major attention to psychoanalytic conceptions of human behavior, and how these explain the presenting difficulties.

Assumptions and the ethnic reality.

The definition of the ethnic reality calls attention to those aspects of the ethnic experience providing sources of pride, a comfortable sense of belonging, various networks of family and community, and a range of approaches to coping that have withstood the test of time. At the same time, it highlights the persistent negation of valued traditions and other turmoils experienced by various ethnic groups as they encounter the majority culture. Particular attention is paid to the effects of discrimination in such spheres as jobs, housing, and schools. Review of the major tenets of psychosocial theory indicates that the roles of ethnicity and social class are incorporated in this perspective. Hollis, Turner, Strean, and others all emphasize the destructive effects of discrimination, poor housing, and poverty. The effect of destructive stereotyping is mentioned by many.

And yet, two major gaps are apparent. First, there is no clear or detailed indication as to how minority status, ethnicity, and class converge to shape individuals and contribute to the problems for which they seek help. This gap is noted by many social work analysts (Fischer 1978; Reid 1978; Turner 1974). A second omission, or perhaps distortion, is the tendency to stress the negative and dysfunctional aspects of the ethnic reality. The disabling effects of discrimination or low socioeconomic status receive a great deal of attention. This is as it should be. However, the unique and often beneficial effects of membership in various groups is often ignored (Mirelowitz 1979; President's Commission on Mental Health 1978).

Good psychosocial practice should be ever mindful of those sources of identity deriving from a sense of peoplehood and those sources of difficulty that stem from systemic inequity. The consideration of past history in relation to present functioning should present positive and negative aspects of the ethnic reality. The classic statements of the psychosocial approach do not help us here. Efforts to make these kinds of connections have been made (Grier and Cobbs 1969). A recent "test" of applicability of psychosocial theory to work with Chicano clients shows its usefulness in work with this group when integrated with cultural insights (Gomez, Zurcher, Farris and Becker 1985).

The American Indians' perspective on time and the priority some give to kin over work relations are frequently cited (Good Tracks 1973). Behaviors related to these perspectives clash with the values of the larger society. When work schedules are not met, jobs can be lost, resulting in much pain and turmoil.

Similarly, some Chinese fathers who, by mainstream standards, remain emotionally distant from their children may well trigger confusion and doubt in those children emerging into adolescence in American society. But there is another aspect to these types of experiences. In a hostile world, or a world that devalues certain subcultural dispositions, kin who act in accustomed ways and transmit powerful belief systems go a long way toward providing emotional sustenance. The loss of job may seem negligible compared to the sense of satisfaction obtained from doing what is expected by family. "Distancing" may be experienced as rejecting and confusing, yet it provides a sense of the past or a clear sense of time honored ways.

Our reading of the best that has been written about the psychosocial approach suggests that insufficient attention has been paid to these matters, despite the fact that Hollis and others take great care to point out that practitioners must be attuned to these subcultural differences.

Interventive Procedures

The methods of intervention embodied in the term *psychosocial* have been characterized in a number of ways. Here particular attention is given to the typology developed and tested by Hollis (1972). In her classic work, she proposes that casework intervention essentially involves the following procedures: (1) sustainment [sustenance] direct influence, and ventilation, (2) reflective discussion of the person-situation configuration, and (3) reflective consideration of dynamic and developmental factors. These are focused on *forms of communication* between client and workers. Also of importance is *milieu* or *environmental work*. This typology of casework *treatment communication* or *casework process* has been tested. Client-worker interactions were systematically examined to determine if they fit the categories described. The work appeared to indicate that much of worker-client communication does proceed as outlined. Milieu and environmental work were not included in the research procedures.

Sustainment, direct influence, and ventilation. Hollis's presentation of the major components of sustainment, direct influence, and ventilation culls out much that is essential both in casework and in other forms of social work practice. She calls attention to the inherent discomfort and anxiety related to needing help, to the fears engendered by self-revelation, and to the doubts concerning the outcome. Sympathetic listening and noncritical acceptance are stressed. The importance of providing reassurance, while not losing sight of those realities which may make reassurance inappropriate, is pointed out, as well as the need to render a variety of concrete services, vital in their own right and symbolic of the worker's interest in the client.

Reflective discussion of the person-situation configuration. This procedure draws clients into discussion focused on their functioning in the major areas of their lives. The practitioner must be alert to distorted perceptions whereby individuals are able to see only one side of persons or situations that have impact upon their present life circumstances. A father, afraid that his son might be "stupid" like his own brother, may not notice his son's positive accomplishments. Or, parents trying to cope with their adolescent in turmoil see only the "negative" behavior and deliberately or inadvertently cut off communication. When using this procedure practitioners may need to consider the possibility that if the client and worker are members of different racial groups, this may interfere with the reflective discussion process. A difference in race between practitioner and client may produce hostility that will need to be identified and clarified (Hollis 1972).

When focus is on decision making, consequences, and alternatives, workers try to help clients think about the effects of their actions on others or themselves. These may be of a practical nature, concerning possible changes to be made in residence or employment. They may involve more intimate, emotional issues including decisions concerning marriage, divorce, or adoption. Always, every effort should be made to enable clients to come to "see," on their own, how typical behavioral patterns affect themselves and others. Helping people to become aware of hidden feelings or to express feared feelings is viewed as helpful.

Reflective consideration of dynamic and developmental factors. In this type of client-worker interaction it is assumed that intrapsychic forces of which people are unaware may strongly influence behavior. Emphasis then is on pursuing some of the intrapsychic reasons for feeling, attitudes, and ways of acting. The worker needs to explore factors in the person's past history that may help to explain the reasons for certain feelings.

Environmental work. Environmental work is essentially focused on intervention within those problematic systems of which the client is a part. All the procedures previously outlined may be employed in various combinations. Diverse resources, including those people with whom the client has emotional relationships, are used.

Varying worker roles are identified: provider, locator or creator of resources, interpreter, mediator, and aggressive intervener. The importance of advocacy is stressed.

Turner (1978) expands on these important distinctions by pointing to significant environments as components of treatment. The network of relationships in which people are involved should be viewed as a component of treatment, not merely as sources of information. Turner also points to the importance of paying attention to the settings within which service is rendered. Such factors as sponsorship and congruence with client values may be crucial. While not all clients are concerned with "ethnic sponsorship," for some this may be most important. Some Black clients may look for the agency endorsed by the Urban League, while a Hungarian client may feel most comfortable in a program sponsored by the Hungarian Reformed Church. Differences in feeling on this matter have been studied by Jenkins (1981).

We have summarized a number of the procedures that serve as the basis for psychosocial practice. Hollis (1972) proposes that workers who become involved in dynamic or developmental matters and pay major attention to these in intervention must have a thorough familiarity with both conscious and unconscious aspects of personality functioning. She also suggests that workers who are not adept in applying casework skills to environmental work will be less able to help clients with intra and interpersonal relationships.

Interventive procedures and the ethnic reality. The review of basic psychosocial procedures as outlined by Hollis suggests that we must answer our question "Does the model guide practitioners in their use of the ethnic reality?" in the negative. In other work Hollis (1965) does propose practice modifications presumed to be more consonant with "working class orientations." She suggests that the differences are in emphasis and cautions against stereotyping. But, in our perusal of many case examples in the major work there is virtually no mention made of class or ethnic group membership. Although "persons-in-situations" are presented, their situations are marital conflict, problematic parent-child interaction, and the life-threatening or fearsome situations related to illness. These are the "gut" and "heart" of the problems with which social workers try to help people. But people in marital conflict are also Black, Italian, Jewish, Chicano, or Puerto Rican. They may be threatened with job loss, not merely making a decision about vocational change, or contemplating the advantages of a promotion, but also struggling with the threat of moving to another part of the country, removing them from kin.

Turner (1970) has demonstrated that clients and workers from different ethnic groups do have different value orientations. These differences affect the outcome of treatment when various aspects of psychosocial functioning are assessed. Despite this awareness, limited if any attention is paid to the possible usefulness of these findings in identifying appropriate treatment.

For instance, *reflective consideration of the situation* and self-disclosure are alien to many Mexican-Americans and American Indians. For some, telling a stranger about weakness or family turmoil runs counter to the core of their being. Some American Indians reject discussion on intimate matters unless there is mutual sharing. Some Indian women, experiencing marital difficulties, will in the course of discussing these with a female social worker believe that she, too, has had similar experiences. Their expectations are that these are to be mutually shared, that perhaps the two can help each other. Certainly there is little in social work education to prepare the social worker for such reciprocal interaction. Quite the contrary, it has been the expectation that social workers will not bring their problems into the encounter with the client. Adaptations of this kind involve more than the kinds of transference relationships commonly thought to effect client-worker interaction. Experiencing of transference phenomena on the part of the worker is not ruled out. But what is at issue here is a major difference in perspective on the circumstances under which it is appropriate to discuss problems, and how the worker is viewed. An issue to which we shall pay some attention is whether practice can be modified to incorporate these kinds of client perspectives.

What emerges from our examination of some classic work on the psychosocial approach is that the approach is congruent with the kind of attention to the ethnic reality with which we are concerned. However, when we review the case examples, and other suggestions for practice, we find that there is a dearth of material to aid in operationalizing this approach.

THE PROBLEM-SOLVING APPROACHES

Rather than pursue the psychosocial approach concentrating on psycho-analytic insights, a significant number of practitioners look to the problem-solving approaches as the framework to be used for the helping process. Prominent among these are Helen Harris Perlman, William Reid, and Laura Epstein. Perlman may be considered the originator of the *problem-solving framework*, presented in her classic work (Perlman 1957). Reid and Epstein have introduced a more structed model termed *task-centered casework* (Reid 1978; Reid and Epstein 1972; Reid 1986).

Common to these approaches is reliance on a wide range of theoretical stances. Few reject Freudian conceptions; they are, however, not as committed to them as are those who proceed from the assumptions outlined in the psychosocial approach. Ego psychology, learning theory, role theory, and communication theory are among the theoretical foundations drawn upon by the proponents of the problem-solving approaches.

The basic problem-solving approach as developed by Perlman and the task-centered system of Reid and Epstein are treated separately. We begin with the basic assumptions put forth by Perlman.

PROBLEM SOLVING FRAMEWORK

Assumptions

Intrinsic is the view that all of human life is a problem-solving process; difficulties in coping with problems are based on a lack of opportunity, ability, or motivation.

In the course of human growth, individuals develop problem-solving capacities as basic features of the personality. To deal effectively with diverse problems, including recurrent life cycle tasks, requisite resources and opportunities must be available. Excessive stress, crisis, or inadequate resources impair coping capacity. Interpersonal conflict, insufficient resources, deficient or dissatisfying role performance, and difficulties in moving through the stages of the life cycle as anticipated are all viewed as problems.

There is less emphasis than in the psychosocial approach on the importance of personal pathology in the etiology of problems. Equilibrium may be restored and optimal functioning regained when competence is restored or strengthened and when needed social and welfare services are provided (Siporin 1975). Past experiences, present perceptions and reactions to the problem, as well as future aspirations join together to form the person with a problem. Of primary importance is today's reality. Knowledge of current living situations by which persons are "being molded and battered" provide the facts necessary for the problem-solving process to be activated (Perlman 1957). Perlman suggests that a major contribution of the model is its ". . . *focus upon the here-and-now*" and the recognition that ". . . each help seeker comes to us at a point of what *he* feels to be a crisis . . ." (Perlman 1986, p. 249).

The person's response to the problem-solving process is influenced by the structure and functioning of the personality that has been molded by inherited equipment as well as interactions with the physical and social environment. However, blocks may impede the process. These may include lack of material provisions available to the client, ignorance or misapprehension about the facts of the problem and ways of dealing with it, or a lack of physical and emotional energy to invest in problem solving.

Culture and its influence on individual development is discussed. In describing the person, Perlman presents the individual operating as a physical, psychological, social entity: a product of constitutional makeup, physical and social environment, past experience, present perceptions and reactions, and future aspirations. Also important is the person as a "whole" (1986, p. 250). "The time schedules that we keep, the way we eat, dress, talk to other persons and respect we show for property and the rights of others and our personal expectations for success are an indication of our incorporation of societal standards and ideas" (Perlman 1957).

The goal in problem solving is to provide necessary resources, restore equilibrium, and promote optimal functioning through a process that places emphasis upon contemporary reality, and present problem-ridden situations. These resources are of both a concrete and an interpersonal nature.

Assumptions and the ethnic reality

There are no contradictions between this model and the concept of the ethnic reality. There is considerable congruence between the notion that effective coping is contingent on the availability of adequate resources and opportunities and our view that, for the most part, the ethnic reality often simultaneously serves as a source of stress and strength. While the dysfunctional effect of personality pathology is not neglected, greater emphasis is placed on restoration of competence and provision of resources in delineated problem areas. This is consonant with our stress on the systemic source of problems often faced by ethnic and minority groups.

Interventive Procedures

Perlman suggests that the problem-solving event has several components: (1) the person, (2) the problem, (3) the place, and (4) a process. More recently she suggests two others: professional person and provisions (1986). It is through the process that problem-solving operations take place within a meaningful relationship. This process includes three essential procedures intended to move people from a state of discomfort to one in which they are able to cope with problems using their own skills (Perlman 1957).

Ascertainment and clarification of facts. This initial step requires that the caseworker establish the facts of the individual's situation, that is, the *why* and *what* factors as they are perceived. These facts include the feelings and behaviors manifested by people as they struggle with the problem and respond to the objective reality in subjective ways. While this is identified as the initial step, it must be recognized that ascertainment and clarification are a continuing responsibility throughout the problem-solving event.

Thinking through the facts. While the problem-solving process places emphasis on collaboration between social worker and client, the professional has a major responsibility in thinking through the facts. This thorough consideration requires that the facts are turned over, probed into, reorganized, and examined in relation to one another while their significance is viewed in relation to various pieces of knowledge gathered from other experiences and disciplines. Enabling clients to speak about the problem with its facts and emotional impact allows for their entry into the thinking process, thus establishing the two-pronged problem-solving approach.

Making some choice or decision. Once the facts are presented and thought through by both parties, decisions must be made. They may take the form of overt action or changes in behavior related to the problem. The question at this phase is, "What will happen if ____?" Often, in order to accomplish this phase, material means or accessible opportunities must be made available to the person, as they are essential to problem resolution.

Perlman contends that, in order to be effective, these modes of action must involve a systematically organized process that is a conscious, focused, goal-directed activity involving client and caseworker.

Interventive procedures and the ethnic reality. The problem-solving approach as delineated by Perlman does call attention to the part played by membership in varying subgroups in influencing behavior. However, little if any explicit attention is paid to the influence of social class. Case examples provide the facts of age, sex, and family composition. Occasional reference is made to social class membership or income.

The practitioner who uses this model as a base of practice must add fact-ascertaining questions dealing with ethnicity if these are viewed as a crucial characteristic of the client. Attention must be paid to the values deriving from ethnic identity and social class position.

The process of thinking through the facts associated with the ethnic reality would add critical information as the decision-making phase is approached.

The procedures proposed provide few guides for the practitioner in use of knowledge concerning varying world views of the many members of various ethnic groups seeking help with the myriad of problems that occur in daily life.

TASK-CENTERED CASEWORK

The task-centered approach was first formulated by Reid and Epstein in 1972. When initially developed it resembled other structured, time-limited approaches geared to alleviation of specific problems (Reid

1978). It drew on components of structured forms of brief casework (Reid and Shyne 1969), aspects of Perlman's problem-solving approach (Perlman 1957), the perspective on the client task put forth by Studt (1968), and the specification of casework methods presented by Hollis (Hollis 1964; Reid 1977).

Since its inception, extensive work has been carried out to test and refine the model (Reid 1977, 1978). Viewed as an evolving approach to practice, responsive to continuing research and developments in knowledge and technology, its basic principles were recently summarized by Reid (1986).

The theoretical system stresses the importance of helping clients with solutions to problems in the terms defined by clients. The worker's role is to help bring about desired changes. The client, not the worker, is the primary agent of change. In keeping with the view presented by Perlman, the system stresses human capacity for autonomous problem solving and people's abilities to carry out action to obtain desired ends. Problems often are indicative of temporary breakdown in coping capacity. The breakdown generates forces for change. These include client motivation as well as environmental resources. The range of problems usually encountered, and delineated in a *problem classificaton* scheme include problems: in family and interpersonal relations, in carrying out social roles, in decision making, in securing resources, and in handling emotional distress reactive to situational factors (Reid 1986).

Intervention is usually brief and time-limited; this derives from the view that most client benefit is derived in a few sessions within a limited time period. Substantial research has documented that: (1) short, time-limited treatment is as effective as long-term intervention, and (2) change occurs early in the process.

Problems take place in the context of individual, family, and environmental systems that can hamper or facilitate resolution (Reid 1986). In contrast to psychosocial theory, problem-oriented theory as defined by Reid and Epstein does not focus on remote or historical origins of a problem but looks primarily to contemporary causal factors. Attention is centered on those problems the client and practitioner can act to change. "Wants," "beliefs," and "effects" are crucial determinants of action (Reid 1978).

The possible role of the unconscious in influencing human action is not ruled out. However, given the emphasis on the present, it is assumed that problems as defined by clients can be managed without efforts to gain insight into unconscious dynamics (Reid 1978). "In this conception the person is seen as less a prisoner of unconscious drives than in the theories of the psychoanalyst and less a prisoner of environmental contingencies. Rather people are viewed as having minds and wills of their own that are reactive but not subordinate to internal and external influences" (Reid 1986, p. 270).

In task-centered casework, theories designed to explain personality dynamics and disorders, the functions of social systems, and other factors aid in problem assessment. However, these provide limited clues concerning how people perceive problems, and do not explain the relationship between personal and environmental factors. Furthermore, there are competing theories to explain similar problems. The worker is left with limited guides for action.

Research-based knowledge has highest priority, and speculative theorizing is avoided (Reid 1986). The approach to personality theory is "pragmatic" and "eclectic." Practitioners are free to draw on any theory or combination of theories if they seem to aid understanding of the situation (Epstein 1977).

Another major set of assumptions discussed by Epstein is important here. These involve views of poverty and characteristics of poor clients, and how these contrast with other perspectives on the poor. As a case in point, Epstein reviews long held views on the "multi-problem family." It is frequently suggested that these families are poor, consist of members of minority groups, and are often headed by women. In her view they are often described as having dirty children and dirty homes and as being uneducated. Their "obdurate tendency to avoid or discontinue contact" and their overriding interest in obtaining concrete services is frequently stressed in the literature (Epstein 1977). These traits are often seen as the result of faulty personality development. Epstein contends that these descriptions and the prescriptions that follow from them, derived from "pseudo explanations," do not lend themselves to the development of treatment technologies capable of effecting desired changes. She suggests that given modern society's persistent and severe inequities that minimize access to resources for so many, "no treatment technology of any kind has the capability of addressing itself to managing or controlling influences so vast" (Epstein 1977, p. 43). Substitution of the term *families with special hardships* for the term *multi-problem family* is proposed. Fundamental resolutions to the problems experienced by these families "rest upon development of social policies to mitigate the oppressive restraints of racial, ethnic, and sex discrimination, poverty, unavailability of quality education, day care, and the like" (Epstein 1977, p. 37).

Assumptions and the ethnic reality. Reid and Epstein point out that much of the impetus for development and refinement of the task-centered model was based on an interest in providing more effective service to the poor. The critique of certain prevailing views of the poor has been noted, as has the emphasis on the delivery of concrete services. The insistence on working with problems in the terms identified by the client is stressed. These thrusts are a major step in the direction of ethnic-sensitive practice as we define it. (See chapter five). When clients truly have the freedom to reject problem definitions that do not concur with their own views, the risk of attributing personality pathology to systemically induced behaviors and events is minimized.

For example, many American Indians feel that responsibility to family takes precedence over responsibility to the workplace. Knowing this, the social worker is unlikely to characterize as "lazy" an American Indian who explains his failure to work on a given day because of family obligations. If the ethnic reality of an American Indian man is understood it is unlikely that he will be characterized as lazy or unmotivated. The extent to which adherence to such subcultural perspectives leads to frequent job loss may become the issue of concern if he chooses to make it so. He is free to define the problem and to deal with it on his terms. In this atmosphere, consideration of various options is possible without labeling him or his behavior pathological. For example, can his need to work regularly be reconciled with the responsibilities to family and friends as these are defined by his own group? In some instances a new client or group of clients can emerge. These may be fellow employees or supervisors who understand the kinds of commitments he has and are able and willing to make adaptations in required work routines.

Interventive Procedures

In this system interventive procedures are referred to as *strategies* and as *practitioner-client activities*.

Based on the theories and assumptions earlier reviewed, the basic strategies involve: (1) helping clients to identify specific problems that derive from unrealized wants, or conditions to be changed, (2) contracting involving specific agreement between worker and client, (3) problem analysis leading to consideration of activities likely to lead to problem resolution, and (4) reliance on tasks as a means of problem resolution. This emphasis is based on the view, earlier presented, that people *act* when they have problems; worker supplementation of client problem-solving action is one way of implementing a strategy of "parsimony" that respects people's rights to manage their own affairs. Action taken toward solving a particular problem will become part of a coping strategy that will serve clients in the future when confronting new problems.

Individuals may be said to be clients only when they have accepted the social worker's offer to help or acknowledge a problem. Considerable thought is given to "involuntary clients," those people referred to social agencies for a variety of situations that have brought them into conflict with the law. (Parents thought to be abusing their children are an example.) Epstein suggests that, where intervention is necessary such as removal of children from their parents' care against their wishes, it should not be termed "treatment;" rather it should be seen for what it is: "authoritative, socially approved coercion to safeguard a child's life" (Epstein 1977).

Reid and Epstein are among a number of theorists who point to the importance of a structure, a framework, and a clearly specified objective of intervention (Fischer 1978; Reid 1978; Reid and Epstein 1972).

In the task-centered model, distinction is made between activities engaged in jointly by client and worker, those done by the worker on the client's behalf, and techniques used by workers. The roles of agency and worker are spelled out. The worker provides professional expertise and help in problem solving; the agency provides resources and confers the authority of office that facilitates the trust required by people seeking help.

In Reid's recent review of *practitioner-client activities* he identifies the following major activities: (1) problem exploration and specification, (2) contracting, (3) task planning, and (4) establishing incentives and rationale (1986).

Problem exploration and specification. In the initial interview, worker and client explore and clarify problems by focusing on what the client wants, not on what the practitioner thinks the client may need. A period of deliberation may alter the client's initial perception of the problem. Important in this model is the view that (1) worker and client come to agree on the problems on which they will work, and (2) problems are discrete, identifiable "entities," and delineated in terms of the conditions in which change is sought. In the process, involuntary clients may realize that they do have problems requiring attention. Research attests to the importance of this problem exploration stage in which new developments and shifts in focus are constantly explored. The example cited by Reid (1977) is a case in point. The child referred for "fighting" thinks he/she is "picked on" and therefore fights. While this may not be an accurate description of the state of affairs, it is a starting point for action intended to help the youngster understand that it is the fighting which may cause him/her to lose friends, be picked on, and the like. The fighting may become the problem requiring change.

Contracting. A number of key principles are identified: (1) a written or oral contract is required, in which both worker and client identify explicit, acknowledged problems on which they will work, (2) the goals and proposed solution may be identified, (3) the contract should include an estimate of approximate number of sessions (an eight to twelve week time limit is usually set), and (4) worker and client must agree on whether and when the contract will be renegotiated.

Task planning. "A task defines what the client is to do to alleviate his problem" (Reid 1986, p. 277). It may provide a general direction for action. As an example, Reid suggests that in a parent-child interaction problem, the parent decides, in general terms, to develop a more consistent approach in response to the child's behavior. Or, a task may be very specific. Examples are making a job application within the next week, or engaging in an activity the client puts off because it is difficult.

Task planning is a major component of the task-centered approach (Reid 1977). Tasks are designated and obstacles to their completion assessed. Much in-session work is focused on rehearsing and planning for activities to be carried on outside the sessions. Crucial is the client's expressed willingness to carry out the tasks. Research suggests that client commitment to the task is the best predictor of progress (Reid 1977). There is great stress on having clients begin to work on the task before the next contact with the social worker, for example, to make some effort to look for a job during that time period. The worker makes sure that the plan for action involves tasks of which the client is capable.

Establishing incentives and rationale. Here stress is on assuring that the involved individuals will view the potential results as being of sufficient benefit to make difficult action worthwhile. That is, a rationale for carrying out the task is established.

In the process obstacles are anticipated. This includes reviewing possible sources of failure, problem and task review, and contextual analysis. In problem and task review progress is reviewed at each session, problems solved, and new task activities specified. Contextual analysis refers to efforts to identify obstacles and resources. These may be internal (as with distorted perceptions) or may involve the external system.

In a recent review Reid expands the model to include work with families and groups, and reviews the results of research on the outcomes of the model (1986). Empirical investigation generally supports the effectiveness of the model, while also pointing to unknowns in the relationship between task accomplishment and problem change. He also addresses the range of applicability and limitations of the model. The latter includes failure to serve: (1) those not interested in taking action to solve problems, but who would rather explore existential issues, (2) those who reject the structure of the model, preferring a more casual, informal mode, (3) those whose problems (e.g., motor difficulties) don't lend themselves to the task approach, and (4) those who don't want help but need to be seen for protective reasons.

Interventive procedures and the ethnic reality. As we have noted earlier, there is little doubt that Reid and Epstein are keenly aware of the debilitating effects of poverty and discrimination. Furthermore, they emphasize the importance of awareness of values and self-perceptions as these arise from ethnic and social class membership. They stress the fact that problems occur in contexts of socioeconomic and ethnic identifications and have pointed out that "unfortunately no effective system has been developed for mapping the context of psychosocial problems" (Reid 1977). While emphasizing these problems, they make no effort to identify the particular coping strategies various cultural, class, and ethnic groups have developed.

In some respects, the focus on structure and time limits may run counter to the perspectives on time held by different groups. Adherence to different time schedules and the discomfort with self-disclosure of American Indians and some Hispanic groups are examples. Time-limited, structured approaches are responsive to the high level of motivation to reduce distress generated by a breakdown in coping capacity. While this may well be true for many groups, we wonder whether the pride so many people have in "managing on their own" should not be given greater attention than we discern. Marital problems of long standing, child neglect that has not reached disastrous proportions, and school problems involving many people are all examples of situations in which extensive time may be needed to build trust. It is not clear whether the research on motivation to act early in treatment touches these types of problems. It is possible that the "failures" in this and other approaches are in some measure related to the fact that insufficient time has been allotted to recognizing particular dispositions to problem identification and resolution that relate to the ethnic reality. The task-centered approach requires a high degree of rationality, which may be incongruent with the world view of some cultural groups.[1] The emphasis on structure and time limits may muffle sensitivity to the "dual perspective" that increases awareness of the possible and actual points of conflict between the minority client's perspective and that of the dominant society (Norton 1978). Clashes generated by the dual

---

[1] Conversation with Professor Daniel Katz, School of Social Work, Rutgers University

perspective may be encountered by worker and client struggling to specify an acknowledged problem.

This may well be the case in the situation described by Jones, in which American Indians are frequently referred to the local child welfare agency because of presumed child neglect. To the outsider it appears that children are left untended while their parents go to the "native drinking center" (Jones 1976). Discussion with the distraught parents may reveal that appearances notwithstanding, the children are not left unattended, for in their housing complex parents arrange to check on each others' children; attendance at the "drinking center" is part of the ritualized and accepted behavior within the group. However, only thorough knowledge of the beliefs and behavior of the group, and their consequences for the children, will enable the worker to make a sensitive judgment as to whether or not child neglect is involved.

Similarly, knowledge of Jewish tradition becomes most important in working with the young Jewish woman who comes to a counseling center, distraught because her parents have threatened to "sit shive" for her should she go through with her plans to marry a non-Jewish man. This threat to consider dead those young people who marry out of the group may be very real, and represent a basic point of conflict between people caught in different worlds.

We doubt whether situations such as these are amenable to the highly structured, time-limited actions projected. We agree that "pinning down the elements of the problem to be changed" may need to proceed quickly. The agency must make a decision as to whether children are in real danger. The young woman needs some quick help in identifying whether her major loyalties are to her parents or to her boyfriend, for she may lose a valued relationship if she wavers too much. But beyond this, we contend that support and examination of the ethnically derived aspect of the problem or response takes time and continued exploration.

As is true with other approaches, we find no explicit effort to adapt the guidelines for task-centered intervention for work with people who may approach their problems from varying class, minority, or ethnic perspectives.

THE SOCIAL PROVISION AND STRUCTURAL APPROACHES

Approaches that highlight social structural inequity as a major source of difficulty have long been an integral part of the social work practice literature. The work of Addams (1910) and Wald (1951) exemplified this perspective. They were followed by Reynolds (1938), Titmuss (1968), Younghusband (1964), and Kahn (1965).[2]

Recent efforts to explicate the relationship between the social context and social work practice principles are exemplified by Germain's (1979) and Germain's and Gitterman's (1980) ecological approach and Meyer's (1976) ecosystems perspective. Germain proposes that: "Practice is directed toward improving the transactions between people and environments in order to enhance adaptive capacities and improve environments for all who function within them." Out of this perspective a number of "action principles" are derived. These relate to: "efforts at adaptation and organism environmental transactions. . . . those transactions between people and environments are sought that will nourish both parts of the interdependent system" (Germain 1979).

A similar theme is presented by Meyer, who suggests that the "interface between person and environment is fluid." Furthermore, it is not possible to make clear distinctions between internal or external cause and effect (Meyer 1976). Meyer identifies a policy-oriented practitioner whose focus is developmental services and who is guided by an ecosystem perspective, a "life model" of practice, and a clear sense of social accountability (Meyer 1976). She pays considerable attention to the "way people live" and identifies life cycle stages and tasks, the potential crises and problems associated with these, as well as institutional resources needed and available.

Common to these approaches is the view that social institutional sources of stress play a major part in generating problems at the same time as interventive actions must be geared to individualized understanding of people in terms of their institutional membership (Siporin 1975).

A detailed model that identifies social institutional sources of stress and specifies social work actions generated by such a perspective is presented by Middleman and Goldberg (1974). They identify theirs as a structural approach, examined here in some detail because both assumptions and related practice procedures are explicitly delineated.

Assumptions

This approach is derived from two basic assumptions: (1) individual problems are perceived as a function of social disorganization and not as individual pathology, and (2) all social workers, regardless of where they work, have an obligation to pursue social change efforts as an integral part of their ongoing assignment.

---

[2]We acknowledge the work of Siporin (1975) in helping us to arrive at this formulation.

In the view of the proponents of the structural model, it is destructive and dysfunctional to define social problems in psychological terms. Many of the people served by social work—minority groups, the aged, the poor—are "neither the cause of, nor the appropriate locus for change efforts aimed at lessening the problems they confront" (Middleman and Goldberg 1974, p. 26).

Much of social work efforts are expended in working with and on behalf of people who do not adequately deal with the situations in which they find themselves. "Inadequacy" is a relative term, essentially referring to the disparity between skills or resources and situational requirements. If it is expected that people ought to be skillful and resourceful in response to the requirements of varied situations, then those lacking the necessary coping skills are perceived as inadequate. On the other hand, when situational demands are inappropriate and not sufficiently responsive to individual or collective need, then the situation is perceived as inadequate. "Thus to say that a given man is inadequate is at one and the same time both a description of disparity between that man and a particular situation, and a value judgment attributing blame for that disparity" (Middleman and Goldberg 1974, p. 26). They put major responsibility for that disparity on inadequate social provision, discrimination, and inappropriate environments and organizational arrangements.

Based on this perspective, they conceptualize social work roles in terms of two bipolar dimensions: "locus of concern" and "persons engaged." Locus of concern identifies the reason for social work intervention. The concern may focus on (1) the problems of particular individuals such as the members of a minority group who confront discrimination in employment, or (2) the larger category of individuals who suffer from the same problem, "a general category of persons identified as sufferers by definition of a social problem" (Middleman and Goldberg 1974, p. 18).

"Persons engaged" calls attention to those people with whom the social worker interacts in response to the problem. Those engaged may be the "sufferer" and/or others. This may involve a process by which the social worker facilitates action by clients and family and community networks to help themselves and each other; or attention may be focused on more explicit social change activity. This can range from effort to effect legislative change, to organizing for specific community services, to marshalling informal community support systems in time of crisis.

The major targets of intervention are always the conditions that inhibit functioning and increase suffering. Social workers intervene in the effort to enhance the nature of the relationship between people and their social environment. They try to use, change, or create needed social structures and resources.

Assumptions and the ethnic reality. The congruence between many of the assumptions of the structural approach and our perspective on the ethnic reality is in many respects self-evident. We have established that a sense of class and ethnicity is strongly experienced in everyday life, and that many ethnic groups and all minority groups are held in low esteem by various segments of the society. We have also suggested that certain culturally derived behaviors are viewed as deviant.

Such interpretations, often arising from mainstream expectations, define culturally derived behaviors as inadequate, and pay insufficient attention to the situations out of which they emerge. Clearly, the basic assumptions of the structural approach are consonant with our view concerning the part played by the ethnic reality in generating many of the problems at issue.

However, like the proponents of other approaches, Middleman and Goldberg leave the implicit impression that matters of race and ethnicity are primarily problematic. They do not call attention to the sources of strength or coping capacity such group idenitification often generates, nor to the different ways in which such factors affect problem identification or manifestation. While they hint at this when they point to the social worker's role in facilitating mutual aid activities, they do not make it explicit.

Interventive Procedures

Middleman and Goldberg identify four basic principles of the approach as well as major social work roles and skills.

In this section we summarize and discuss these principles.[3] The *principle of accountability to the client* is based on the assumption that people are capable of defining their own needs, and that the social worker's major task is reduction of pressures felt by the client. The primary tool for putting this principle into action is the contract established between the practitioner and client. Through the agreement a practitioner and client may identify a point of stress, determine how it ought to be relieved, and take on the tasks that will accomplish the goal. Stress may emanate from problematic interpersonal relationships, illness, social structural flaws, or the very nature of tasks to be accomplished, such as learning in school. The plan for action may fail. The contract may then be revised or activity halted.

---

[3]In chapter five, many of the procedures identified draw on the work being reviewed here.

The *principle of following the demands of the client task* is based on the view that client need and not worker skill or disposition determines worker activity. In their discussion of this principle, Middleman and Goldberg delineate the practice implications that flow from a perspective that views the environment as the primary target of change. At the same time, indidivual problems are approached with sensitive awareness to uniqueness. By suggesting that workers "look beyond each client to see if there are others facing the same task," they highlight the fact that problems are often of a collective and structurally induced nature. Their contention that workers must take different roles at different times points to the importance of being guided by client need rather than worker need, or agency or other institutional constraints. Their focus on the worker roles of broker, mediator, and advocate suggests that inadequate service structures often militate against adequate problem resolution. The various activities designed to carry out the terms of the contract called for by this principle require work with clients (1) in their behalf, (2) in behalf of themselves and others, and (3) with others in behalf of the clients. At times all three may be necessary. For example, a child who feels hurt because of racist slurs in school needs help in talking about this to a teacher. At the same time, efforts to involve school personnel in creating a less racist atmosphere may be indicated. Confrontation or social action may be necessary if there are other children having similar experiences. Inherent in this conception is role flexibility.

The *principle of maximizing potential supports in the client's environment* points to the need to modify established structures or create new ones. Viewed as the essential thrust of the structural approach, this principle points to a number of needed activities. For example, on finding that a group of adolescents in a school have not learned to read, the worker must try to get a special reading program started. Or, when agency intake procedures delay service delivery, action aimed at altering and speeding up the intake process is called for. Workers, though central at key points of stress, should continually be aware of and help to maximize the use and development of diverse support systems in the community.

The *principle of least contest* directs the worker to exert the least pressure necessary to accomplish the client task. Specifically it is proposed that, when an environmental source of difficulty is identified, effort is made to change the environment before engaging in more vigorous protest activities.

In summary, the structural approach views systemic inequity as the major source of client stress, and effort to modify or create less dysfunctional structures as the social worker's major obligation.

Interventive procedures and the ethnic reality. A review of the basic principles of the structural approach highlights its keen sensitivity to matters of concern to members of minority groups. Many of the examples center on people suffering the effects of deprivation or racism and target interventions geared to minimize their negative consequences. More than any approach we have reviewed to this point, the principles, if consistently followed, would of necessity generate ethnic-sensitive practice. It seems unlikely that workers who truly adhere to these principles would negate the needs for protection for intimate disclosure of many American Indians, the various pain responses of certain ethnic groups, "Black pride," or stoicism in the face of adversity, which is the hallmark of Slavic groups. However, we do not find any specific suggestions as to whether or how these principles might be modified to deal with varied ethnically based responses.

THE SYSTEMS APPROACH

Most of the models we have reviewed in the preceding section are to varying degrees based on substantive theoretical orientations, which in turn shape and give focus to interventive procedures.

In the introduction to this chapter, the reader's attention was called to the fact that some social work theoreticians have sought to identify approaches to social work practice that are independent of various substantive theories derived from other domains of interest; indeed, they seek to identify a "social work frame of reference," related to the basic values, function, and purposes of the profession.

Pincus and Minahan (1973) present such a model. They define social work practice as a "goal-oriented planned change process." The model uses a general systems approach as an organizing framework. It is intended for application in a wide range of settings. They make an effort to avoid the often noted dichotomies between person/environment, clinical practice/social action, and microsystem/macrosystem change. In their view, "the strength of the profession lies in recognizing and working with the connections between these elements" (Pincus and Minahan 1973).

Assumptions

Two basic concepts form this approach—*resources* and *interaction* between people and the social environment. A resource is defined as "anything that is used to achieve goals, solve problems, alleviate distress, accomplish life tasks or realize aspirations and values." Resources are usually used in interaction with others. Thus, there is interdependence between resources, people, and varying informal and formal systems. The former include family, friends, and neighbors; the latter include the societal, governmental, and voluntary health, educational, and social welfare services.

This perspective helps to identify five areas of concern to social work: (1) the absence of needed resources, (2) the absence of linkages between people and resource systems or between resource systems, (3) problematic interaction between people within the same resource system, (4) problematic interaction between resource systems, and (5) problematic individual internal problem-solving or coping resources.

Assumptions and the ethnic reality. This approach derives its basic thrust from the values and purposes of social work, focusing attention on the many gaps in institutional life that prevent people from reaching their full potential. There is no question that the gaps related to discrimination and cultural differences have always been recognized by our profession. The emphasis on resources and environment implicitly calls attention to those problems and strengths related to the ethnic reality. Pincus and Minahan do not devote explicit attention to these issues; however, their examples do point to problems experienced by minority people as they confront mainstream institutions. The assumptions on which this system or generalist approach are based are, like all the others we have reviewed, congruent with a view that takes account of the ethnic reality. However, no explicit attention is paid to these matters.

Interventive Procedures

Pincus and Minahan refer to the social work "mode of action" and discuss several components. *Helping people enhance and more effectively utilize their own coping capacities* is identified as a unifying aspect of the systems approach committed to joint effort with clients to change those aspects of their lives that are causing discomfort.

Establishing initial linkage between people and resources, a primary social work responsibility, is the location of those individuals or institutions with ability to assist the worker and client in their planned change effort. Once located, they are enlisted to join in the effort. Needless to say, this effort is not always successful, but the investment is an essential procedure.

Facilitating interaction within resource systems. In this process the social worker looks within the resource system to ensure that resources are being used in a manner congruent with client need. Concretely, this involves efforts to minimize bureaucratic red tape and to examine policies to ensure that they maximize rather than minimize client functioning.

Influencing social policy is an aspect of micropractice that is often not clearly articulated. Since practice is carried out within agencies serving needs generated throughout the life cycle—from early childhood to old age—the agency's workers possess knowledge about and access to data on social problems, environmental conditions, and responses of social service delivery systems to those who require support. This access places social work in a position to influence public policy.

Dispensing material resources is a concrete service that is the backbone of practice in many areas. Food, clothing, employment, and shelter may be all that an individual or family needs to be able to cope with life. Lack in these areas may be the major problem with which people need help. Given the assurance of regular meals and sufficient snacks, acting out school children may become the vivacious, motivated, above-average students they were meant to be.

Serving as agents of social control. Despite desires to the contrary, there are those persons labeled as deviant. They have had experiences in prison, mental hospitals, or a variety of other psychiatric treatment centers. Society often requires that their activities be supervised and/or monitored. Children who live in situations in which they are threatened with abuse and/or neglect have need of protection. Adequate care must be provided.

Interventive procedures and the ethnic reality. There is no quarrel with the validity of the "mode of action" as an approach to practice. However, much like the other approaches reviewed here, it gives little recognition to the impact of ethnicity upon the lives of clients.

In their elaboration of data collection skills, Pincus and Minahan (1973) suggest that much may be learned by a walk through a community in the process of change. Such a walk does provide information. Food stores and newspapers on newsstands give clues to ethnicity, as do converted religious structures. But they fail to describe methods for interpretation of such data and its significance in the daily lives of individuals and the community at large. To view the "ethnic street" without considering its residents' responses to their ethnicity and social class is to omit important variables in the data collection process. A concise systems approach to practice is presented, but no procedures that would make use of the various areas of knowledge a practitioner may need to acquire related to ethnicity, social class, and the wide variations of life-styles emerging from the impact of the ethnic reality.

ECOLOGICAL PERSPECTIVES

We began this chapter by pointing to the two major streams of thought on person-environment relations that have long been an integral part of social work theory and practice.

The *ecological* or *life model* approach developed by Germain (1979) and Germain and Gitterman (1980) is a response to this long standing dialogue and an attempt to develop a conceptual framework that provides a simultaneous focus on people and environments (Germain and Gitterman 1986). Some analysts view ecology as a useful "practice metaphor" that seeks to further understanding of the reciprocal relationships between people, the environment, and how each acts on and influences the other. The ecological perspective is an " . . . evolutionary, adaptive view of people and their environments." (Germain and Gitterman 1986, p. 619). An important concept is that of *person-environment fit*.

The present discussion reviews the basic assumptions of the ecological or life model approach as developed by Germain and Gitterman in 1980 and summarized in 1986.

Assumptions

The ecological framework is an important and useful way of thinking about social work's societal function. Key concepts are *ecology*, *adaptation-stress-coping*, *human relatedness*, *identity/self-esteem*, *competence*, and the *environment* including its "layers and textures."

Ecology is a useful concept because of its focus on the relationships between living organisms and all elements of their environments. Integral is an effort to examine the *adaptive-balance* or *goodness-of-fit* achieved between organisms and their environments. All forms of life are involved in the process of achieving this *adaptive balance*. In order to develop and survive, all living forms require stimulation and resources from the environment. In turn, these living forms act on the environment, which becomes more differentiated, complex, and able to support more diverse forms of life.

Under positive environmental circumstances, individuals grow and develop in a positive manner. But the reciprocal organism-environment interactions may occasionally be at the expense of other organisms. A damaged environment may no longer be capable of supporting human or physical life forms; or conversely, failure of the environment to support individual life forms may threaten their survival. For example, social environments may become damaged or "polluted" by poverty, discrimination, and stigma.

Adaptation, *Stress*, and *Coping*. *Stress*, defined as "an imbalance between a perceived demand and a perceived capability to meet the demand through the use of available internal and external resources . . ." (Germain and Gitterman 1986, p. 620) develops when there are upsets in the usual or desired person-environment fit. Stress may be positive, in the sense associated with positive self-feeling, and anticipation of mastering a challenge. Or, it may be experienced negatively. *Coping* refers to the adaptive effort evoked by stress and usually requires both internal and external resources. Internal resources refer to levels of motivation, self-esteem, and problem-solving skills. Problem-solving skills are in part acquired by training in the environment in family, schools, and other institutions.

Human relatedness, identity, self-esteem, and competence. Human relatedness is essential for biological and social survival. Infants and children require extended periods of care, and opportunities for learning and socialization. The family, peers, and the institutions of the larger society are the context in which such learning takes place. Deprivation in key primary relationships with other people is painful and may lead to fear of relationships because of their association with loss and pain. Human relationships are crucial and give rise to a sense of *identity* and *self-esteem*. This process begins in infancy and expands to include the increasing range of social experiences that usually accompany growth. Included among the experiences that shape identity and self-esteem are experiences accompanying gender, race, and social class. *Competence* has been defined as ". . . the sum of the person's successful experiences in the environment" (Germain and Gitterman 1986, p. 622). A sense of competence is achieved when individuals have the experience of having an effect on the social and physical environment. Important in the development of competence are curiosity and explorative behavior. If competence is to be developed and sustained, appropriate conditions must be provided by family, school, and community.

The *environment* consists of "layers and textures" (Germain and Gitterman 1986). The former refers to the social and physical environment, the latter to time and space. The physical world includes the natural and the "built" world. The social environment is the human environment of people "at many levels of relationships." These environments interact and shape each other. Technological and scientific developments shape norms in social behavior. Illustrative are the changing sexual norms influenced by the development of contraceptive technology. How the society appraises certain groups is evidenced by elements of the "built" environment. Germain and Gitterman (1986) make an important point when they suggest, for example, that design differences between a welfare office and a private family agency often reflect societal values. These in turn impact on daily life and self-perception.

Key elements of the social environment are bureaucratic organizations and social networks. The structure and function of bureaucratic organizations have potential for positive or negative impact on person-environment fit. Social networks often occur naturally—though not always—in the life space of the individual. Whether occurring naturally, or whether formed (as in the case of organized self-help groups) they often serve as mutual aid systems, providing resources, information, and emotional support.

The physical environment is the context within which human interaction occurs. The sense of personal identity is closely related to "a sense of place." The importance attached to the degree of "personal space" and what is defined as crowding is influenced by culture and gender, as well as physical, emotional, and cognitive states.

The life model views human beings as active, purposeful, and having the potential for growth. In the course of ongoing interchange with the environment there is the potential for problems. These are termed, in the model, *problems in living*.

Problems in living are encountered in the course of managing *life transitions* and dealing with *environmental pressures* and, in some, are caused by *maladaptive interpersonal processes*. Life transitions can become problematic under a number of circumstances including conflicting role demands related to status changes. Problems also occur when life transitions and developmental changes don't coincide. Marriage may present women with demands to be "wife" in the traditional sense at the same time as an occupational role must be played in more contemporary terms. The unmarried teenage mother is often not developmentally prepared for the parenting role.

Environmental pressures may result from: (1) the unavailability of needed resources, (2) people's inability to use available resources, or (3) environments and resources that are unresponsive to particular "styles" and needs. The last point is well illustrated by the highly structured elements of many of our health and welfare systems that fail to take account of the ethnic reality of particular groups. For example, the sterile, private atmosphere of a contemporary delivery room may not be congruent with the communication and presence of female relatives to which some Chicano and American Indian women are accustomed.

Maladaptive interpersonal processes can arise in efforts to cope with significant aspects of the environment, illness, and other stresses.

Social work purpose. The distinctive professional social work purpose is helping people with problems in living, that is, improving transactions between people and their environments, or improving the *goodness-of-fit* between needs and resources. This effort provides social work with a core function. These three major types of problems in living are particularly suited to social work interventions.

Assumptions and the ethnic reality. This important contribution to the practice literature goes a long way toward helping social workers recognize and understand the complex person-environment interactions that have long been of central concern to the profession. It recognizes that problems result from the interactions of many factors and abandons the search for a single cause or cure.

Clearly, there are no contradictions between the ecological perspective and the view of the ethnic reality developed in this book. The focus on person-environment fit, and on the reciprocal relationships between people and their environment is congruent with the view that ethnicity, minority status, social class, resource availability, and societal evaluations give shape to problems in living, and affect the capacity to cope with these problems. The authors repeatedly stress that matters of culture and class are critical elements in the person-environment interaction. The congruence between this model and ethnic sensitive practice has been noted by Devore, who suggests that the proponents of the model ". . . have encouraged practitioners to move beyond practice models that look within the individual for the cause of problems to one that encompasses the many facets of life" (1983, p. 525). Clearly, this model and its assumptions can only facilitate the work of the ethnic-sensitive practitioner.

Interventive Procedures

Germain and Gitterman make the point that the techniques of the life model are "not prescriptive," and are those held in common with most models. Differences may be in "the ends toward which the procedures are directed, as well as the areas of the ecological context where action takes place" (1986, p. 633). Attention is paid to social work purpose, function, and roles in a number of areas.

Strengthening the fit between people and their environments. In the effort to effect this goal, people's inability to use available resources may be encountered. The roles of facilitator, teacher, or enabler are utilized to help overcome this inability. Where the problems lie with environmen-

tal difficulties, the worker *coordinates*, *links* the client to available resources, *mediates* (where perhaps transactions are distorted), and helps
to *connect* the organization, the client, and the social network. Advocacy
roles are called for when other roles fail, and as *innovator* the worker fills
gaps in services, programs, and resources.

Client and worker roles involve *contracting* on how to define the
problem on which they will work, the objectives of the work, and
planning how to achieve the objectives.

Engaging will vary depending on whether clients present themselves
voluntarily or as the result of a mandate. Always there is concern with
an "ethical balance" between the client's right to refuse service and
protecting the vulnerability of clients and those involved with them.

Exertion of *professional influence* extends case advocacy to focus on
recognition of the impact on clients of agency policies, and to propose
and introduce new services.

Interventive procedures and the ethnic reality.

Devore (1983) analyzes the life model in respect to the degree to which
it helps incorporate understanding of Black families in practice. Her
comments are useful in helping to assess the extent to which the model
guides practitioners' efforts to incorporate the world views of different
groups into their practice.

Devore points out that the model: (1) recognizes the impact of social
class, ethnic group membership, life-style and culture (more so than
most other models), (2) lacks specificity in presenting cases about
Blacks, and (3) uses information about Blacks "descriptively" without
proposing how these descriptions serve to guide problem assessment
and resolution. An example cites a case presentation in which there is
mention that the Black mother is "light skinned" and the father "dark
skinned." Given societal standards which value lighter skin, it would be
important to note how such standards become internalized and affect
self-concepts.

Similar criticisms are made of Germain's and Gitterman's discussion
of the problems faced by an abused Black adolescent (1980). Though
they address adolescent development theory, the special understanding
required to help her cope with her ethnic reality is virtually not
considered. Issues that should be included are helping the youngster to
question "white norms" for beauty, develop a sense of self, and develop
a growing sense of identity with her people. If an adolescent is also
poor, the "moratorium" on growth described by Erikson may be
"speeded up."

The life model then, though attentive to matters of class and ethnicity, does not incorporate guidelines for how workers seek and use information about the client's ethnic reality in their day-to-day application of the model.

APPROACHES FOCUSED ON CULTURAL AWARENESS AND MINORITY ISSUES

CULTURAL AWARENESS AND HUMAN SERVICE PRACTICE

Assumptions

Green and his co-workers (1982) developed an approach focused on cultural awareness because, in their view, social work had paid limited attention to the concerns and interests of minority clients. In approaching this task, Green reviewed a number of concepts of culture, race, ethnicity, and minority groups. He rejects use of the concept of race because he believes it has pejorative connotations. He also proposes that the concept *class* is difficult to apply in pluralistic societies. Based on his review of the concepts *class*, *minority*, and *cultural differences* he suggests that there are terminological and conceptual problems in efforts to define these concepts. He asks whether there is a "concept of cultural variation that could be . . . useful in understanding cross-cultural social service encounters, regardless of the social characteristics or the relative power of the groups or individual involved?" (1982, p. 8). He answers his own question by suggesting that the concept of ethnicity as developed by anthropologists is useful.

Two views of ethnicity are contrasted. One, termed categorical, attempts to explain differences between and within groups and people by the degree to which distinctive cultural traits such as the characteristic ways of dressing, talking, eating, or acting are manifest. These distinctive traits "are not significant except to the extent that they influence intergroup and interpersonal cross-cultural relationships" (1982, p. 11). These elements of cultural content may become important as political and cultural symbols used when a group makes claims for resources or commands respect.

The second view, termed transactional, focuses on the ways in which people of different groups who are communicating maintain their sense of cultural distinctiveness. It is the understanding of the manipulations of boundaries between distinctive cultural groups that is crucial to understanding ethnicity and its impact on life. Ethnicity may be defined in terms of boundary, and boundary maintenance issues. The importance of ethnicity surfaces when peoples of different ethnic groups interact.

Green adopts a transactional approach to ethnicity. He suggests that in interaction between groups it is not "the descriptive cultural traits" that are important, but "the lines of separation and in particular how they are managed, protected, ritualized through stereotyping, and sometimes violated that is of concern in a transactional analysis of cross-cultural diversity" (1982, p. 12). Those persons who mediate intergroup boundaries are critical "actors" in cross-cultural encounters.

Social workers assume an important role as boundary mediators, given the part they play in the communication of information and regulation of resources pertinent to various groups.

Four modes of social work intervention within minority groups serve to identify the implications of ethnicity for the characteristic key social service activities. The first, *advocacy*, points to the inherent conflicts in minority-dominant group relationships. Dominant institutions dominate minority people, and advocacy identifies with clients who are subjects of domination.

In *counseling*, the individual is the target of change. Culturally sensitive counseling is not well developed. A *regulator* role is also identified. This role is used in work with those usually termed involuntary clients, and the role is often viewed as unfair and unjust by ethnic community leaders. An example is the removal of American Indian children from their homes following allegations of social deprivation. As *regulators*, social workers are in a position to define deviance in ways that may denigrate important group values.

In the *broker* role social workers intervene both with the individual and with society. This role represents a "necessary response to the failure of established social service organizations to meet the legitimate needs of minority clients" (1982, p. 21). Each of these roles has different destructive or liberating consequences for minority clients.

A Model of Help-Seeking Behavior

Green suggests that there is a lack of cross-cultural conceptualization in social work, and therefore turns to a medical/sociological/anthropological model of help-seeking behavior. This model focuses on (1) culturally based differences in perceiving and experiencing stress, (2) language and how it crystallizes experience, and (3) the social as well as personal experience of a problem.

Client and professional culture are distinct. Components of the model, as they pertain to cultural differences are: (1) the recognition of an "experience" as a problem by the client, (2) the way language is used to label a problem, (3) the availability of indigenous helping resources, and (4) client-oriented criteria for deciding whether a satisfactory resolution has been achieved. There is a basic contrast between the values and assumptions of the client and those of the service culture. Culturally aware practice requires an ability to suspend agency and professional priorities in order to be able to view services from the perspective of the client. This requires much learning and effort on the part of the worker.

Ethnic Competence

A number of ways of acquiring *ethnic competence* are proposed. Ethnic competence refers to a performance level of cultural awareness that involves more than the usual patience, genuineness, and honesty in client-worker relationships. It is the ability to conduct professional work in a way consonant with the behavior and expectations that members of distinct groups have of each other. Use of cultural guides and participant observation in diverse communities are means of acquiring ethnic competence.

Congruence of the Model with Prevailing Approaches to Social Work Practice

The model of cultural awareness reviewed here presents a useful way of looking at social work's past tendency to minimize and neglect ethnic and cultural differences. It draws on key social work roles as a way of illustrating some of the real dissatisfaction with which social work is viewed by some minority groups.

Green's disenchantment with the profession's neglect and distortions of ethnic group life leads to his identification of a model of help-seeking behavior drawn from disciplines outside of social work. The key elements of that model are potentially congruent with prevailing approaches to social work practice. However, Green does not make the linkages. Each of the elements of the model could be readily integrated by the approaches reviewed here, assuming the kind of commitment and *ethnic competence* described.

The Model as a Guide for Practice

The model contributes conceptual insights on ethnicity, highlights the profession's historical neglect of this area, and presents some important guidelines for acquiring sensitivity to various ethnic groups. Ethnographic interviews, participant observation, and study of ethnographic documents are all useful mechanisms to help workers understand the lives of clients.

Limited if any attention is paid to how the constraints of time and agency function impact on the worker's ability to take the steps that in Green's view are needed to acquire ethnic competence. A related question is how workers can acquire ethnic competence in the ways proposed when they work in a multiethnic community.

THE PROCESS STAGE APPROACH

Assumptions

Lum (1986) "aims to break new ground" by focusing on key differences between current social work practice emphases and minority characteristics, beliefs, and behaviors. He believes that social workers' professional orientation must be re-examined from the viewpoint of ethnic minorities, and presents a framework for ethnic minority practice by proceeding from the assumption that there are "universal principles of situational predicament, value beliefs, and practice protocols that are applicable to minorities" (1986, p. x). He points to the relative lack of attention in social work to "minority practice," defined as "the art and science of developing a helping relationship with an individual, family, group, and/or community whose distinctive physical/cultural characteristics and discriminatory experience require approaches that are sensitive to ethnic and cultural environments" (1986, p. 3).

The terms *people of color* and *ethnic minority* are used interchangeably throughout this book, and basically refer to Blacks, Latinos, Asians and Native Americans. The common experiences of racism, discrimination, and segregation "bind minority people of color together and contrast with the experience of white Americans" (1986, p. 1).

A number of commonly held minority values are postulated. It is proposed that social work values and the code of ethics of the National Association of Social Workers need modification to incorporate collective minority values that emphasize family unification, recognition of the leadership of elders and parents, and mutual responsibility of family members for one another. Certain "Western values" and interventive theories and strategies are centered on individual growth in contrast to kinship and group-centered minority cultures. Minority family values revolve around corporate collective structures including maintenance of ethnic identification and solidarity. Extended family, religious, and spiritual values have extensive influence in the minority community. There are a number of generic principles of feeling and thought that cut across groups despite the known differences in values and culture between varied groups.

Minority knowledge theory has its own intrinsic concepts. Drawing implications for practice with minorities from existing social work knowledge theories is not sufficient. Nevertheless, most social work practice theories can be adapted for use with people of color.

The framework for the model discussed here assumes: (1) etic goals (focused on principles valid in all cultures), and (2) *emic* goals (focused on behavioral principles within a particular culture). There are a series of practice process stages. In each stage there are (1) client-system practice issues and a series of worker-client tasks, and (2) identified worker-system practice issues.

Interventive Procedures

Detailed attention is devoted to the stages of (1) contact, (2) problem identification, (3) assessment, (4) intervention, and (5) termination. In considering these stages, focus is primarily on (1) issues requiring attention in meeting the needs of the minority community, (2) practice issues, (3) client-system practice issues, and (4) a series of worker-client tasks.

Contact. In the *contact* stage, worker-system practice issues focus on delivery of service, understanding of the community, *relationship protocols*, *professional self-disclosure*, and communication style. An agency self-study and gathering of data on the minority community are important as is design of services that takes minority needs into account. These include such factors as location in the minority community, bilingual staffing, and community outreach. Identifying the protocols that are characteristic for establishing relationships in minority communities is important, as are communication styles that include a pleasant atmosphere and the presence of bilingual staff. Client-system practice issues relate to recognition of the resistance with which minority people often approach social services. Workers must overcome this resistance by establishing relationships of trust. This may involve establishing personal as well as professional relationships (e.g., professional self-disclosure) because many minority people are reluctant to disclose problems to strangers. Also important is identification of helping networks and establishment of linkages with minority organizations.

Problem identification. In this stage, client system practice issues revolve around (1) evaluating problem information as found in the patterns of the minority client's sociocultural environment, and (2) recognizing the shame and hesitation that many minority people experience in the early part of the helping process. The worker must understand the client's perception of the problem, and how culture influences behavioral response. Task recommendations are concentrated on facilitating discussion congruent with the cultural meaning of the problem and relating the problem events to cultural dynamics. Worker-system practice issues tend not to be focused on problems of internal origin as the assumption is made that minority problem issues are rooted in a racist society. Task recommendations include discussing oppressive environmental factors confronted by minority people, identifying theories that examine these factors, and learning to uncover the social causes of problems.

Problem levels include problem typologies such as those proposed by Reid (1978), as well as identification of stress areas to which minority people are especially prone: (1) culture conflict, (2) minority group status, and (3) social change. Problem themes focus on (1) racism, manifest in various ways, (2) oppression, (3) powerlessness, (4) acculturation, and (5) stereotyping. Task recommendations include: (1) identification of how oppression and related factors affect ethnic minorities, (2) consideration of socioeconomic/ political factors that have a negative impact on minorities, and (3) identification of strategies to cope with oppression, powerlessness, and other problem themes identified.

Assessment. Focus in *assessment* is on client-system practice issues: (1) socioenvironmental impacts and (2) psycho-individual reactions. The first seeks to discover how the range of socioenvironmental factors affect minority clients. This is focused on such matters as: (1) attribution of many problems of minority people to socioeconomic stresses, (2) the ecological perspective on illness thought to be held by most ethnic groups, (3) basic survival issues, and (4) ethnic identity conflicts. Psycho-individual reactions involve marshalling of coping strategies. Some people experience failure, while others develop a strong collective identity and creative coping skills. Also included are psychosomatic reactions. In many minority cultures self-control and avoidance of expressing feelings are stressed. Psychosomatic illness may be more acceptable than mental illness. Many minority cultures have acceptable ways of expressing psychosomatic symptoms related to disharmony and interpersonal stress. Worker-system practice issues focus on the search for strengths of individual and family systems and creative use of client's cultural strength. Included are (1) health, (2) motivational levels, (3) client assets, and (4) natural support systems. Task recommendations focus on assessment of resources, strengths, and clinical problems.

Intervention. Client and worker-system practice issues relate to (1) identification of goals, (2) use of problem-solving behavior, (3) identification of past and present dimensions of the problem, and (4) demonstration that change is a function of the clinical contact. Ethnically related goals of intervention engage both the minority client and worker. Intervention strategies or themes related to the minority experience include: (1) oppression versus liberation, (2) powerlessness versus empowerment, (3) exploitation versus parity, (4) acculturation versus maintenance of culture, and (5) stereotyping versus unique personhood. Micro, mezzo, and macro levels of intervention are identified. The first focuses on individuals and small groups, the second on ethnic/local communities and organizations, and the third on complex organizations and geographic populations. Task recommendations include: (1) identifying and using appropriate ethnic community resources, (2) worker serving as broker between minority clients and helping resources, and (3) identifying ethnic social needs if ethnic services are lacking.

Termination. *Termination* is identified with completion "in the sense of accomplishment of a goal" (Lum 1986, p. 198). In this process stage model, one of the client and worker-system practice issues involves "reunification with ethnic roots" (1986, p. 199). A new sense of what it means to be a member of one of the minority groups is important motivation for coping with the problems of living that have been part of the problem-solving encounter with the social worker. Linkage to significant others who now will play a major role in the client's life may well mean linkage with kinship and neighborhood ethnic networks.

"Termination as recital" reviews the changes that have occurred, and "termination as completion" involves questions about whether the intervention has had an impact on the problem. Task recommendations include asking whether there was effort to connect the client with a positive element in the minority community.

Congruence of the Model with Prevailing Approaches to Social Work Practice

Effort to answer the question, "Is the process approach congruent with prevailing approaches to social work practice?" must be divided into at least two segments: (1) review and analysis of the basic assumptions, and (2) consideration of how the process and stages of practice are in keeping with social work practice procedures.

The Basic Assumptions

Lum proceeds from the assumption that all people of color presently living in the country—Latinos, Asian Americans, American Indians and Blacks—are bound together by the experience of racism, which contrasts with the experience of white Americans. He further proposes that these groups share collective minority values that emphasize family unification, recognition of the leadership of elders and parents, and mutual responsibility of family members for one another. Also important are values of "corporate collective structures" and maintenance of ethnic identification and solidarity. Extended family, kinship networks, spiritual values, and the importance of a vertical hierarchy of authority are said to have extensive influence. Social work ethics as embodied in the code of ethics of the National Association of Social Workers, are currently oriented toward individual client rights. This code should also address and incorporate collective minority values.

In the discussion of ethnic minority values and knowledge base limited attention is paid to the concept of or influence of social class (see elaboration in chapter one of this book). Lum suggests that:

> For ethnic minorities, social class is influenced by racial discrimination and socioeconomic constraints. Although people of a particular minority group may occupy different social class levels, coping with survival and the reality of racism are forces that bind people of color together (1986, p. 55).

We agree with Lum that racism is a factor shared by the groups he identifies. However, the degree to which they hold in common the "minority values" identified is subject to considerable question. The degree of adherence to these types of values by any group, or any individual member of a group, remains a matter of empirical question and exploration with the individual member. Thus, to suggest that all people of color, in contrast with all "whites," value a hierarchy of authority, certain corporate structures, and the same spiritual values runs counter to much of the reality of life experience in these groups. The view neglects substantial empirical evidence that degree of adherence to these values is a function of recency of migration and of social class (e.g., Masuda, Hasegawa, and Matsumuto 1973; Furuto 1986). Indeed, the accelerating current debate about the nature and source of the Black underclass casts serious doubt on the contention that issues of survival and racism "bind" to the degree that the conceptualization presented here would suggest (see our discussion in chapter one and Wilson 1985; Lemann 1986). Our concept of the ethnic reality takes account of social class and suggests a framework for understanding the ethnic and class-related differences that "bind" as well as those that pull people away from identification with core ethnic values.

The major difficulty in identifying a "minority value base" that is shared by all people of color is that the effort to unify can have the effect of minimizing and distorting the important unique and rich cultures and values characteristic of each of the groups identified as people of color. To attribute a common set of values to diverse people already beset by racism risks negation of uniqueness, special needs, and stereotyping.

Surely, even a brief review of the values adhered to by such groups as Navajo Indians, urban Blacks who live in the ghetto, and third or fourth-generation Japanese women casts doubt on the view that they share common spiritual values, beliefs about vertical hierarchy of authority, or sense of the importance of corporate collective structures. Actually, many of these and related values—to the extent that they prevail—are or have been held by many white ethnic groups. For example, the emphasis on family and group solidarity is often discussed as an attribute of Jewish people and of many Italians.

The fact that people of color are the objects of racism and suffer its consequences is a reality. It is critical that the profession of social work takes this fact into account and evolves practice strategies that sensitize practitioners to its consequences and, at the same time, seeks to minimize its destructive effects.

In the eagerness to overcome the profession's neglect of this area, attribution of common values to distinct groups can have the effect of minimizing important elements of culture, and culturally derived need in the practitioner-client encounter.

Practice stages. The discussion of practice stages is a carefully thought out, useful addition to the social work practice literature as it pertains to the delivery of ethnic-sensitive social work services. Pointing to such matters as the special kinds of reluctance experienced by some minority people in seeking help, recognizing that many people don't make the distinction between "professional" and "kin" so important in social work, is an important reminder of how ethnic and cultural factors need to be considered in practice. Constant reminders of how language and culture impact on problem definition are important as is focus on externally induced sources of difficulty. The practitioner can learn much from application of these strategies. The process stage approach presents useful guides for practice with diverse minority groups if caution is exercised in assuming value commonalities.

SUMMARY OF APPROACHES TO PRACTICE

This review of some of the major approaches to social work practice indicates that, with few exceptions, the assumptions on which practice is based are not in contradiction with prevailing understandings of cultural, class, and ethnic diversity. Our summary of a number of well established interventive procedures highlights the point we have made repeatedly, that for too long limited attention was paid to modifying or generating procedures to heighten the practitioner's skill in working with sensitivity with people who are members of various ethnic, class, and minority groups. This work, as well as that by Green and Lum, are efforts to fill this gap.

The models reviewed share adherence to basic social work values. The dignity of the individual, the right to self-determination, the need for an adequate standard of living, and need for satisfying, growth enhancing relationships are uniformly noted. Differences emerge about what social workers need to know and do in order to achieve these lofty objectives for their clients.

It is quite apparent that those social workers who believe past personal experience and nonconscious factors have a major bearing on how people feel in the present structure their practice differently from those who emphasize the importance of institutional barriers, both past and present. Both groups draw on a wide range of psychological and sociological knowledge. However, their theoretical differences influence the manner by which these are incorporated into practice. These differences are reflected in how problems are defined, what kinds of needs are stressed, the structure of the worker-client relationship, and the types of activity undertaken.

Our View of the Theory Practice Relationship

Based on our review and experience, we have little question that knowledge, theory, and values guide problem definition and affect the kinds of assessments that are made. For example, accurate understanding of ethnically derived responses to illness, aging, or education will affect assessment when problems surface. These assessments in turn have bearing on interventive principles and strategies selected. The Slavic mother who appears to neglect childhood illness may not be neglectful but simply adhering to an ethnic dictum in which apparently minor illnesses are to be endured. Given this knowledge, one is less likely to define her as a neglecting parent. Whether intervention is focused on her feelings about being a mother, education to help her to recognize dangerous symptoms, or support to help her live comfortably in a culture that permits indulgence of minor symptoms is, in our view, a function of the theory of human behavior to which one subscribes. At the same time, all social workers would share the goal of maximizing the mother's and the child's physical and emotional well-being. Adherence to the view that racism and denigration of the life-style and culture of many minority groups is a major cause of the problems affecting members of these groups clearly must guide our assumptions and thinking about their problems and the interventive procedures that we use in our daily work.

REFERENCES

Addams, Jane. 1910. *Twenty years at Hull House*. New York: The Macmillan Co.

Devore, Wynetta. 1983. Ethnic reality: the life model and work with Black families. *Social Casework* November, pp. 525–531.

Epstein, Laura. 1977. *How to provide social services with task-centered methods: report of the Task-Centered Service Project*, Vol. I. Chicago: The School of Social Service Administration, University of Chicago.

Fischer, Joel. 1978. *Effective casework practice: an eclectic approach*. New York: McGraw-Hill Book Co.

Furuto, Sharlene B.C.S. 1986. Multigenerational profiles of Japanese American women: Implications for social work education and practice. A paper, presented at the Annual Program Meeting of the Council on Social Work Education, Miami.

Germain, Carol B., ed. 1979. *Social work practice: people and environments*. New York: Columbia University Press.

Germain, Carol B., and Gitterman, Alex. 1980. *The life model of social work practice*. New York: Columbia University Press.

Germain, Carol B., and Gitterman, Alex. 1986. The life model approach to social work practice revisited. In *Social work treatment*, edited by J. Turner. New York: The Free Press.

Gomez, Ernesto; Zurcher, Louis A.; Farris, Buford E.; and Becker, R. E. 1985. A study of psychosocial casework with Chicanos. *Social Work* 30:477–482.

Good Tracks, Jimm C. 1973. "Native American noninterference." *Social Work* 18:30–34.

Green, James W. 1982. *Cultural awareness in the human services*. Englewood Cliffs, NJ: Prentice-Hall, Inc.

Greir, William H., and Cobbs, G. 1969. *Black rage*. New York: Bantam Books.

Hollis, Florence. 1965. Casework and social class. *Social Casework* 46:463–471.

Hollis, Florence. 1972. *Casework: a psychosocial therapy*. 2d ed. New York: Random House.

Jenkins, Shirley. 1981. *The ethnic dilemma in social services*. New York: The Free Press.

Jones, Dorothy M. 1976. The mystique of expertise in social services: an Alaska example. *Journal of Sociology and Social Welfare* 3:332–346.

Kahn, Alfred J. 1965. New policies and service models: the next phase. *American Journal of Orthopsychiatry* 35:652–662.

Kahn, Alfred J. 1973. A policy base for social work practice: Societal perspectives. In *Shaping the new social work*. Edited by A. J. Kahn. New York: Columbia University Press, 3–25.

Krause, Corinne Azen. 1978. *Grandmothers, mothers and daughters: an oral history study of ethnicity, mental health, and continuity of three generations of Jewish, Italian, and Slavic-American women*. New York: The American Jewish Committee.

Lemann, Nicholas. 1986. The origins of the underclass. Part I. *The Atlantic* June, 257(6), 31–61; and Part II, *The Atlantic* July, 258(1), 54–68.

Lum, Doman. 1986. *Social work practice and people of color: a process-stage approach*. Monterey, CA: Brooks/Cole Publishing Co.

Masuda, M., Hasegawa, R.S., and Matsumoto, G. 1973. The ethnic identity questionnaire. *Journal of Cross Cultural Psychology* June, 229–245.

Meyer, Carol H. 1976. *Social work practice*. 2d ed. New York: The Free Press.

Middleman, Ruth, and Goldberg, Gale. 1974. *Social service delivery: a structural approach to practice*. New York: Columbia University Press.

Mirelowitz, Seymour. 1979. Implications of racism for social work practice. *Journal of Sociology and Social Welfare* 6:297–312.

Mostwin, Danuta. 1972. In search of ethnic identity. *Social Casework* 53:307–316.

Norton, Dolores G. 1978. *The dual perspective*. New York: Council on Social Work Education.

Perlman, Helen H. 1957. *Social casework*. Chicago: University of Chicago Press.

Perlman, Helen H. 1986. The problem-solving model. In *Social work treatment*, edited by J. Turner. New York: The Free Press.

Pincus, Allen, and Minahan, Anne. 1973. *Social work practice: model and method*. Itasca, IL: F. E. Peacock Publishers, Inc.

President's Commission on Mental Health. 1978. *Task Panel Reports*, Vol. 3, Appendix.

Reid, William J. 1977. *A Study of the characteristics and effectiveness of task-centered methods*. Chicago: The School of Social Service Administration.

Reid, William J. 1978. *The task centered system*. New York: Columbia University Press.

Reid, William J. 1986. Task-centered social work. In *Social work treatment*, edited by J. Turner. New York: The Free Press.

Reid, William J., and Epstein, Laura. 1972. *Task-centered casework*. New York: Columbia University Press.

Reid, William J., and Shyne, D. 1969. Brief and extended casework. New York: Columbia University Press.

Reynolds, Bertha C. 1938. Treatment processes as developed by social work. *Proceedings, National Conference of Social Work*. New York: Columbia University Press.

Siporin, Max. 1975. *Introduction to social work practice*. New York: The Macmillan Co.

Strean, Herbert S. 1974. Role theory. In *Social work treatment*, edited by F. J. Turner. New York: The Free Press.

Studt, Elliot. 1968. Social work theory and implication for the practice of methods. *Social Work Education Reporter* 16:22–24.

Titmuss, Richard. 1968. *Commitment to welfare*. New York: Pantheon Books.

Titmuss, Richard. 1969. *Essays on the welfare state*. Boston: Beacon Press.

Turner, Francis J. 1970. Ethnic difference and client performance. *Social Service Review* 44:1–10.

Turner, Francis J. 1974. Some considerations on the place of theory in current social work practice. In *Social work treatment*, edited by J. Turner. New York: The Free Press.

Turner, Francis J. 1978. *Psychosocial therapy*. New York: The Free Press.

Turner, Francis J. 1986. Theory in social work practice. In *Social work treatment*, edited by J. Turner. New York: The Free Press.

Wald, Lillian. 1951. *The house on Henry Street*. New York: Holt, Rinehart, and Winston.

Wilson, W. J. 1978. *The declining significance of race*. Chicago: University of Chicago Press.

Younghusband, Eileen. 1964. *Social work and social change*. London: George Allen and Unwin.

CHAPTER
5

Assumptions and Principles for Ethnic-Sensitive Practice

In this chapter, principles for ethnic-sensitive practice are developed. These principles are built on (1) the conception of the ethnic reality and its relationship to the life cycle, (2) the layers of understanding, and (3) the view of social work as a problem-solving endeavor. The perspectives presented in the preceding chapters suggest that social work practice must be grounded in understanding of the diverse group memberships people hold. Particular attention must be paid to ethnicity and social class and how these contribute to individual and group identity, dispositions toward basic life tasks, coping styles, and problems likely to be encountered. These, together with individual history, and genetic and physiological disposition, contribute to the development of personality and group life.

Prior to the presentation of the principles prominent in ethnic-sensitive practice, we identify a set of assumptions that guide such practice. These assumptions are delineated and illustrated in some detail because of our conviction that a group's history, values, and perspectives markedly affect the present concerns of individuals and of the group as a whole.

In our view, these assumptions provide more than background knowledge; together with various theories of behavior they become an integral component of the basic principles that guide practice and serve to shape practice skill and technology.

Basic Assumptions for Ethnic-Sensitive Practice

1. Individual and collective history have bearing on problem generation and solution.
2. The present is most important.
3. Ethnicity has significant influence on individual identity formation.
4. Ethnicity is a source of cohesion, identity, and strength as well as a source of strain, discord, and strife.

PAST HISTORY HAS BEARING ON PROBLEM GENERATION AND SOLUTION

Theorists differ in their views concerning the relationship between the origins of a problem and the mechanisms that presently sustain or diminish that problem (Fischer 1978). Nevertheless, there is little question that individual and group history provide clues about how problems originate and suggest possible avenues for resolution.

Group History

In the review of the persistence of ethnicity as a factor in social life, the history of oppression to which many groups have been subjected was noted; also important is the fact that these groups attempt to develop strategies to protect and cushion their members from such oppression. Culture, religion, and language are transmitted through primary groups to their individual members and serve to give meaning to daily existence.

Crucial to a group's past is the history of the migration experience or other processes through which the encounter with mainstream culture took place. Some, like American Indians and many Chicanos, view themselves as having been conquered.[1] Others, including the early Anglo-Saxon settlers, fled religious oppression. Many came for both reasons. These experiences continue to have bearing on how their members perceive and organize life and how they are perceived by others. Howe (1975) suggests that the earlier generations of Jewish immigrants, fleeing oppression and economic hardship, thought it necessary to "propel sons and daughters into the outer world—or more precisely, to propel them into the outer world as social beings while trying to keep them spiritually within the Jewish orbit." The sons and

---

[1] Today, many American Indian tribes view themselves as nations negotiating on a basis of equality with the American Nation (President's Commission on Mental Health 1978).

daughters of street peddlers, and of "girls" who had worked in the sweatshops of the Lower East Side, were encouraged to become educated. "The fathers would work, grub, and scramble as petty agents of primitive accumulation. The sons would acquire education, that New World magic the Jews were so adept at evoking through formulas they had brought from the Old World" (1975 pp. 51–77). And so, many Jews went to college and substantial numbers of them quickly moved into the middle class. Jews' traditional respect for learning, and the particular urban skills in which they had been schooled—a function of anti-Semitism in eastern Europe whereby they were not permitted to work the land (Zborowski and Herzog 1952)—converged to speed their entry into middle-class America. Education, success, and marriage were the serious things in life. Sensuality and attending to the needs of the body were deemphasized.

There was a deeply ingrained suspicion of frivolity and sport. "Suspicion of the physical, fear of hurt, anxiety over the sheer 'pointlessness' of play: all this went deep into the recesses of the Jewish psyche" (Howe 1975 pp. 51–77).

There may be little resemblance between Jews living on New York's Lower East Side at the turn of the century and the contemporary urbane Jew. And yet, the emphasis on intellectualism persists, as does the haunting fear of persecution. There is a lingering suspicion of things physical, and a tendency to take illness quite seriously. Jewish men are still considered good husbands, kind providers who value their families.

Following the Japanese attack on Pearl Harbor in December, 1941, 110,000 Japanese-Americans were removed from their homes and detained in relocation centers. The relocation experience exposed many to work for the first time. (Many had previously been denied employment opportunities.) Following the incarceration, the Japanese went about reconstructing their lives. Despite the horror of the relocation experience, many of the second generation found they were capable of doing a greater variety of work than they had recognized. It has been suggested that the relocation experience actually speeded the process of absorption into the mainstream by turning over the leadership to the second generation (Nisei) at a much faster pace than is usually the case.[2] As a group they have been highly successful; when comparisons of education, occupation, and income are used, Japanese-Americans exceed the national average in the professions (Knoll 1982).

For many ethnic groups the collective history is viewed from a distance as events long past. The experiences are related by others, older

---

[2]Interview with Dr. Shozi Oniki.

members of the family or community. This may be the experience of third-generation Japanese (Sansei) as they learn of the history of the Japanese in America from their elders, first-generation Issei. There are other Asian populations, however, whose arrival as refugees—persons who flee for safety—is directly related to recent historical events. They have been the victims of atom bombs, defoliants, and napalm. Others are the victims of oppressive governments. Many can recall these events as part of their lives (Knoll 1982).

While many Asian groups share these more recent historical experiences of war and oppression, one must be aware of their differences related to past history. Koreans, often labeled "silent immigrants," come from a country continually besieged by the Chinese and Japanese. The country has been divided into North and South, the North controlled by Soviet commanders, the South by American commanders (Knoll 1982).

Vietnamese have come from a country of harsh land, difficult climate, and frequent wars, earlier with the Chinese and later resisting French domination. It is only recently that they have chosen to leave in great numbers, resisting religious and political oppression and the ravages of war (California State Department of Health 1981; Knoll 1982).

Each of these groups and Filipinos, Laotians, Chinese, and Cambodians have been the victims of the oppression of racism. There are the early accounts of shooting and lynching of Chinese laborers in the West and more recent accounts of tension between Vietnamese and whites as they compete in the fishing industry in the South.

However, unifying trends are part of their collective and individual histories; the family is most important, parents are to be respected, education is important, and family resources are pooled to create employment.

Mexican revolutions early in the 1900s, together with American conquests, generated much family disruption among Mexicans. Conscription of men into the armed forces was common. Poor Mexicans migrating into the larger cities of Texas left behind a history and way of life among homogeneous folk societies. In these societies "God-given" roles were clearly assigned. Women did not work outside the home, except in the fields. Each individual had a sense of place, of identity, of belonging. Work was to be found tilling the soil. Education in the formal sense did not exist. Rituals of the church were an intricate part of daily life (West 1980). These rural immigrants, whose language and belief systems were so different from the frontier mentality, were not welcomed.

The history of Blacks in this country has become well known. They arrived in bondage; the institution of slavery held them for 200 years. Yet, the astute social worker must know that their history began, as Bennett (1964) has stated, "before the Mayflower," on the African continent, where they developed a culture that reflected skills in agriculture, government, scholarship, and the fine arts. Unlike the other ethnic groups mentioned, Blacks were unable to openly preserve their customs, religion, or family tradition in the new land. The institution of slavery actively sought to discourage this process. Their past history of oppression, imposed by the mainstream society, continues to generate problems in the present, and the oppression continues in more subtle ways.

The experience of West Indians in America differs from that of American Blacks initially in that as immigrants they were British citizens. They share an earlier history of slavery. There are indications that conditions were worse for slaves in the West Indies. Infant mortality rates were higher, sexual exploitation of women slaves greater, and self-denigration among Blacks more pervasive than in the U.S. (Sowell 1978, 1981).

However, while American slavery fostered a total dependency upon the white owner, the West Indian slaves, within the context of a brutal system, were issued food rations for the family, were fed from common kitchens, assigned land, and given time to raise their own food. Income from the sale of surplus provided a resource for the purchase of items for themselves. Sowell (1981) suggests that this particular experience in slavery, whereby West Indians took care of themselves to a significant degree, as well as their experience in buying and selling, provided them incentives and experience in the marketplace denied American slaves. These skills provided the West Indians with a greater ability to survive in the urban American community. The regimented dependence of American slavery held no opportunity for a marketplace experience (Sowell 1979).

There are 1.5 million Americans who are natives of the West Indies. Another 1 million have parents who were born in the Caribbean (Whitaker 1986). Despite the small numbers, the successes of West Indians in the United States are significant. They have been frugal, hardworking, and entrepreneurial. Their children, much like the children of Asian immigrants, work harder in school and outperform American-born children, Black and white (Sowell 1981). A value system that places family and friendship before wealth and career is said to lead to this success (Whitaker 1986).

These are but a few examples of how the nature of migration and the values the immigrants brought converge with mainstream America and affect present functioning. Intervention strategies must take these into account.

The collective experience of a group affects individuals differently. Personality and life history serve as filters and determine which facets of ethnic history and identity remain an integral part of a person's functioning, which are forgotten, and which are consciously rejected. Nevertheless, it is unlikely that any Jew would not emit a particular shudder when reminded of the Holocaust. Japanese-Americans, no matter of which generation, recall the relocation experience. In a racist society they can never be sure how they will be received, for their difference is physically visible.

Individual History and Group Identity

Individual members of groups have a sense of their group's history. For some it is dim and for others it is clearly articulated; for each it provides a sense of identification with the group. Such identification becomes a component, an integral part of the personality.

Events in the present that remind one of a past ethnic history may affect decisions made. Such was the experience of a young Jewish woman who considered her group's past and its implications for her future. The dim memories were called forth in response to a class assignment on exploring family origins. However, this vague identification with Jewish tradition influenced actions in the present.

> Education was of prime importance to him [my father], followed closely by social class, religion, and background. Most of my parents' teachings influenced me in other ways. It was understood that I would attend college . . . This push toward the pursuit of education and the importance of proper background influenced me in the rearing of my daughters.

In this example the personality of the mother has been influenced by a clearly identifiable ethnic history. She recognizes that her ethnic experiences influence the way she relates to her children today.

Another example highlights the integration of ethnic tradition into the personality and life-styles of two generations. In this instance the writer has adult children who are somewhat removed from their Italian background. Nevertheless, she notes:

> My grown son on occasion will request that I "make one of them ethnic meals." When my daughter visits, she always tries to time her trip to coincide with some ethnic event. She will be coming home this weekend and we will be going to New York to the Feast of San Genaro in Little Italy. We will partake of some Italian cooking specialties and atmosphere. On these occasions I always feel proud of being Italian.

Each individual has an ethnic history with roots in the past. Traditions, customs, rituals, and behavioral expectations all interface with life in America. These aspects of the past have the potential for affecting perceptions of problems in the present. For those Slavics who were reared with the expectation that intergenerational support is or should be available, its absence may be particularly disquieting and, in the extreme, devastating. The individual and collective histories of Blacks suggest that there are resources available in times of trouble. Families across the social classes respond to the needs of kin, both emotional and financial needs. The response in either instance may rest upon an awareness, articulated or not, of the past (Stack 1975; Krause 1978).

In any situation the social worker should assume that part of the response to that situation derives from the client's sense of past history as it is intertwined with personal history. Experience with the ethnic reality is an integral part of the sense of the past.

THE PRESENT IS MOST IMPORTANT

The past gives shape to problems manifest in the present. Social work's major obligation is to attend to current issues, with full awareness that the distribution and incidence of problems is often related to the ethnic reality. The divorce rate among American Indians is increasing, crimes of violence are increasing in American Indian communities, and children are continually placed in boarding schools (Wilkinson 1981). These problems are added to the well-known problems of alcoholism and suicide. These problems require attention in the present. Family and community life are being threatened. The contact with urban America has had particularly negative effects on American Indians. The pride and noble sense of self and tribe so intrinsic to American Indian life must be used to serve as sources of strength for dealing with current problems.

The Black underclass demands attention in the present. This urban population remains in the ghetto after the flight to the suburbs of the Black middle class. Evidence of racism is overshadowed by problems of out-of-wedlock childbirth, unemployment, crime, and poor educational achievement that have persisted for more than half a century (Lemann 1986). These social class phenomena must be understood, as they foreshadow the future of these families.

Knowledge and understanding of a group's history, customs, and beliefs are required for effective practice, both at the individual and institutional level. Appreciation for customs and beliefs is essential in understanding responses to diverse problems. These are manifest in the wishes of members of many ethnic groups to "take care of their own" in times of trouble. For an example, when the infant daughter of a paranoid schizophrenic Italian woman needs placement, it is the grandfather's wish that a cousin adopt the child, thereby keeping her within the family. The ethnic-sensitive worker will realize that the grandfather's effort to keep the infant in the family may well be founded on the sociopolitical history of southern Italy. In the midst of political turmoil the family was the only social structure upon which an individual could depend. Survival depended on this strong interdependence between family members. It was also a bulwark against those who were not blood relatives (Papajohn and Spiegel 1975). Cousins may not be in a position to offer care in the "old country way" envisioned by the grandfather. At the same time, workers must not only recognize his disposition, but make every effort to help the family explore those family resources that will minimize an already traumatic situation.

The current problem must always receive primary attention. However, the practitioner must recognize that ethnic group history may affect present perception of the problem and its solutions.

ETHNICITY HAS SIGNIFICANT INFLUENCE ON INDIVIDUAL IDENTITY FORMATION

Earlier we spoke of the "routine and habitual dispositions to life which become so thoroughly a part of the self that they require no examination." These dispositions, not articulated, become part of the core of the self. The rhythm of Polish community life may be conveyed through the sounds heard by children as they grow. The sounds become routine, an accepted part of life; they are not examined for meaning. They may evoke joy or sadness for reasons unknown to the listener. "The Polish experience is a language, music and shouts . . . We were a rather emotional and demonstrative family. Laughter and tears, anger and affection were fully given vent . . . We were often headstrong, hasty, sinning, repenting, sinning and repenting again" (Napierkowski 1976).

When Erikson (1968) suggests that identity is a process "located" in the core of the individual and yet in the core of his or her communal culture, he explains the Polish experience described here. There are many ethnic experiences that are among the many personal experiences "hidden" in our vague and obscure thoughts and memories (Hollis 1972). These experiences provide us a sense of belonging and historical continuity essential to our psychological development. They become a part of our identity. Persons who are secure in their ethnic identity have a greater potential for personal success. They are not burdened with negative or distorted views (McGoldrick 1982). But developing an ethnic identity is not easy as the group becomes more American.

Tricario (1984) writes of the struggle to develop a "new" Italian-American ethnicity and the possibility that this is already waning; nevertheless, ethnicity maintains identity and other ethnic symbols resurface. Perhaps the struggle originates from a yearning for the "sights and the sounds" described by Napierkowski (1976). These sights, sounds, and smells can be integral parts of an individual's ethnic reality.

THE ETHNIC REALITY IS A SOURCE OF COHESION, IDENTITY, AND STRENGTH OR OF STRAIN, DISCORD, AND STRIFE

In chapter one, the effects of ethnicity and social class were broadly sketched. Attention is now focused on those specific components of the ethnic reality that serve as sources of cohesion, identity, and strength, as well as sources of strain, discord, and strife.

The Family

As one of the major primary groups the family is responsible for the care of the young, transmission of values, and emotional sustenance. It is a source of strength, identity, and cohesion. All families are expected to carry out such tasks.

The value placed on the family and the extent of commitment to solution of diverse family problems varies by ethnicity and social class. Family values may also produce strain or conflict with the demands and prejudices of the larger society. Particularly cohesive family structures may be observed in the response of Navajo Indians to family problems. It is expected that aunts, cousins, sisters, and uncles will all share in the burden of child rearing and help with problems. Relatives usually do not live far away from one another. Older people give guidance to their children and grandchildren (Jimison 1977). There is strength in this bond. The family becomes a resource when the courts have questions related to child neglect and custody. Chicanos, Puerto Ricans, Asians, and many Eastern Europeans have similar attitudes toward family obligations.

The sense of family cohesion often diminishes in the second and third generations of immigrants or migrants. The family as transmitter of old values, customs, and language is often seen as restrictive by members of the younger generation.

> Zaidia Perez is a single parent, estranged from her family. She has violated a family expectation by refusing to marry the father of her children. Her Puerto

Rican extended family withholds the support usually offered a daughter. The result is a life of loneliness and isolation. There is the additional turmoil of Ms. Perez's struggle with her ethnic reality. She is a poor Puerto Rican. It is her conviction that her Spanish heritage and dark coloring have denied her entrance into the middle class. In response, she attempts to reject her background by refusal to associate with other Puerto Ricans in the neighborhood.

Zaidia's struggle with the ethnic reality denies her those supports that come from affable relationships with family and neighbors. Some of that support is provided by ritual and other celebrations.

Rituals and Celebrations

As Puerto Ricans celebrate "Nuech Buena" (Christmas Eve) there is a feeling of relaxation, of caring, and of temporary retreat from problems. The extended family gathers with close friends to celebrate "The Good Night." The regular diet of rice and beans becomes more elaborate; yellow rice and pigeon peas are most important, as is the pernil asalo (roast pork).

The ethnic church is a place where those with similar histories and problems gather to affirm their identity and beliefs, for example, Italians, Polish, Blacks or Jews. Feast days are days of celebration that combine reverence with ethnic tradition.

The Academy Award–winning film *The Deer Hunter* vividly depicts how rituals and the church serve to buttress and sustain. A wedding takes place in the "Russian Orthodox Church with its spirals that might well have been set in the steppes of the Urals" (Horowitz 1979). The old Russian women carry cake to the hall for the wedding of one of three young men about to go off to war. There is joyous celebration, Russian folk singing, and "good old-fashioned patriotism." The second-generation, working-class, Russian-Americans have strong allegiances to this, "their native land." The wedding provides the occasion for the community's show of love and support as their young men go off to war.

There is excitement in rituals and celebrations. For weeks or days before the event family members in many ethnic groups prepare for Rosh Hashanah, Yom Kippur, Christmas, weddings, and saints' days. Yet, on each of these occasions there is the potential for stress. Each participant does not have the same perception of the event.

Sax (1979) describes his return to his parents' home for the Jewish holidays. No matter what his age, he is always assigned a seat at the dining room table. He is a single male, and at shul fellow worshipers offer condolences to his parents, who try to be stoic on the matter. But it is time he was married. Proud to be a Jew, he returns to his home for the celebration of Yom Kippur. But he has not fulfilled a communal obligation and this causes tension in the family even on this holiest of days. For, just as the ritual is an occasion for joy and celebration, it is also a time when the young are reminded of their transgressions or departures from tradition. Perhaps the David Saxes will think twice about returning for the next celebration.

Ethnic Schools and Parochial Schools

The Hebrew school, the Hungarian or Ukrainian language school, and the parochial school are examples of mechanisms for the preservation of language, rituals, and traditions.

Some, like the after-school language programs, are used to supplement the education provided in secular public schools. Many Jewish children go to Hebrew schools sponsored by synagogues in the afternoons and on weekends. There they prepare for the bar or bas mitzvah and learn Hebrew, Jewish history, and the details of ritual. Many Americans of Eastern European descent offer after-school programs in which the native languages are taught. The buildings where these are held often become social centers. Not infrequently these are located in old city neighborhoods. Second and third-generation families who have moved to the suburbs provide the financial support by which these schools and the ethnic churches are sustained. The tie to the ethnic group of origin and its values is often maintained through such schools.[3]

The young do not always feel the need for such an experience. While they attend after-school programs, other children are involved in a variety of activities from which they are excluded. The feeling of strain is expressed by a young adult as he recalls his childhood experience: "I went to Hebrew school and felt left out of things that went on in the neighborhood. Hebrew school was two afternoons a week and Sunday morning. So, I couldn't belong to Little League, or play Pop Warner football and do the normal things other kids did."[4]

Parochial schools in many neighborhoods are expected to transmit ethnic tradition and values, as are the many secular ethnic schools. They assure a continuation of the faith as well as a place in which morality and social norms may be reinforced.

---

[3]For example, New Brunswick, New Jersey, is the center of an old Hungarian community. Although the number of Hungarian-American families that continue to live there is small, and those who do are aging, there are flourishing Hungarian banks, churches, and schools. The city is viewed as a regional center for Hungarian America in three surrounding states.

[4]Conversation with David Jacobson.

With these schools there are inherent conflicts as ethnic neighbor-hoods change. Gans's (1962) study of the Italians of Boston's West End describes such a neighborhood in which the church and its school were founded by the Irish, who slowly moved away and were replaced by Italians. The church, however, retained Irish priests and lay leaders. Dedicated Italian Catholics often complained that the school was indoc-trinating their children in Irish Catholicism. Rather than providing the solace they expected from association with church-related institutions, the school caused much discord.

An example of the stress that may come from such a conflict is provided by an Italian who attended such a school:

> I like being Italian. I grew up in a mixed neighborhood. But it wasn't mixed in terms of what the authority was in relation to church and school if you were Catholic. It was Irish . . . I went to a parochial school run by Irish nuns and priests. That is important to mention because there was an insensitivity to our cultural needs at the time . . . The Americanization of the Italians was a cultural genocide, at least when I grew up. St. Patrick's day would come and we would all celebrate . . . Obviously, there were other saints who were Italian but the cultural aspects, the cultural pride was not brought in the way St. Patrick was.[5]

As the church combated the tensions described by Gans "national parishes" were established to serve the needs of various immigrant groups. Italian parishes were served by Italian priests or others who spoke Italian and were sympathetic to the Italians' cause. Through this process Italians, and other ethnic groups, were able to worship accord-ing to their own traditions (Alba 1985).

This Catholic response to ethnicity did not assure continued devotion to the church. Some Italian Catholics have joined protestant denomina-tions, others have remained in the Catholic church and resisted reform. Still others have accepted the Irish-American norms of the church. Second and third-generation families no longer resist sending children to parochial schools for fear of Irish influences (Alba 1985). Yet, when parochial schools connected to the national parish are available, families may be willing to take extraordinary steps to provide their children with an Italian Catholic education. Johnson (1985) cites a girl who lived with her grandparents in order to be closer to the Catholic school connected to the national parish. Her experience will be more comfortable than the one described earlier. Here she will find a continuation of tradition that affirms her faith and ethnicity.

---

[5]Interview with Frank Becallo.

Language

Most immigrant and migrant groups are identified with a past that includes a language other than English. That language is variously used by or familiar to first, second, and third-generation children of immigrants. Each language generates a unique ambience and contributes to a group's "Weltanschaung" (Sotomayor 1977). Although language can serve as a self and group-affirming function, and the bilingual individual is to be admired, the continued use of the second language often generates problems. This is particularly true in those institutions that refuse to listen to anything but mainstream words. Yet, as has been suggested, the language can function as "solution" in an alien place. For Chicanos, Puerto Ricans, and many others, linguistic identification and affirmation can serve to ease internal stress imposed by political, economic, and social degradation.

The number of Hispanic and Asian immigrants has sharply increased in recent years (Reinhold 1986; Vidal 1980). Many groups, especially many Hispanics, reject the notion that they should abandon their language and its associated culture. Bilingual education that facilitates the acquisition of skills needed for participation in the economic sector of society is strongly supported. Many minorities view this as essential, refusing to relinquish this basis of uniqueness. Nevertheless "talking funny" attracts attention and increases the risk of being called "dumb" wop, Polack, spick, or Chink.

Language—the sounds of discord. The effects of mainstream negation of native language have already been noted. There are those group members who consciously deny their native language as a way of "losing" their ethnicity. To speak Italian, Polish, Hungarian, Chinese, or Spanish may well cause strain for those who feel this inhibits their efforts to become American. Richard Rodriguez (1982) tells of his childhood struggle with language; Spanish was the private language of home and English, the public language. The insistence of nuns, his teachers, propelled the family into the use of English for private as well as public life. As an adult Rodriguez defines himself as "a middle-class American man Assimilated."

In her struggle to become American, Rose Mary Prosen (1976) did not speak Slovenian, the language of her birth, from the time she entered high school until she reached womanhood. When addressed in the language, more often than not she did not respond.

In each instance children are confronted with the discord caused by their language. Language that does not conform to the mainstream at times suggests that one is not American. There are those who are fearful of the day that "the immigrants' native tongue becomes the first language for any community or—a state". They quote Theodore Roosevelt's cry against hyphenated Americans and calling for one language, the English language. To print ballots and voting material in language other than English "reverses the main American movement,—to meld many people into one" (Cooke 1986). There are others who claim that the melting pot did not happen, perhaps in the future but not yet (Glazer and Moynihan 1970).

Still, names like Franzyshen, Bastianello, and Turkeltaub attract attention. Teachers, employers, and new acquaintances stumble and often resist attempts to learn how to pronounce these names, yet many maintain these names with pride, often lamenting their inability to speak the language of their forebears.

PRINCIPLES FOR ETHNIC-SENSITIVE PRACTICE

An eclectic theoretical framework focused on various measures of human functioning has been developed. Particular attention has been paid to those components of theory that serve to heighten attention to the roles of social class and ethnicity, The Ethnic Reality.

The framework provides the foundation for two essential practice principles. The first calls attention to the fact that the paths to social work services are varied. We refer to these variations as *The Route to the Social Worker* and suggest how that route affects problem definition and intervention.

The other relates to the need for simultaneous or sequential attention to individual and collective concerns, as these emerge from client need and professional assessment. Both reflect the view that "private troubles are examples of public issues, the public issues are made up of many private troubles" (Schwartz 1985).

The Route to the Social Worker

During the past decade social work theoreticians have increasingly stressed the need to focus on problems as they are perceived and defined by clients. This is a response to some once common aspects of practice in which worker, rather than client definitions were given major attention in problem solving. In the view of many theoreticians, psychodynamically oriented workers were particularly prone to emphasize "nonconscious" factors and to minimize those concerns consciously articulated by clients. The following is illustrative: A woman seeks help from a family counseling center because of continuing tensions and quarrels between herself and her husband. An assessment may suggest that she is constantly seeking from her husband the affection she never received from her father, or that her husband is responding in adverse ways to her demands that he reconsider alternatives to her traditional woman's role. Neither was the problem as presented by the client. Such problem definition deflects attention from the current aspects of her life situation that may be sustaining the problem. These may be mainly emotional tension or concrete problems such as inadequate housing in which to raise a family or insufficient income.

Another area of concern in past practice is a certain degree of paternalism. The assumption is made that the worker's definition of the problem is more legitimate, more valid than the client's. In this sense problems are sometimes attributed to clients that they neither experience nor articulate.

Consider the following common situation: A young woman turns to the public welfare department for Aid for families with Dependent Children after her husband deserts her and their newborn child. Her request is for financial aid. In the assessment phase the worker assumes that the problem is one of immaturity, and that the young mother is unable to care for her infant child adequately. This can be "corrected," however, by participation in a counseling group for young mothers.

This is not an uncommon assumption. Indeed, Mullen, Chazin, and Feldstein (1970) carried out a major investigation to test whether intensive professional casework services would decrease rates of disorganization *presumed* to be associated with entering the welfare system. Reid and Epstein (1972) have grappled with these and related issues by making the distinction between attributed and acknowledged problems (see chapter four). In their view the mother described above should receive counseling services *only* if she feels in need of them or if her child is in danger. If the latter is the case, a social control, not a treatment function, would be exercised.

This is an important distinction that highlights the need to work with people on issues they define as important. Nevertheless, the continuing discussion about the distinction between real and presenting problems and the debate about the difference between attributed and acknowledged problems does not fully address the reality. People get to service agencies through various routes. Their problems, for the most part, are very real. Whether or not they perceive the social worker as a potential source of help in the terms defined by social work practice is another issue. Much of service is rendered in contexts that have a coercive or nonvoluntary component. This is illustrated by a continuum of *Routes to*

TABLE 1. Routes to the social worker

Routes to the Social Worker	Clients	Fields of Practice
Totally coercive	Clients assigned by the courts to probation, parole, or protective services	Child welfare Corrections
Highly coercive	Welfare clients expected to enter job training or counseling in order to maintain eligibility; person assigned to drug rehabilitation center or Job Corps as an alternative to jail	Public welfare Corrections
Somewhat coercive	Patient involvement with hospital social worker for discharge planning; student in interview with school social worker to maintain child's presence in school; client in alcohol treatment program suggested by employer	Health services Schools
Somewhat voluntary	Husband entering marriage counseling at wife's request	Mental health Family services
Highly voluntary	Family enters into treatment at the suggestion of the clergy	Mental health Family services
Totally voluntary	Individual presenting self for family counseling; individual in psychotherapy	Family services Private practice

the Social Worker that range from total coercion to totally voluntary requests for service.

In presenting this first principle for practice we examine the extent to which practice is initiated by coercion or by those who seek help voluntarily.

As Table 1 shows, whether involvement with social work services is voluntary or coercive is in large measure related to the context in which service is rendered, or to what is often termed the social work field of practice. This does not negate the fact that there are voluntary and coercive elements in all fields of practice. Parolees do request social work services; by the same token, many people seek family counseling under stress.

In addition to the components of practice depicted in the table there are others including outreach, social work-initiated community development activities, and certain preventive efforts to combat problems identified by professionals rather than articulated by clients.

There are clear-cut differences in the initial approach to the client-worker encounter related to the variations along the coercive-voluntary continuum. These differences relate to whether intervention is mandated by legal authority, encouraged or required by the workplace, the needs of various social institutions such as hospitals, schools, and the family, or by individual discomfort. Additional work has further illuminated these distinctions and related practice strategies. Epstein (1980) refers to "mandated target problems" as those "which originate with a legal or social authority, whether or not the client is in agreement . . . Mandates to act in a certain manner imply that there is an obligation placed on the client and the agency to change a situation . . . by retraining or curbing identified actions." Legislation, actual or threatened court orders, professional opinion, or public opinion as to negative behavior are the sources of mandated behavior changes.

Epstein's (1980) view is related to our conception that those whom we would term "somewhat" coerced or "somewhat" voluntary clients are unlikely to work on problems as they are identified by typical referral sources. For these reasons, the problems as perceived by clients should be the central focus of the interventive process. Where a totally coercive or legal mandate is at issue, as with the parolee or abusing parent, work on the mandated problem should be accompanied by efforts to work simultaneously on issues identified by the client.

Professional perspective on origin or solutions of problems affects the initial client-worker encounter. A structural perspective would focus on environmental rather than individual change (Middleman and Goldberg 1974). Activities designed to change environments are not easily classified as coercive or voluntary. They often involve the assumption of professional responsibility for populations at risk.

The route to the social worker takes many forms. Whatever the route, working with problems in terms identified by clients is an essential dictum of ethnic-sensitive practice. The initial worker-client encounter, wherever it falls on the continuum, must be focused on efforts to help clients formulate the problem in terms manageable to them.

Together these perspectives point to the range of possibilities for expanding the scope of client self-direction even under the most adverse authoritative conditions. For the truly voluntary client, the potential for using the momentum generated by the process of seeking help is considerable. This is suggested by a body of evidence that has linked the act of help seeking to accelerated problem-solving capacities (Reid and Epstein 1972).

It is clear that many people become involved with social welfare delivery systems whether or not they acknowledge a problem. Given this, the following formulation is proposed:

1. Initial problem definition and formulation is in large measure related to the route to the social worker.

2. Regardless of the route, the social worker's responsibility is to cast the problem in terms of professional values and the client's understanding of the problem.

This suggests that, no matter who initiates the process of service delivery, the interface between private troubles and public issues is usually evident. The fact that some people are in need of public assistance is in large measure a function of societal forces that contribute to economic inequity. The insistence on job training for unemployed or underemployed persons reflects the societal value on work and on economic independence.

Social workers are obligated to be aware of the origins of such problems, as well as the route to the social worker, as they function in these various arenas.

Simultaneous Attention to Interpersonal and Institutional Issues

The interface between private troubles and public issues is an intrinsic aspect of most approaches to social work practice. All models identify systemic change efforts or "environmental work" as a component of professional function. The integration of individual and systemic change efforts is a basic component of ethnic-sensitive practice. Such integration is essential if practice is to be responsive to the particular needs and sensitivities of various groups and individuals. Attention must be focused on the structural sources of problems and on those actions that"adjust the environment to the needs of individuals" (Middleman and Goldberg 1974).

Practice is a problem-solving endeavor (Perlman 1957). Problems are generated at the interface between people and their environments. Many of the problems with which social workers deal involve economic and social inequity and their consequences for individuals. This inequity is frequently experienced at the individual and small group level.

Ethnic-sensitive practice pays particular attention to the individual consequences of racism, poverty, and discrimination. Examples are internalization of those negative images the society holds of devalued groups, or learning deficits that are consequences of inadequate education for minorities.

Members of all groups experience some difficulties in their intimate relationships, become ill, and struggle to master the varying tasks associated with different stages of the life cycle. Simultaneous attention to micro and macro tasks focuses the social worker's attention on individual problems at the same time as the systemic sources and possible solutions. Support for personal change efforts and help in altering dysfunctional behaviors is crucial.

A useful framework for highlighting the process of simultaneous attention to micro and macro tasks is the one presented by Middleman and Goldberg (1974). They identify practice as bounded by locus of concern (the problem calling for social work intervention) and persons engaged (persons and/or institutions involved as a consequence of the problems being confronted). This formulation suggests an approach to intervention that in their terms, "follows the demands of the client task." (See chapter four.)

In a reconsideration of the Middleman and Goldberg framework Jackson, Macy, and Day (1984) have provided a model for practice that draws on systems language, situational analysis, and concepts of interactional and analytical tasks. Practice falls into areas of interpersonal practice, social action, policy practice, and social treatment. Tasks are interactional (management of a professional relationship between worker and client) or analytical, in which the worker examines the social situation. Particular emphasis is paid to the need for practitioners to respond in more than one area of practice simultaneously.

In both the structural and simultaneity models the social worker must look beyond the problems presented by individual clients to see whether others are suffering from the same problem. The perspectives serve to call attention to those community and ethnic networks in which people are enmeshed and which can be called upon to aid in problem resolution.

Problems, as identified by the client or social worker, have diverse sources and call for a variety of systemic and individual action. This may be seen in the following example: A Jewish boy may feel torn between a parental injunction not to become involved in celebration of Christmas and his need to join the children in his public school as they trim Christmas trees and sing carols. The turmoil may result in the child's becoming withdrawn and searching for reasons to stay home from school. Support and counseling from the school social worker may be needed. This may be particularly true if there are few Jewish children in the school, and if alternate sources of support and identity affirmation are not available. Actions may be designed to enhance respect for and knowledge of diverse customs. Suggestions that the school incorporate celebrations unique to various groups as part of the holiday celebration are part of the plan for action. The results provide an opportunity for Jewish children to tell about the tradition of Chanukah and Greek Orthodox children may share the unique ways their holiday is celebrated.

Social workers must be attuned to interpersonal and institutional levels of intervention as they go about the task of helping people who are caught in a clash between varying cultures.

Many of the problems with which social workers deal involve inequity and discrimination. Systemic actions are often called for by the "presenting problems." If successfully carried out, such actions can forestall or minimize similar problems for other people.

A number of cases are presented to illustrate how practice is enhanced when there is simultaneous attention to micro and macro level tasks, coupled with sensitivity to the ethnic reality.

A Mexican-American woman accustomed to delivering her babies at home, surrounded by family and friends, suffers greatly when placed in the Anglo maternity ward. The sounds are unfamiliar to her and the strangers do not speak her language. She is denied privacy when she is placed in the labor room with other women. Wrapped in a towel, she gets up searching for familiar faces and more familiar sounds. Physical force may be used to return her to bed. She may be termed an uncooperative, unappreciative patient (Brownlee 1978).

Little consideration has been given to the possibility of adapting hospital procedures to meet the needs of a large Mexican-American community in the area. Understanding of Chicano childbirth rituals could help hospital personnel to enhance the experience rather than induce terror in an alien setting. A variety of actions are required in this situation based on the assumptions and theoretical formulations previously discussed: (1) sociological insights call attention to the ethnic reality and suggest an explanation for the action of wandering out of the labor room, though the possibility of pathology must be explored, (2) the patient needs help to avoid a crisis, and (3) alternatives to the alien delivery room structure need to be explored. "Birthing centers" may provide a more comfortable structure, one in which family members participate in the delivery process. This Chicano mother is an "involuntary" social work client. Yet, institutional and individual needs require the social worker's attention. The crisis nature of the situation compels quick action. Subsequent efforts to modify delivery procedures should involve Chicano women in the planning process.

In the midst of a city, hidden within a Hispanic population, is a community of Russian Orthodox Jews. Their life is barren. Their housing is substandard. The few clothes that they own are threadbare. Many basic necessities of living are missing from their lives. Language separates them even more from the mainstream. A Russian-speaking outreach worker, from a community senior citizen program, discovers that a significant number of adults are in need of health care. A particular need is nutrition. They do not get enough to eat. As a relationship develops they are able, with the worker assuming a broker role, to obtain the services of a local Nutrition for the Elderly Program that will respect their dietary tradition. Such an accommodation is accomplished with the rabbi of the community. Together they attempt to work this out, realizing that the nutrition program has no requirement to provide services for members of this religious group, despite the fact that the program's mandate is to meet the nutritional needs of the elderly. Special meals for the Orthodox add to the program's workload. However, success means that not only will this group be fed but other ethnic groups will be more likely to have their requests heard.

The activity has provided regular, nutritious meals that meet dietary tradition as a result of cooperation among the elderly, their rabbi, and the various staff members and administrators of the Nutrition for the Elderly Program. The outreach worker began from a point of sensitivity to the ethnic reality. Application of the principle of "following demands of the client task" was successful in beginning a process of change in the policy of a community service program.

Christine Taylor is a small, thin, Black woman in her middle years. She receives AFDC for herself and her two children, who are ten and eight years old. Her sister, Florence Jackson, lives in the same community.

During the past few years Ms. Taylor has had a number of medical problems, including a hysterectomy and a cerebrovascular accident, which caused paralysis of her left side. For some time she was bitter about her condition, feeling that she was being punished for her past wrongdoing, and suspected that the doctors were persecuting her. Her worker has assisted her in getting the resources necessary for her continued therapy and educational programs to meet the children's needs. Although the worker is unable to effect any increase in the family's meager income, she is aware that they have sufficient food and the children are well clothed. She suspects a community process known as "swapping." The primary participants are Christine, her sister Florence, and their close friends. These women have lived on welfare for some time and have had little ability to accumulate a surplus of goods. They share food, clothing, and daily necessities. The limited supply in the community is continually redistributed among family and close friends. Without this system the sister, their friends, and neighbors might not survive.

The practitioner who is aware of this survival technique, which has grown out of the reality of the Black experience, would not have assumed that defiance, illicit relationships, or fraud were at work. Knowledge of the existence of such support systems minimizes premature suspicion and harassment on the part of the worker.

Hidden in the community is another support that enables Ms. Taylor to cope with the guilt and anger she feels about her handicap. Sister Sawyer is an African healer. She claims to have been born in a little village in South Africa and believes a special blessing has been given to her that enables her to remove evil spells, change luck from bad to good, ease pain, and remove unnatural illness. From Sister Sawyer Ms. Taylor receives comfort and reassurance that she is indeed a special person, as well as potions and scriptures, which will assist in her need for affirmation.

In this situation two environmental supports of the type often overlooked or considered illegitimate have been identified. If the principle of maximizing potential supports in the client's environment is to be applied, then ethnic coping practices must be viewed as valid. More extensive knowledge of these practices may enable the practitioner to enhance the established structures. "Swapping" is a well-established custom but may be enhanced if the network is enabled to purchase in bulk from a local cooperative, known to the practitioner and used by the entire community. This would make more commodities available to the group at lower prices, thus maximizing the benefits of a useful custom.

A young probationer was under court supervision and had strict orders to remain with responsible adults. His counselor became concerned because the youth appeared to ignore this order. The client moved around frequently and, according to the counselor, stayed overnight with several different young women. The counselor presented this case at a formal staff meeting, and fellow professionals stated their suspicion that the client was either a pusher or a pimp. The frustrating element to the counselor was that the young people knew each other and appeared to enjoy each other's company. Moreover, they were not ashamed to be seen in public with the client. This behavior prompted the counselor to initiate violation proceedings (Red Horse et al. 1978).

This counselor is unaware that these young women are functioning as a support system for his client. They are in fact his first cousins, who are viewed in the same way as sisters. He has been obeying the orders of the court and staying with different units within his family network, which includes over 200 people and spans three generations. With this knowledge of this client's ethnic reality, the worker can recognize and encourage the system. Appropriate family members may be enlisted to participate in plans for the future.

Many additional examples could be given. Individual problems often bring to the surface the need for changes in agency policy and administrative practices. Client concerns continually highlight the need for change in existing legislation, the development of new public policy, and research on appropriate service delivery.

The examples have illustrated the need for sensitive awareness of unique cultural patterns, whether the service rendered involves one-to-one counseling with individuals or developing community programs consonant with the ethnic reality. Each of these and other types of services call for an extensive repertoire of skills. The principle of "following the demand of the client task" suggests that client need shall determine the nature of the service rendered. In the example of the pregnant Chicano woman who runs out of the labor room searching for a familiar face, a number of interventive tasks are suggested. "On-the-spot intervention" calls for the ability to help her to minimize her fears and avert a crisis. A long-range perspective points to the need to adapt hospital routines in a manner congruent with both the perspectives of other Chicano women like her and good medical practice. If practitioners are to respond to diverse consumer needs they must be aware of the range of activities commonly suggested by any one problem.

All of these activities involve extensive skill, which will be considered in the next chapter.

SUMMARY

The basic assumptions of ethnic-sensitive practice are:

1. Individual and collective history have bearing on problem generation and solution.
2. The present is most important.
3. Ethnicity has significant influence on individual identity formation.
4. Ethnicity is a source of cohesion, identity, and strength as well as a source of strain, discord, and strife.

In addition to these assumptions, ethnic-sensitive practice is based on a particular set of principles, which include:

1. Simultaneous attention must be given to individual and systemic concerns as they emerge out of client need and professional assessment.

2. The *Route to the Social Worker* affects problem definition and intervention.

REFERENCES

Alba, Richard. 1985. *Italian-Americans into the twilight of ethnicity.* Englewood Cliffs, NJ: Prentice-Hall, Inc.

Asian Community Mental Health Services. 1981. *Vietnamese in America bamboo in the wind.* Oakland: California Department of Mental Health.

Bennett, Lerone, Jr. 1964. *Before the Mayflower: a history of the Negro in America 1619–1964.* Rev. ed. Chicago: Johnson Publishing Co., Inc.

Brownlee, Ann Templeton. 1978. *Community, culture and care—a cross-cultural guide for health workers.* St. Louis: The C.V. Mosby Co.

Cooke, Alistair. 1986. Letter in behalf of US English.

Epstein, Laura. 1980. *Helping people, the task-centered approach.* St. Louis: C.V. Mosby Co.

Erikson, Erik H. 1968. *Identity, youth, and crisis.* New York: W.W. Norton and Co., Inc.

Fischer, Joel. 1978. *Effective casework practice: an eclectic approach.* New York: McGraw-Hill Book Co.

Gans, Herbert J. 1962. *The urban villagers.* New York: The Free Press.

Glazer, Nathan, and Moynihan, Daniel P. 1970. *Beyond the melting pot, the Negroes, Puerto Ricans, Jews, Italians, and Irish of New York City,* 2d ed. Cambridge: M. I. T. Press.

Hollis, Florence. 1972. *Casework: a psychosocial therapy.* 2d ed. New York: Random House, Inc.

Horowitz, Irving Louis. 1979. On relieving the deformities of our transgressions. *Society* 16:80–83.

Howe, Irving. 1975. Immigrant Jewish families in New York: the end of the world of our fathers. *New York* 8:51–77.

Jackson, Eugene C.; Macy, Harry Jed; Day, Phyllis J. 1984. A simultaneity model for social work education. *Journal of Education for Social Work* 20:17–24.

Jimison, Leonard B. 1977. Parent and child relationships in law and in Navajo custom. In *The destruction of American Indian families,* edited by Steven Unger. New York: Association of American Indian Affairs.

Johnson, Colleen Leahy. 1985. *Growing up and growing old in Italian-American families.* New Brunswick, NJ: Rutgers University Press.

Knoll, Tricia. 1982. *Becoming Americans Asian sojourners, immigrants, and refugees in the western United States.* Portland, OR: Coast to Coast Books.

Krause, Corinne Azen. 1978. *Grandmothers, mothers, and daughters: an oral history of ethnicity, mental health, and continuity of three generations of Jewish, Italian, and Slavic-American women.* New York: The American Jewish Committee.

Lemann, Nicholas. 1986. The origins of the underclass. *The Atlantic Monthly.* 258:54–68.

McGoldrick, Monica. 1982. Ethnicity and family therapy: an overview. In

Ethnicity and family therapy, edited by Monica McGoldrick, John Pearce, and Joseph Giordano. New York: The Guildford Press.

Middleman, Ruth, and Goldberg, Gale. 1974. *Social service delivery: a structural approach to practice*. New York: Columbia University Press.

Mullen, Edward; Chazin, Robert; and Feldstein, David. 1970. *Preventing chronic dependency*. New York: Community Service Society.

Napierkowski, Thomas. 1976. Stepchild of America: growing up Polish. In *Growing up Slavic in America*, edited by Michael Novac. Bayville, NY: EMPAC.

Papajohn, John, and Spiegel, John. 1975. *Transactions in families*. San Francisco: Jossey-Bass.

Perlman, Helen Harris. 1957. *Social casework: a problem-solving process*. Chicago: University of Chicago Press.

The President's Commission on Mental Health. 1978. Task Panel Report Vol. III, Appendix.

Prosen, Rose Mary. 1976. Looking back. In *Growing up Slavic in America*, edited by Michael Novac. Bayville, NY: EMPAC.

Red Horse, John G.; Lewis, Ronald; Feit, Marvin; and Decker, James. 1978. Family behavior of urban American Indians. *Social Casework* 50:67–72.

Reid, William R., and Epstein, Laura. 1972. *Task-centered casework*. New York: Columbia University Press.

Reinhold, Robert. 1986. Flow of 3rd World immigrants alters weave of U.S. Society. *New York Times*, June 30.

Rodriguez, Richard. 1982. *Hunger of memory the education of Richard Rodriguez*. Boston: David R. Godine.

Sax, David B. 1979. A holiday at home, a widening gulf. *New York Times*, September 27.

Schwartz, William. 1985. In Schulman, Lawrence. *The skills of helping individuals and groups*. Itasca, IL: F.E. Peacock Publishers, Inc.

Sotomayor, Marta. 1977. Language, culture, and ethnicity in the developing self-concept. *Social Casework* 58:195–203.

Sowell, Thomas. 1978. Three Black histories. In *American ethnic groups*, edited by Thomas Sowell, with assistance of Lynn D. Collins. The Urban Institute.

Sowell, Thomas. 1981. *Ethnic America—a history*. New York: Basic Books.

Stack, Carol B. 1975. *All our kin—strategies for survival in a Black community*. New York: Harper and Row.

Tricario, Donald. 1984. The new Italian-American ethnicity. *Journal of Ethnic Studies* 12:75–94.

Vidal, David. 1980. Living in two cultures: Hispanic New Yorkers. *New York Times*, May 11–14.

West, Richard. 1980. An American family. *Texas Monthly* 8, March.

Whitaker, Charles. 1986. The West Indian influence: Caribbean Blacks enrich life in the U.S. *Ebony* 41:135–144.

Wilkinson, Gerald Thomas. 1980. On assisting Indian people. *Social Casework* 61:451–461.

Zborowski, Mark, and Herzog, Elizabeth. 1952. *Life is with people: the culture of the shtetl*. New York: Schocken Books.

PART TWO
ETHNIC-SENSITIVE PRACTICE

Part Two is designed to illustrate the assumptions and principles of ethnic-sensitive practice in action.

Chapter 6 identifies four stages of social work activity. Generic skills associated with these stages are reviewed and defined. A series of suggestions (termed "adaptation to the ethnic reality") focus on the information needed before involvement with clients, the importance of understanding the community context, the need to be sensitive to peoples' concern about discussion of emotional issues, and the use of contracting, concrete services, and community action.

Chapters 7, 8, and 9 focus on work in three fields of practice: social work practice with families, social work with recipients of Aid to Families with Dependent Children, and social work in health care. We suggest how the assumptions and principles of ethnic sensitive practice can be integrated into the body of concepts and themes relevant for any field of practice. In these and other areas of practice the third layer of understanding applies, indicating that social workers should be familiar with prevailing policies and resources and how services are organized. Case examples illustrate how understanding the impact of social class, ethnicity, life cycle stages, self-awareness, and specialized knowledge converge to aid in assessment and suggest directions for intervention. Attention is called to how the "route to the social worker" constrains and enhances practice.

CHAPTER
6

Adapting Strategies and Procedures for Ethnic-Sensitive Practice

This chapter emphasizes those social work strategies and interventive procedures most commonly used by social workers and how these may be adapted to take into account the various ethnic and class dispositions to seeking and obtaining help. These procedures and strategies are drawn from a wide range of approaches. For, as was pointed out in chapter four, the elements of the helping process are essentially the same, regardless of the particular theory or approach to practice adopted by any worker or agency.

It is important to note that for many years considerably less attention was paid to the *what* and *how* of practice than to the theories and philosophy of intervention. Recently, major strides have been made in filling this gap. Middleman and Goldberg (1974), Egan (1975), Fischer (1978), Shulman (1979, 1984), and others have variously described important components of skills. Most important, considerable research has been carried out to determine how the characteristics of worker-client relationships affect problem resolution (Fischer 1978; Shulman 1978, 1979; Truax and Mitchell 1971). Less attention has been paid to how strategies and procedures need to be modified to conform to cultural and ethnic dispositions, although here, too, some progress has been made (e.g., Green 1982; Lum 1986; Gomez, Zurcher, Farris, and Becker 1985). We suggest such modifications and build on the work of these and other writers. For, just as we have not "invented" a new form of social work practice, we do not presume to generate a new body of practice strategies and procedures. Rather, we present a composite of those repeatedly identified in the social work literature, and suggest how they might be adapted in keeping with the ethnic reality.

In reviewing elements of the helping process and their adaptation to the ethnic reality, focus is on various stages of the intervention process. All encounters have a beginning and take place within certain contexts. At some point the work proceeds, sometimes falteringly, only to move forward again. Usually, there is a point of termination. Different writers use somewhat different words to describe the same elements of the process. We suggest that the process takes place in overlapping stages identified as follows:

1. The work prior to involvement
2. The work of finding out what the problem is
3. Work on the problem
4. Termination

Identification of these stages of the interventive process does not imply that clearly distinct procedures, strategies, and skills are called for in each stage. Indeed, there is more overlap than uniqueness. However, the skills involved in meeting with an individual or group for the first time do differ from those needed when a relationship has been in process for some time. And the act of termination is not the same as assessing the problem.

Ethnic-sensitive practice is first and foremost good social work practice. Therefore, the basic procedures or guidelines for any one phase of practice are first reviewed and identified as generic skills and principles. Where applicable, these are followed by suggestions for adaptation to the ethnic reality.

WORK PRIOR TO INVOLVEMENT

There is much work to be done before contact is initiated. This phase of work, though important, often does not receive explicit attention in the literature. One level of that work involves learning about the community where service is rendered, acquiring knowledge about the particular types of problems that usually come to the attention of the agency, and developing self-awareness in relation to these types of problems. Another aspect of the work focuses on the types of data that can or should be gathered prior to meeting with any individual or group.

Understanding of the Community

Knowledge about the community in which services are rendered is essential. Population characteristics, availability of resources, type of government, availability of transportation, and prevailing community and ethnic networks are but a few of the factors bearing on the ability to render service. A variety of tools exist to facilitate the process of becoming familiar with the community. Census materials, publications about the community, and interviews with community leaders are but a few of the available resources. It is incumbent upon agencies and practitioners to make use of these in order to develop a community profile.[1]

Lum (1986) makes some important suggestions by identifying a series of tasks that go beyond the development of a community profile. These include conducting a study of the needs of minority clients, developing service programs, and staffing patterns. It is essential to determine whether the network of social agencies and other institutions have sufficient staff who, if necessary, are bilingual, and sensitive to the needs of the diverse community groups served.

Knowledge of Human Behavior and Self-awareness

The social worker has an obligation to be familiar with the general knowledge of human behavior that has been identified as the first "layer of understanding" and to assess how this interfaces with insight into the particular constellation of problems usually addressed in an agency and community. Knowledge about the feelings typically generated by the kinds of problems encountered in a setting is crucial. Practitioners should be familiar with the prevailing trends in family life and with the concerns of those who find themselves in troubled family situations. The daily traumas of marital conflict may be compounded by a sense of personal failure, hostility, threat of desertion, or economic strain. Work with people who are ill requires knowledge of the fact that many fear death, desertion, or limits on their mobility. Those who work in schools need to be familiar with theories of learning disabilities and who is at particular risk for developing school-related problems. These are examples of the kinds of knowledge social workers must have.

Also important is the effort to learn how others who work in a system think, feel, and behave. This is particularly relevant in interdisciplinary settings. Workers employed in school systems in which they function on

---

[1]See Appendix for guidelines for developing such a profile.

teams of psychologists, teachers, and consulting psychiatrists must familiarize themselves with the kinds of problems usually brought to the team and how each discipline views its role. They should be aware of the important linkages between school, home, and other resources. They need to be aware of how they may have experienced problems in their own school work. If, as children, they had difficulty, are they likely to "overidentify" with clients having difficulty in school? Or, conversely, if their own school careers were extremely successful, how can they use this experience to help those in trouble? How can they *learn* to understand?

Those who provide service in the criminal justice system need to know something of the adversary system, the law, and how people experience encounters with these awesome institutions.

The young, inexperienced worker with a middle-class background who sets out to organize tenants for better housing services needs to understand the tenants' fears of being evicted, their long-standing distrust of authority, and the anger and hostility of landlords who believe they have given "these folks" more than enough for the little rent they already pay.

Such orientation must become part and parcel of workers' thinking, acting, and feeling as they embark on work in varous contexts. A *generic* definition of the work that must be carried out before any client or situation is addressed can now be presented:

> Skilled use of the accumulated knowledge of the types of problems and issues with which workers usually deal in this setting, including knowledge of the community, the prevailing responses and concerns of people facing certain problems, and workers' own emotional responses to these issues.

What is involved is an emotional and intellectual awareness and a readiness to listen, evoke meaningful responses, and draw on diverse resources. This readiness is derived from experience, from a conceptual stance that aids in thinking about the problems, and from awareness of the range and types of reactions usually evoked.

Adaptation to the ethnic reality. In dealing with problems in the work situation, the particular class and ethnic dispositions related to those issues that regularly surface in the work setting must always be considered. There is a substantial literature on the impact of race in the helping process. Though the research findings are equivocal, there is some suggestion that communication is enhanced when workers are members of the same group (e.g., Jones 1978; Turner and Armstrong 1981; Atkinson, Mervin, and Matsui 1978).

Social workers must consider how their own ethnic and class backgrounds affect responses. Efforts to achieve ethnic competence as described by Green (1982) and reviewed in chapter four are pertinent here. The reader will remember that the emphasis is on "a . . . level of cultural awareness . . . that surpasses the usual injunctions about patience, genuineness, and honesty in client-worker relationships" (see p. 52). If workers are themselves members of the ethnic groups usually served in the setting, they may have much "inside" knowledge. At the same time, they must be aware of and guard against the possibility of overgeneralizing from their own experience, or holding out particularly stringent expectations for behaviors they believe are related to their own ethnic group. For example, Puerto Rican workers in school systems may have a particular awareness of the strain evoked by bilingualism. They may understand the special comfort the children experience in speaking Spanish to their peers, or know the taunts of teachers who admonish children to speak only English. As young people they may have accompanied their own mothers to the school, the welfare board, or the landlord to serve as translators. They may have experienced the frustration of trying to convey accurate meaning in a different language.

They must guard against approaching the situation with an attitude such as, "I made it, why can't you?" Such tendencies are not uncommon. Irish social workers have told us that, because they know alcholism is a particular problem for some Irish people, they expect Irish alcholics to "shape up." Also instructive are the experiences of one of the authors of this book, Elfriede Schlesinger.

Shortly after beginning practice as a young hospital social worker, I was asked to talk with the Orthodox Jewish mother of a child admitted to the hospital because of an infected rash on the leg. The doctors thought that the rash may have begun or been exacerbated by dirt. They thought the child was seldom bathed.

I immediately informed them that I would check, though it was most unlikely because Jews weren't dirty. This was indeed a unique referral involving a Jewish family. I told them that Jewish mothers fussed over and bathed their children a lot.

Subsequent discussion revealed that the doctors had been correct. Not only did I feel chagrined but insulted that Jews should treat their children so.

The initial stance, derived from my perception of "proper Jewish behavior," slowed the process of helping the mother to come to grips with the problem, for her Jewish neighbors and relatives had a disposition similar to mine. To help her deal with the problem I should have projected special sensitivity to her perception of herself as having failed as a mother.

When workers are not members of the ethnic and class groups usually served they have the obligation to familiarize themselves with the culture, history, and ethnically related responses to problems of all groups served. Among the suggestions made by Green (1982) about the processes that may prove useful in developing ethnic competence are strategies of participant observation in communities of interest and studying ethnographic material about the community.

Just as workers are responsible for learning basic principles of human behavior, they must become aware of how their own ethnic backgrounds impact on their behavior. We refer here to the "third layer of understanding" as considered in chapter three.

Gathering Data Prior to the Encounter

The worker usually knows much about a particular situation before contact begins. The generic work of gathering data prior to the encounter can be defined as the process of reviewing, synthesizing, and ordering information—both factual and emotional—concerning the client(s), the problem, and the route to the agency.

The nature and amount of information available varies. Where "on-the-spot" crisis intervention is rendered, little more may be known than the fact that someone has appeared at the welfare office alone and disoriented. The only information available may be the sex and race of the person and his or her approximate age. On the other hand, there are the extensive referral letters exchanged between agencies and other facilities. Considerable information may be conveyed in cases of neglect or abuse or in a referral from a physician or school for assessment of a child believed to have a developmental handicap. Where much information is available a number of generic skills and processes can be identified: (1) review of available materials to obtain a picture of the problem, (2) review of the "route to the social worker" (Chapter five contains considerable discussion of the meaning, to both clients and practitioners, of the process involved in getting to the agency. Those people who come on their own may have expressed an eagerness to get to work on a problem. Where the route has been involuntary, as much information as possible concerning clients' feelings about coming to the agency should be obtained.), and (3) efforts to distinguish the client's perception of the problem from the way others perceive it. The latter involves the distinction between "attributed" and "acknowledged" problems as this has been discussed by Reid (1978). Attention should be paid to such statements by referral sources as: "This child acts out a great deal in school. His mother, Mrs. Jones, insists the teachers 'have it in for him' and find fault readily. Discussion with the teachers reveals that the child comes to school unkempt, looks tired, and on occasion has minor bruises on the arm." Child abuse is clearly implied; whether it is present or not, the mother does not acknowledge this problem. This difference in perception must be kept in mind by workers in their approach to the mother. Before beginning work the workers must exert much effort in "thinking through," synthesizing, and analyzing available facts and feelings. Are bruises really indicative of abuse, or does this family consider hitting appropriate punishment for perceived misbehavior? In processing data prior to the encounter workers inevitably make a preliminary or tentative assessment of what may be operative.

Adaptation to the ethnic reality. It is crucial that workers integrate such ethnic and class data as are available and be aware of gaps in the information. Some basic principles can be stated as follows:

1. Information on the ethnic reality should be obtained. Thus, if available information indicates that a client is white, it is important to have information on the particular ethnic identity. From previous discussions about the differences between Jews, Polish-Americans, and other whites of European ethnic origins it should be evident that specific group membership may affect disposition to the problem at issue.

2. Social class information should, when possible, be supplemented with information about the nature of the work people do. This is imperative for a number of reasons. Chapter one describes the relationship between the type of work people do and the way they might feel about their ability to be autonomous and to control their lives. The images people have of themselves and those held of them by others may have great bearing on how they approach problem resolution. Certainly, class data usually gives clues about socioeconomic wherewithal, always an important element of information.

3. In processing information about ethnic and class identity, the worker should be aware of the fact that many people are extremely sensitive about these matters. When the requisite information is not readily available, workers should be careful not to "jump in with all fours" to get it; rather, they might wait for clues, asking as it seems appropriate.

4. The fear of racist or prejudiced orientations is never far from the minds of most minority or other disadvantaged people. Practitio-

ners must constantly be alert to this possibility. This is particularly important when the clients are members of minority groups, and when worker and clients belong to different racial or ethnic groups (Brown 1950; Curry 1964; Gitterman and Schaeffer 1972).

With this work done, attention can be focused on the encounter with the client.

THE WORK OF FINDING OUT WHAT THE PROBLEM IS

In this process, often referred to as "problem identification," there are a number of steps that facilitate the process of engaging clients and helping them to clarify the nature of the difficulty.

Those strategies involved in "launching the interaction process" may be referred to as *entry skills* and are focused on those activities designed to create a comfortable environment for the interview or other form of interaction (Middleman and Goldberg 1974). These are known as (1) stage setting (2) "tuning in" (Middleman and Goldberg 1974), (3) attending (Egan 1975), and (4) "preparatory empathy" (Shulman 1984).

Stage Setting

Stage setting involves attention to the physical setting in which the interaction is going to take place and takes account of positioning vis-a-vis clients. The purposive use of space to enhance comfort and communication is basic. There is little question that the prevailing norms of American society suggest that privacy is urgent. It is assumed that most people will feel more comfortable discussing their problems if they are not likely to be overheard by strangers or other family members. By and large, people are more comfortable if there is sufficient physical space to permit them to maintain some physical distance from each other; they may move closer together if the situation warrants. Settings providing at least a minimal degree of physical comfort are thought to be essential. Comfortably cushioned chairs, pleasantly painted, cheerful rooms, and a place to stretch one's legs are seen as highly desirable, if not essential.

A mental review of many of the places where social workers meet their clients quickly leads to the realization that these generic guides to stage setting are often breached. Hospitalized patients who are unable to leave their beds usually share rooms with others. A curtain is the most deference to privacy that can be offered. When clients are visited in their homes relatives, friends, or neighbors may be present. Large segments of the client population—particularly those served by underfunded public agencies—often encounter workers in large offices occupied by many other people. At best they may be in glass-enclosed cubicles in which the partitions do not reach the ceiling. Visits may be made in community center playrooms, libraries of prisons, or empty cafeterias of residential centers. Each of these spaces is likely to be frequented by others. Many of these regrettable structural facts emerge from society's low regard and lack of respect for those at the "bottom of the ladder."

There are circumstances in which interaction is most comfortable if carried out in "natural" or "convenient" settings. These include seeing the child in the playground or concerned relatives in a parking lot or restaurant during a lunch hour. Social workers who are sensitive to the facts of space will learn to make adaptations. When the interview with the hospitalized patient calls for as much privacy as possible, workers will draw the curtain and sit close. This closeness may be a compromise with the desire to maintain a comfortable physical distance, usually important in the early stages of building a relationship. Other examples of compromises with privacy are talking with youngsters in the community center lounge or with the residents in the institutional cafeteria. Workers will try to gauge to what extent they can create a "do not disturb" ambience by positioning, but by doing so, they must be careful not to embarrass those who are seeking or being offered service. Privacy should be guarded, but not at the expense of avoiding needed contact, or in a manner that publicly singles out a particular person. A conversation between two or more people in the midst of a crowded room can be more private than one held in a distant but readily spotted part of a public room.

Adaptation to the ethnic reality. The degree to which the worker should adhere to the tenets of privacy will vary considerably by the ethnic group membership of the client. Many Eastern Europeans (e.g., Czechoslovakians, Estonians, Hungarians, Poles, and Ukrainians) are particularly "shamed" at having to ask for help (Giordano and Giordano 1977). For members of these groups and others with similar dispositions, particular effort should be made to assure privacy and/or anonymity. When people who share these feelings are seen in the hospital, it would be wise to take off the white coat, if it is customarily worn. After people have been engaged in a private conversation with the curtain drawn, they may decide how to answer a neighbor's queries about who that "nice young woman was" who came to see them. They are then free to identify her as a family member, neighbor, or the social worker.

When the pain of getting help is almost as intense as the problem that necessitates it, a number of other concessions to privacy should be considered. Is a prearranged home visit for an intake interview for public assistance feasible? Can workers park their cars "around the corner?" Can workers dress in a manner that does not readily identify them? Can the mother of a disturbed youngster be seen in the school courtyard amidst a crowd? Is the sign on the van advising all that this is the "Senior Citizens' Nutrition Project" or the local "Economic Opportunity Corporation" really necessary?

Not all possible concessions to privacy and anonymity can be spelled out. However, it is crucial that workers be aware of these possibilities and behave in a manner that keeps options open. Some Slavics, Asians, and others may feel quite comfortable about being interviewed within earshot of their neighbors. However, unless people are given a choice on these matters, workers may find that despite sincere offers to help plan for care or other problems, their clients are most uncommunicative.

Indeed, there are people who do not seem to mind discussion of certain private matters when others, unrelated to them, can hear. Many Jewish and Italian people are quite voluble and seem ready to express discomfort and pain publicly; some are given to reaching out for a sympathetic, interested ear (Zborowski 1952). Dominick and Stotsky (1969) describe Italian nursing home residents who are always ready to converse with visitors about rooms, belongings, "anything at all." It is possible that people with this kind of orientation may gain some satisfaction from the public visibility provided by the social worker's concern and attention. However, the possible satisfaction gained by visible attention to physical problems may not carry over to the situation in which an application for public assistance, food stamps, or publicly subsidized housing is to be filed or in which a youngster has developed problems with the law. These may represent loss of face or highly valued financial independence. In such situations generic rules of privacy apply. Workers must make an effort to learn with which people privacy and anonymity are crucial.

Tuning In

"Tuning in" has been defined as "development of the worker's preparatory empathy" (Shulman 1984). Citing Schwartz, Shulman suggests that the worker must make an effort to "get in touch with those feelings that may be implicitly or directly expressed in the interview." Although the process should begin before the encounter, it is ongoing and continues throughout the interaction. Shulman suggests that "tuning in" can take place at several levels. Some of these have been noted in other contexts. They include the acquisition of basic knowledge of human behavior, articulation of that knowledge with the problems at issue, and the unique responses of worker and client. The following case situation illustrates the articulation of several levels.

> A male school social worker knows that a thirteen-year-old boy has been referred because he is disruptive in school and is reading several years behind his grade level. The boy has recently transferred to the school as a result of moving into his third foster home this year.
>
> In synthesizing, "tuning in," and processing these facts, the worker draws on his general knowledge about the possible reasons for learning difficulty, family systems and how families absorb new members, and the dynamics involved in foster parent-foster child relationships.
>
> In "tuning in" to the situation of this child he should consider the possibility that the reading deficit may be a function of poor education, perceptual difficulty, or emotional distress. He needs to "think and feel" in advance about how alienated, isolated, lonely, and rejected this boy might be feeling. Perhaps the worker can recall an analogous experience he may have had. Did he go to summer camp when he really didn't want to? Was there ever a time when he was afraid his own parents had abandoned him? Did he ever experience a similar school failure?

These and many other examples indicate the varying processes involved in developing preparatory empathy.

Adaptation to the ethnic reality. Processes similar to these are involved in "tuning in" to the meaning of the helping encounter for members of various ethnic groups. In the example cited, it is important to know that the young client is a Black child of underclass background whose foster parents are Black, middle-class professional people living in a community composed predominantly of white people.

If he is a white male, the worker needs to review his knowledge about the Black community and what he understands about how class differences within that community manifest themselves. He needs to recognize that Black people living in a predominantly white neighborhood may be experiencing substantial strain. At an emotional level he needs to "feel through" his reactions to Black people, particularly adolescent boys. Is he afraid of physical aggression and does he associate Black youngsters with aggression? Does he tend to expect "less" academically from a Black man? Is he perhaps feeling that the white middle-class school has been invaded? Does he have a "feel" for how Black children might experience the white world? Does he understand the particular sense of distrust, inadequacy, and fear of not measuring up that many young Blacks feel?

Other illustrations of the various levels of "tuning in" to ethnic dispositions can be given. Repeated reference has been made to the frustrations of those whose command of the English language is limited.

Many approach human service agencies fearing that their culture and way of life are not respected. There may be distrust of practitioners, particularly those who are not members of their own group. Such matters should always be "tuned into" before and during an encounter.

Attending

Generically, attending refers to purposeful behavior designed to convey a message of respect and a feeling that what people are discussing is important. Attending skills include the ability to pay simultaneous attention to cognitive, emotional, verbal, and nonverbal behaviors. Attending involves perceiving and selecting verbal and nonverbal stimuli, deciding "what is the main message," and focusing attention on that message (Middleman and Goldberg 1974, p. 100). In the process of focusing on the key elements of the situation it is important to be aware of and refrain from communicating inappropriate judgmental attitudes.

Appropriate use of body language and dressing in a manner considered appropriate by clients are also examples of attending. Egan (1975) identifies the following aspects of "physical attending." The client should be faced squarely, an "open" posture should be adopted, and good eye contact maintained. The practitioner should lean toward the other. These aspects of physical attending let the others know of the worker's active involvement and aid the practitioner in being an active listener. These postures help in picking up both verbal messages and nonverbal clues. Under most circumstances it is important to maintain a relaxed, natural, comfortable posture and to use those spontaneous head, arm, and body movements that come naturally to workers in most interactive situations. Maintaining comfortable eye contact is customary in many contexts.

In professional as well as personal interaction the use of friendly greetings is expected. Put simply, when the encounter begins—whether with individual clients or with legislators whose aid is sought in supporting an important bill—it is crucial that initial approaches are made in a professional but human manner that is attentive to the concerns of the other.

Adaptation to the ethnic reality. There are some groups whose members find it difficult to respond to the type of spontaneity and physical posturing described above. Toupin (1980) suggests that even acculturated Asians are likely to consider eye to eye contact shameful. This is particularly true for women who believe "only street women do that." American Indians view the matter similarly. Eye contact may be indicative of lack of respect.

There are situations that call for modification of other aspects of attending. Those groups (e.g., many working and underclass minority people) who view workers as authority figures may, in the initial contact, be more comfortable when there is more formality than Egan's proposals imply. This is also true for those who are most uncomfortable about expressing feelings or who feel ashamed about needing help (for example, some Slavics and Asians). It is important for workers to understand that for many people failing to respond to eye contact, sitting demurely, or not readily revealing feelings are not necessarily indicative of pathology or "resistance."

Practitioners who truly attend will modify their behavior according to the knowledge they gain about the dispositions of various groups.

At the time of the initial meeting, worker and clients usually have some information about the issue that has brought them together. Such additional data as are needed to proceed must then be obtained.

The Nature of Questioning

At this point some comments about the nature of questioning and listening are in order. These will be discussed here only briefly. There are many excellent works that treat the matter in detail, including the effects of race on the interview process.[2]

Two basic types of questions are identified: open and close-ended. The former are used to explore and get a wide-ranging perspective on an issue; the latter "focus attention on key issues and clarify information provided" (Middleman and Goldberg 1974).

For example, a client may say: "Things are really awful at home." In an open-ended question, the worker may reply: "Tell me more about that." At some point after a series of complaints have been aired and a lot of feeling ventilated, it may be appropriate to focus on what appears to be a key issue.

> A male college student who has been doing poorly in his studies tells the worker that his instructors keep asking questions he doesn't understand, that he studies as hard as anyone else but doesn't seem to catch on. With sadness in his voice he says, "My mother was right when she said going to college was a bad idea."
>
> The worker replies, "What's really bothering you is that you think you're not smart enough to go to college, isn't it?"

Open and close-ended questions are usually alternated in an effort to get a clearer image of what the person is feeling and experiencing.

---

[2]See Kadushin (1972), and Benjamin (1969).

Adaptation to the ethnic reality. There are few ethnically relevant differences in the nature of questioning other than awareness of the kinds of questions different people can and cannot tolerate. Those who don't readily share feelings may be more comfortable with a series of close-ended questions that don't require a more spontaneous, free floating response.

Reaching for Facts and Feelings

It is difficult, and often inappropriate, to separate the effort to obtain "facts" from that involved in understanding and gauging the associated feelings. In addition, obtaining information about facts and feelings is a two-way street. Workers need to know what the problem is and how people feel about it. Clients need to know what information and resources are at the worker's disposal to help them with their problems. Will the worker give them money, help them find a job, tell them how to handle their children? They will want to know how the worker is likely to respond to their fears and aspirations, and to the problem itself. For example, youngsters in trouble with the law, people who have engaged in extramarital affairs, and those suffering from mental illness may be afraid that their behavior will be negatively judged.

In the course of obtaining information about facts and feelings workers convey a sense of acceptance (to the degree that ethics and law permit) and set a comfortable tone.

Reaching for feelings. The process of helping people to express and cope with feelings is an integral part of every professional endeavor. For social workers, the process of seeking expression of feelings about self, others, and the institutions in which people are enmeshed is a basic and fundamental component of their work. Indeed, there are many situations in which the bulk of the problem identification and problem-solving effort is devoted to listening to and exploring feelings. When other concerns exist, it is frequently impossible to proceed without first paying attention to feelings. If a neighborhood group is feeling outraged over the closing of a local health service, suggestions that a meeting be planned with the administrator are likely to go unheeded until the members have had the opportunity to express their rage. Feelings, particularly those of a negative nature, must often be expressed before people can move forward to consider facts or suggestions for action.

Marital partners may not be able to talk about how to improve their strained relationship until they have ventilated their anger. Frustrated tenants may not be able to consider participating in a rent strike until they have "blown off steam" about poor conditions.

Many times during the first as well as subsequent encounters people will find it difficult to express what they are really feeling or to tell the worker what it is they really want to know. Often they may not know. People do not always express feelings that seem appropriate to the situation at hand. Workers need to be sure they understand what is being expressed.

The generic skills of "reaching for" or obtaining expression of feeling are encompassed in what are known as the core conditions of warmth, empathy, and genuineness. Essentially, what is involved is the ability to "hear" and respond to tone, mood, absence of expression of feeling, and activities that have the effect of diverting from the painful and difficult situations at hand. For example, the hospitalized woman who is uncommunicative when the worker tries to interview her in her husband's presence may be letting the worker know that she does not want to discuss certain matters while her husband is there. Returning when the woman is alone, the worker may find she is quite verbal. The person who fidgets a great deal, fusses about the location of chairs, or makes sure a door is closed may be fearful. The well-dressed young man who tells the worker matter-of-factly that he has been sent by his doctor to make arrangements for care of his severely handicapped young child may be harboring a great deal of shame and sadness. In these and like instances it is most important that the worker *reach for feelings*, obtain and give information.

Middleman and Goldberg (1974) define reaching for feelings as the process of asking others if they are experiencing a particular emotion presumed to be evoked by the situation at hand. A number of generic skills, focused on (1) obtaining information on facts and feelings, and (2) providing information on facts and feelings can be delineated.

1. *Draw on such information as is available prior to the encounter. Avoid repeating basic questions that have already been asked*. For example, if it is known that a recently widowed woman lives alone, seems depressed, and does not know what to do with her time, it may be appropriate to ask whether she has children. If she says, "yes," perhaps she perks up as evidenced by her facial expression; or, she may seem even more sad. Either response provides some clues. The first suggests that she may be helped to overcome her sadness by encouraging involvement with her children. The second suggests further exploration about the nature of her relationship with her children.

   A newly formed group of parents of developmentally disabled adolescents may be trying to identify how participation in the group might help them. The worker may ask them to describe their problems with the children. As the parents talk about their children's disabilities, it is clear from their voices and facial expressions that they feel some sadness.

In these types of situations, the alternation of expression of facts and feelings is evident and illustrates a second skill.

2. *Elicit, via appropriate alternation of open and close-ended questions, as much description and discussion of the facts and feelings of the situation as possible.* The worker may ask the widowed, depressed woman where her children live, how many she has, and how frequently she sees them; or the worker may ask the parents of the developmentally disabled adolescents for a description of how the children spend their time, under what circumstances taunts from others take place, and the kinds of activities of which they are capable.

3. *Reflect or "get with" the facts and feelings that have been expressed.* Middleman and Goldberg (1974) make some important comments in this connection. They suggest that saying "I understand" is not enough. Workers must try to see the world as the client sees it and accurately state their own understanding of the client's emotional experience.

If the widowed mother says in a rather strained manner that her children live only a few miles away but are too busy to come and see her, the worker responds to the apparent feeling of rejection. "You wish they weren't so busy, don't you? Sometimes you wonder if they really care." As the parents of the developmentally disabled adolescents speak, it appears that they are worried about what might happen should they become ill and unable to care for their children. The worker can help them put this into words. "A lot of you are wondering how you might plan for your children when you can no longer care for them."

4. *Share feelings. This refers to the process whereby workers share with clients those feelings appropriate to the situation.* There is increasing evidence that it is appropriate for workers to share their experiences and emotions when such sharing is thought to contribute to clients' comfort or resolution of the problem. This may involve such "basically human acts" as crying with a person who has experienced a great loss (Shulman 1984) or expressing frustration about bureaucratic intransigence. "I've had no better luck than you in getting those s.o.b.'s upstairs to budge on those regulations."

In another vein, it must be noted that workers often hear clients express prejudiced or racist feelings about groups of people, and assume their feelings are shared by the worker. "You know those 'spics,' they're always stealing." In our view, the ethics and value system of the profession are such that workers should never convey the impression that they share such sentiments. A comment such as "No, I don't know," or "I know what you're saying, but I don't believe in that kind of prejudice," disassociates workers from such a stance, and allows them to move beyond, by making a comment such as "I think you're really troubled about having things stolen, no matter who does it."

Intergroup tension may be the basis of the problem being considered, as is often the case in schools, community centers, or community action programs. The worker's basic stance on the issue must be conveyed. At the same time, people must be allowed to convey their feelings and to express their perceptions. "What makes you think that all of the white students are out to get you? What happens when you talk to them? Are there times when you can work together, have fun together?"

Sharing facts and giving information. This is such a crucial and essential part of practice at the problem-solving and other stages that it is frequently not discussed. People come needing information about how to apply for public assistance or housing, or how to process forms. Others have been "told" what their medical problems are but "don't understand." Clear-cut factual statements go a long way toward clarifying the situation.

"The welfare office is at 310 Main Street."

"Now here's a list of what you need to take with you when you go to the Housing Authority."

"Let's be sure you understand what the doctor told you. He says you have hypertension; that means you have a disease involving your blood pressure. I suppose the doctor told you that taking your medication regularly cuts down the chances of bad side effects."

The basic skill involved here is:

5. *Sharing facts and offering such opinions or ideas as may increase knowledge of a situation or event* (Middleman and Goldberg 1974). In beginning the encounter, the principle of "honing in on feelings and facts" about the problem at hand is crucial. For the most part, efforts designed to convey warmth and empathy should proceed quickly, on the assumption that people will feel better and more motivated to move on with the process if they find the worker to be in tune with their feelings and to be giving important information.

Adaptation to the ethnic reality. Reaching for facts and feelings often means knowing when to move slowly and cautiously, when to concentrate on facts *or* feelings, when to focus on sharing feelings, and when to emphasize the process of providing facts.

It has been noted that some Chinese clients are unlikely to ask for help with emotional problems without, at the same time, asking for concrete assistance (Chen 1970). The reluctance of many American Indians to engage in consideration of emotional issues with a stranger has been observed (e.g., Lum 1986).

Many people don't perceive problems as "belonging" to the individual, as most do in mainstream culture. Problems may be seen as "belonging" to the family or the community. If something is wrong, the family is shamed (e.g., many Asians). A large number of groups tend to perceive emotional problems in physical or other concrete terms. Somatic problems are more respectable than mental health problems in many groups (for example, among many Asians, Slavics, and Poles). If these kinds of ethnic dispositions are known, the likelihood that certain requests or attitudes are interpreted as resistance, lack of insight, or inappropriate displacement of feelings is minimized.

Rather, these dispositions must be understood in their cultural context and respected. A number of additional approaches are important.

1. *Respect requests for concrete services and be as responsive as possible in meeting such requests.* Lum (1986) and others make an important point when they stress the fact that many of the problems that bring members of minority groups to social agencies are triggered by environmental deficits. Coping is clearly enhanced when deficits are reduced.

2. *Move slowly in the effort to actively reach for feelings.* People who find consideration of feelings painful need to have time before they can or want to move in this area. There are repeated references in the literature to the reluctance associated with sharing feelings with a stranger. Lum (1986) proposes that after initial friendly conversation, some minority group members will confer "family status" on the workers as a way of legitimating the process of sharing intimate matters.

3. *Convey facts readily.* Most people who come for services, despite their reluctance to "engage emotionally," need and want information.

4. *Be imaginative in efforts to learn what the problem is.* We have already addressed the issue of stage setting, and noted that efforts to talk to people "on their ground" are important.

Lewis and Ho (1975) describe a situation in which some American Indian school children were brought to the worker's attention because of frequent school absences. Since the worker lived near the family she volunteered to transport the children to school. Sensing some difficulty in the family, she simply let the mother know that she was available to listen. After some time had elapsed, the mother sadly told the worker about her marital problems.

Many people view home visiting as an indication of respect and caring and welcome such visits. They may not venture to the agency. Perhaps a psychiatric clinic is perceived as a place where "they lock you up." Unannounced home visits are to be discouraged, however, until or unless a situation of trust has been developed. On the other hand, if the worker has been accepted in a community where people freely move in and out of each other's homes, the formality of prearranged visits may strike a discordant note.

5. *Be sure to understand who the appropriate "actors" are.* In many groups some issues are dealt with only by men, others only by women. Frequently matters of housekeeping are "women's work." Among Puerto Ricans it may be appropriate to involve distant relatives in efforts to mediate intrafamilial conflict over matters such as property. In some families it is believed that close relationships should not be risked over such issues (Ghali 1977).

There is increasing evidence that social agencies minimize the role of the Black male, both as service user and as provider. Leashore (1981) makes a strong point about the importance of adjusting agency hours and service delivery patterns to facilitate the key part Black men can and do play in helping their families cope with problems. Current emphases minimize the likelihood that the Black male's role as problem solver will be readily identified.

It is in these early efforts to find out what the problem is that attention to the ethnic reality is most important, for the client may not return if early efforts are not met with sensitivity. Lum (1986) makes some important suggestions bearing on ethnic-sensitive processes of problem identification. Helping clients to express those concerns they believe are related to their ethnic minority status is important. For example, a worker may sense that a parent feels a minority child is being discriminated against in school but that the parent is fearful to express this to the nonminority worker. The worker may tune in and state this as a possibility. Recent empirical investigation shows a significant correlation between the satisfaction with service as expressed by Chicano clients and the workers' "culturally oriented behavior" (Gomez, Zurcher, Farris, and Becker 1985). This behavior includes inquiry about culturally based beliefs as they relate to problems being addressed in mental health centers.

Specifying the Problem

Problems seldom surface in neat, clearly defined packages. At the point at which help is sought, or offered, people may be experiencing the cumulative effects of extensive periods of emotional distress, economic deprivation, or long-standing pain and other physical discomforts. After the initial phase during which workers and clients talk about the basic problems, a number of other steps follow. These include (1) particularizing or rank-ordering the problem and (2) identifying the source or locus of the problem.

Particularizing or Rank-ordering the Problem

Whether practice is approached from a psychodynamic or a structural stance, it is usually necessary to particularize problems into component parts. If environmental pressures are extreme, what are the specific manifestations? Do they include inadequate income, dissatisfying work, violence in the neighborhood, inadequate housing, or lack of space for adolescents to meet? Are the senior citizens isolated as a result of depression or senility, or because they cannot reach the local shopping areas? And, if both emotional strain and inadequacy of environmental supports are interacting problems, which can and which should be given prior attention?

Is it impossible for a couple to look at their own fighting and harsh treatment of their children until their welfare allotments are increased? Or, will they continue to use already meager allowances to punish, deride, and blame each other unless they come to understand and change their negative behavior? "I'll show her. I'll go on to play cards and lose money if she doesn't stop nagging me the minute I walk in the house."

Shulman (1984) suggests that one way of tackling complex problems is to break them down into component parts and address one at a time.

During the preassessment phase the protective services worker has learned that Mrs. Ignazio's four children were forcibly removed from the family's custody when the young ones were thought to have burns and bruises inflicted by the mother. Further, Mrs. Ignazio had spent two years in the reformatory following sentencing for the death of a fifth child. Although Mrs. Ignazio claimed that the child had hit his head on a table edge, the courts thought there was sufficient evidence that she had inflicted the blow that led to his death.

At the time the new worker sees Mrs. Ignazio she comes in because she wants her children back. In the interview she continues to insist that the removal of the children and her incarceration were unjustified.

She says, "Sure, I hit them once in a while, but who wouldn't with five screaming little kids, a husband who spends all his time and lots of money in the bar, and won't lift a finger even to get a kid a glass of milk? Besides, he hits me, and then I take it out on the kids. He says his job is earning the money and protecting me from all of those stray men that hang around this rotten neighborhood."

After this outburst she cries, and says, "I really want to be a good mother. That's all that matters to me."

The worker says: "That's what you really want, isn't it—to learn how to become a better mother?" Behind her tears, Mrs. Ignazio nods. The worker asks whether she thinks she's ready yet to have her children back. Mrs. Ignazio, still crying, says "No," both she and her husband would have to learn to control their tempers. The worker suggests that they might talk about how to decide what needs to be done first. Mrs. Ignazio nods, and says, "Maybe you can help me figure out how to stop hitting the kids when they come to visit."

From the massive number of problems confronting this family, worker and mother have isolated a major issue. In this or subsequent discussions they may identify other problems to be tackled, including how Mr. and Mrs. Ignazio interact and how the children feel about coming home.

A twelve-year-old boy is referred to the juvenile justice system because he has been running away from home and sleeping in doorways. During discussions preliminary to the hearing, the boy is quite uncommunicative. He sits with his eyes averted and says little when court personnel ask him why he's been running away from home and whether there has been trouble at home. Interviews with the parents evoke a somewhat similar response, uncommunicative with one-word responses. He's been running away. They don't know why; they will take care of him. Everything is fine at home. When the court worker suggests that perhaps there are tensions at home, and ways in which the court worker could help, there is minimal response.

With this kind of "resistant client" it is most important to clarify purpose in the process of particularizing. Perhaps a simple, gentle statement to the parents such as "We will have to talk, since the judge says that's a condition of keeping your son in your custody," clearly identifies the major issue confronting this family. They may not be ready for more at this point.

In these and many other situations the client's ethnicity may have bearing on how particularization is approached.

Adaptation to the ethnic reality. In neither of the cases described was the ethnic background of the people identified. The Ignazios are Italian; therefore, it is likely that the importance of being a good mother is something Mrs. Ignazio has heard about all of her life (Gambino 1974). She has indeed failed. Abusing her children, she is also an abused wife. The offer to try to help her to "stop hitting the kids" is a beginning step toward helping her regain some control over family life, a matter that is crucial to most people. The importance of family to Italians is well known and deeply embedded in Italian women. As she begins to struggle it will be necessary to review with her, her images of family and motherhood. Is there a generational history of abuse, or has she somehow gone astray? Is there an Italian church, a priest, an ethnic community to support her struggle?

The twelve-year-old boy described is second-generation Chinese. It is most likely that his particular reluctance to communicate derives from an overwhelming sense that he has shamed his family (Toupin 1980). His averting his eyes may be related to the fact that the worker is an authority figure. Even if there is marital strain, the family is likely to feel strongly that this is a matter to be handled within the confines of the home.

The boy and family are in trouble; court action has been taken. The broad-based, exploratory, nondirective interview style has not evoked a meaningful response. The authoritative nature of the setting and the involuntary route to the worker may serve as useful starting points in choosing an approach. A clear-cut statement by the worker to the effect that (1) the son is in trouble, (2) he is expected to stop running away, and (3) he is expected to report to the worker regularly, suffices at this point.

Some general principles in adaptation to the ethnic reality are suggested by these and similar cases. Basically, they involve the effort to make a connection with the client in terms that are culturally relevant or syntonic. These may be conveyed via subtle nuances that give the encounter more meaning.

Identifying the Source or Locus of the Problem

Both factual information and theoretical perspectives play a part in identifying the source of the problem. In the review of approaches to practice in chapter four divergent theoretical views were summarized. Although these differences exist, a number of basic principles cut across the divergent perspectives.

1. *The client's perspective on the source of the difficulty should be given primary consideration.* Putting this principle into action requires much skill, patience, and holding back judgment. Workers are trained to think in theoretical terms, to synthesize, and to make assessments. It is not easy to be nonjudgmental when people attribute all of their difficulties to external matters or, perhaps, to supernatural forces. Workers who are eager to "put their knowledge to work" need to be self-disciplined. Sensitive workers will ask and listen before they make judgment.

2. *Where the problem is sytemically based, individuals should not be held responsible for the situation.* The list of resources inadequate to deal with problems is endless. When clients complain about welfare budgets, workers must acknowledge the trauma of trying to survive with so little; perhaps they even need to cry with people before going on to help with budgeting designed to stretch the unstretchable. The budgeting process may be necessary as a survival technique. But to suggest to such people that they are not getting along because they do not know how to budget is "blaming the victim." The instances in which meager funds are grossly misused or mismanaged are rare.

3. *Effort must be made to ascertain the link between individuals' functioning and the social situation in which they find themselves.* Most people's problems are related to the social structures in which they find themselves and to the coping skills they have developed to function within those structures.

   The situation in which increasing numbers of middle-aged women find themselves is illustrative. Most such women were reared to value the roles of wife and mother. With the advent of the women's movement, many have moved out into the world of work, some aspiring to and achieving responsible business and professional careers. Not infrequently, considerable conflict ensues. Consider the following situation:

   Mrs. Willey, a thirty-five-year-old mother of three adolescents, recently graduated from college and is enrolled in graduate school. One of her children, Mary, is having difficulties in school. Mrs. Willey is frequently asked to come to school to meet with the teachers, but her own school schedule interferes. She and her husband spend much time in the evening going over Mary's homework and talking with her about her problems.

   Mrs. Willey tells the social worker: "I guess I'll have to give up school. I feel so guilty when I sit there, knowing that Mary's school wants me there."

Much from her own socialization tugs at her to put the needs of her children first. And yet the worker might ask the following kinds of questions: Is it ever possible to meet with Mary's teachers in the evening? What is it that has to be done during the day? Could you and your husband consider taking turns going during the day?

This is not an easy conflict to resolve. The social system has a long way to go before fully adapting to the needs of working mothers. But even if schedules were adapted, there are many changes in feeling about oneself and one's responsibilities which go to the core of the personality as people get caught up in the throes of social change. These take more time to alter. Both systemic and individual concerns must be balanced.

Adaptation to the ethnic reality. The principles and associated skills discussed apply in work with all people. They become even more important when dealing with ethnic, minority, and other oppressed people.

The ethnic-sensitive worker has a particular responsibility to be aware of the systemic sources of many problems. Attributing systemically induced problems—those derived from racism, poverty, and prejudice—to individuals is harmful. It adds to their burden. Lum (1986) identifies many of the systemically induced problems that bring minority people to social agencies. Racism manifest in negative reactions to minority people in a wide spectrum of situations is a case in point. Blacks are disproportionately unemployed and underemployed, contributing to negative self-images, and interpersonal problems. These experiences of low status, low income, and exploitation yield feelings of powerlessness. The relatively high levels of depression found among Black men may be related to the high frequency of stressful events they are likely to encounter (Gary 1985). These include residential changes, job changes, physical illness, and arrests, all found among Black men with greater frequency than among other groups. Recent immigrants (e.g., Vietnamese and Laotians) experience dislocation as they try to make sense of the new culture. Helping to identify the links between systemic problems and individual concerns is a crucial component of ethnic-sensitive practice. With some notion of the nature and source of the problem established, worker and client begin to consider how they will work on the problem. Contracting is an important move in that direction.

Contracting: Some Preliminary Considerations

The literature on contracting is extensive (Fischer 1978; Maluccio and Marlow 1974; Middleman and Goldberg 1974; Pincus and Minahan 1973;

Reid and Epstein 1977; Seabury 1976; Compton and Galaway 1984). At the core of much of this work is the assumption that people can contract to explore their interpersonal relationships, to confront dysfunctional systems, and to make use of health and welfare systems as these are currently organized.

The concept of contracting has evolved from Western, rational conceptions of time, reciprocity, and assumptions of trust in formally organized helping institutions. In many ways the concept is viewed as corrective of the long-prevalent mode of practice in which worker and client came together for extensive periods of time, frequently lacking a clear focus and purpose for the interaction. Moreover, goals were often imposed by workers.

From many perspectives contracting is a most useful concept. Nevertheless, when viewed within the context of ethnic-sensitive practice, some of the assumptions inherent in traditional views of contracting must be reconsidered. Many groups do not share the rational conceptions of problem solving implicit in the concept. Many lack trust in the available health and welfare delivery systems. Some are particularly loathe to accept the designation of "client," which some views of contracting imply. Indeed, Reid (1986) suggests that some people cannot and will not engage in this form of worker-client interaction.

Many American Indians view any act that may be considered manipulative with mistrust. This applies to psychological as well as physical behaviors. Good Tracks (1973) points out that suggestions concerning appropriate behavior, whether conveyed subtly or in the form of an outright command, may be viewed as interference, and interference in other's behavior is considered inappropriate. This holds true for the ways parents teach their children as well as demands made by organized institutions. Good Tracks suggests that for these reasons many major social work techniques are ineffective with many American Indians.

Contrast this with certain dispositions common to many Asian Americans. Several themes recur in the literature. According to Toupin (1980), some general characteristics of the "model Asian personality" can be identified. Many are likely to express deference to others, to devalue themselves and their families to others, and to avoid confrontation. Shame for insensitive behavior, for behavior subjecting the family to criticism, or for causing embarrassment is emphasized in Asian socialization practices. The family honor is preserved by not discussing personal problems outside the family. Expression of emotions may not bring an Asian relief, as it may reflect negatively on the family. There is deference to authority, and therapeutic personnel are viewed as authority figures.

In commenting on the social worker's potential ability to be helpful to American Indians without violating cultural precepts, Good Tracks suggests: "Patience is the number one virtue governing Indian relationships. A worker who has little or no patience should not seek placement in Indian settings. . . . The social worker's success may well be linked with his ability to learn 'Indian time' and adjust his relationships accordingly." He points out that the workers will be closely observed, and clients may seem indifferent. But workers' efforts to provide a variety of concrete services will be observed, and, at some point a member of the community may bring a problem of a more personal nature to a worker. It may take considerable time, perhaps a year or more, before they are ready to trust the workers. Technique alone will not speed up this process. This holds true for many ethnic groups.

The principle of contracting is crucial when it is related to client autonomy and self-determination. When viewed primarily as a technique for rapid engagement of clients in the helping process, the danger exists that class and ethnic dispositions will receive insufficient attention.

Approaches to Contracting

The approach to contracting that follows is guided by the preceding considerations.

Contracting refers to the process by which workers, clients, and others engaged in problem-solving activities come to some common agreement about the work to be done, the objectives sought, and the means by which these are to be attained. By its very nature the process involves clients and others in setting the terms by which the work of problem solving is to be carried out. Various writers have stressed the fact that contracting involves "a partnership" (Compton and Galaway 1984). When social worker-client interaction is approached from this perspective, workers are less likely to impose their definition of the problem or task on the client.

Many definitions of the contract have been offered. In social work and other interpersonal helping endeavors the contract may be viewed as a consensus between concerned persons about why they are working together, how they will work together, and what they hope to achieve. Translated into the "gut and heart" of day-to-day practice, what does this mean? It means that workers and clients deliberate—often struggle—to come to decisions about the focus of the work to be done. This is affected by the various contexts in which services are rendered, and the point in time when decisions about the work to be done are made. Some people can make such decisions quickly; others waver, and need considerable time.

The Service Context and Contracting

For the most part, workers and clients meet under the auspices of an agency within the health and welfare delivery system. These differ in many respects by the nature of the service offered, whether people arrive willingly, and whether social work is an ancillary or primary service (e.g., the welfare office, the protective services agency, or the hospital). The very fact of being present in these contexts may result from coercion (See chapter five). The poor tend to predominate among those served. Their socioeconomic circumstances usually leave them little choice about using the services of a social worker. It is in these contexts that the search for consensus should proceed in a forthright manner.

Shulman (1984) makes reference to the "search for the elusive common ground" and suggests that a simple, nonjargonized statement about what the social worker can do is a good starting point. With the prisoner soon to be released, the social worker may say:

> Jim, I'm a social worker. The parole board said that you and I should talk about the things you might do when you get out of here. I've been able to help guys think ahead about what it might be like to get back to the family and friends. Please come down to my office a couple of times a week.

Or, to the mother whose children have been removed from the home because of suspected abuse:

> Mrs. Jones, I'm a social worker. I know you're feeling low right now with the kids going into that foster home. Other women who've been in the same position have found it helpful to talk about that, and after awhile to think about what they have to do in order to have the children returned.

The service has been offered and the client given some options. Nevertheless, the authoritative nature of the worker's role inherent in the setting is not forgotten. The parole board says workers and prisoner *should* talk; the protective services agency sends the message that Mrs. Jones *has to do certain things* if she wants her children back.

These contexts differ sharply from the psychiatric clinic or the family counseling agency. People who come to these types of agencies are also likely to feel stressed or bewildered. Yet the process of getting there may be more volitional.

When people know why they've come to the service center, the social worker can begin to move more quickly to engage the client in contracting on the *how* of the process to be pursued.

> Mrs. White has indicated that she is contemplating separation from her husband because they fight a lot over her desire to go back to work. An

exchange between Mr. Jones, the worker, and Mrs. White, the client, may go something like this:

Worker: Mrs. White, you've said you want to talk about your plans for separating from Mr. White. Have you pretty much made up your mind that that's the best thing, or are you still wondering?

Mrs. White: Oh, I'm about 75% decided. But I do want to talk with you a little about whether you think there's any way we could make it work.

Worker: How would you feel if we spend the next couple of sessions reviewing the bad and the good parts of your marriage? Perhaps you want to review for yourself how you both have dealt with differences in the past, and consider whether there are things you could do that would make it comfortable for you to stay together.

Here much of the focus is on the worker's *enabler* role. The worker begins to contract with people to look at their own behavior, their conflicts, and the kinds of changes they can and want to make. Many of these contexts generate a variety of other roles that can be contracted early. In the prison, the hospital, or the welfare board, mediating, brokerage, or advocacy roles can be suggested.[3] New applicants for public assistance may ask whether they can be helped to find a job. The prisoner may ask the worker to play an advocacy role. He may suggest that his release is too far off.

Jim: Mr. Brown, they got me staying here another six months. Do you think you could help me get a new hearing before the parole board?

Worker: I'll look over your record, and we can talk about why you think you should get out sooner. If it makes sense to both of us I'll go to bat for you. I can only do that if I agree and it makes sense to me.

Mrs. White, in conflict about whether to remain in her marriage, may ask the worker whether he can play a mediating function.

Mrs. White: You know, if he only wouldn't fuss and fume so when I talk about finding a job I think we could make it. Do you think you could get us both in here, and we could talk about it together?

---

[3]Many practice texts spell out the components of these roles (e.g., Compton and Galaway 1984; Hepworth and Larsen 1986).

Maybe you could convince him that it's not going to take anything away from him.

The social worker assigned to the outpatient clinic of a hospital is asked to find out why so many people do not keep essential follow-up appointments. In exploring the matter she learns that people are "fed up" with being told to be there at nine in the morning and then not being seen until eleven or twelve. They lose time from work, as well as patience. In checking to find out what happens elsewhere, the worker finds that people with similar needs come much more regularly if there is a staggered appointment system. In this instance she first contracts with the hospital administration to explore the issue. She then shares her information with the administration and patients. Does the administration want to institute a staggered appointment system? Should she ask her patients how they would feel about it? In this process, effort is made to maximize the possibility of involvement in problem solving by those concerned, the patients and hospital administration.

In considering the relationship between the context and contracting, a number of generic principles can be stated:

1. When clients have little or no choice about being there a clear-cut statement about the help and the options available, despite the constraints, is essential.

2. The range of services available should be spelled out clearly, with an emphasis on the role the client and worker each will play.

3. The contract should not focus on *people* changing where *system* changing is in order (e.g., only if the staggered appointment system in the outpatient clinic is not successful should the social worker talk to patients about their appointment-keeping behavior).

4. The limitations of time and agency function should be clearly spelled out (Compton and Galaway 1979).

Adaptation to the ethnic reality. There is little doubt that members of minority groups, those who do not speak English, and those who have a long history of negative experience with health and welfare institutions are particularly sensitive and fearful about what might happen when they get there. Continuing attention and sensitivity to these matters on the part of the worker is essential. The skill of helping people who feel particularly defeated to recognize and believe that they can play a part in determining why and how something is to be done is one that should be continually sharpened. Gomez, Zurcher, Farris, and Becker (1985) have demonstrated the positive effects with some Chicano clients.

The injustice done to American Indians by massive removal of children from their homes to boarding schools has been repeatedly documented (Byler 1977). The assumption that minorities and the poor are not articulate and cannot constructively engage in therapeutic encounters involving active verbalization has been challenged. The difficulty of conveying affect and sensitive factual information through an interpreter is well known. Despite this, some American Indians abuse their children, and some poor minority people need help with basic survival needs before they can engage in the process of examining interpersonal relationships. Bilingual or indigenous workers are not always available.

The basic rules of contracting must then be *expanded* to include the following kinds of considerations:

1. Consider the basic meaning that involvement in this setting is likely to have for different people. For instance, an American Indian family may be quite ready to consider placement of a child with someone in the extended family, once assured that the child is not going to be torn from the fold of the community.

2. Consider the implications of what is being suggested, given the client's ethnic reality.

Groups respond differently to their members' deviant behavior. While all experience some sense of shame, or of being disgraced, some Poles, Asians, and Chicanos find it particularly difficult to deal with the assault to group pride caused by delinquency or crime (Lopata 1976). In contracting with the prisoner referred to previously, the fact that he is Polish is important. In thinking with him about his release and engaging him in contracting, recognition of this aspect of his life may be extremely important.

As one plans for care for the elderly, it should be remembered that institutional care is still anathema to many Blacks and Puerto Ricans, especially those at the lower rungs of the socioeconomic ladder.

Studies have shown that working-class people are less prone to institutionalize their retarded children than are middle-class people (Mercer 1972). In suggesting institutionalization to such families, the worker must bear this in mind.

Turning *compadres* into paid foster parents may help Puerto Rican families to feel more comfortable about out-of-home, publicly paid child care.[4]

---

[4]Study the practice of using parafoster parents, developed by the Division of Youth and Family Services, State of New Jersey.

Contracting, then, must take into account the particular sensitivities generated by the problem and the context in which service is rendered.

The Timing of the Contract

When the social worker and client begin to talk and the relationship is being developed, an ongoing, albeit shifting, consensus about the nature of the interaction is being established. Timing in contract development is an extremely variable process that will depend on a number of factors. The way in which these factors converge has major impact on *when* the process of contracting is used or initiated.

Many services are time-limited and by their nature focus on the provision of concrete services. Most welfare clients need money. Some people require information about their eligibility for Medicaid or food stamps. Services such as these do not call for extensive contracting. At the same time, in order to make use of these services, people must fill out forms and give permission for release of information.

Even for the provision of such seemingly simple services the principles of contracting—and the implication that worker and client are working together on something—apply. Such contracts are usually formed early and quickly.

If the major basis for the contact is for public assistance, day care services, homemaker services, or other concrete services, contracting is usually done early in the encounter. As is always the case, careful attention must be paid to the previously identified skills of stage setting, attending, tuning in, and finding out what the problem is. Sensitivity about the need for these services must be ever present.

In many instances, people in need of concrete services are also in need of supportive casework or group work services. Those who apply for public assistance may feel defeated or fearful that they will not be able to obtain sufficient food or pay their rent or other bills.

The process of offering and contracting for services beyond those of a concrete nature is delicate and requires much skill. On the one hand, there is the danger of "seeing" and "looking for" emotional problems where none may exist. Lum (1986) repeatedly makes the point that the problems of minority people often have a systemic and not a psychological base. On the other hand, people requiring supportive services are frequently troubled. In weighing these issues, skillful workers will first attend to the problem presented before attempting to contract for anything beyond this.

In many situations, the concrete service, courteously and warmly rendered, may be all that the client wants or is able to deal with at that point.

There are many differences in the nature, duration, and intensity of services. Parents may come to a school social worker or those in child guidance clinics expecting workers to provide discipline for unruly children. Others may come distressed about the embarrassing behavior of a psychotic family member. Tenants may ask the social worker to intervene with the landlord to get them more heat or needed repairs. A group of institutionalized children may come and ask the social worker to get cottage parents "to change their nasty ways."

In each of these situations people may expect the social worker to intervene on their behalf to effect a change in others' actions. Frequently they do not perceive their own role in attaining the desired changes: parents may become defensive when effort is made to explore how they discipline the children, tenants feel powerless with the landlord, families coping with an emotionally distressed member feel fatigued and hopeless.

Facts and feelings about these matters are usually expressed in the problem identification stage. There is evidence that if people are to move from a sense of distress and powerlessness to the point of some resolution of the difficulty, their active participation in goal setting is crucial (Seabury 1976; Reid 1986).

The various approaches to social work (see chapter four) differ in their views as to how quickly clients are to be engaged in contracting, setting priorities, and defining tasks. Nevertheless, some generic guidelines can be presented.

1. *When appropriate, suggestions should be offered early as to how client and worker might proceed.* For example, when parents begin to understand the circumstances that trigger a child's difficult behavior, workers may suggest that the parent's talk about how to modify their own behavior. Early in the contact the worker may suggest that parents try firmness rather than a wavering "No" to a seemingly unreasonable demand. This begins the contracting process, and sets into motion the idea that all have an obligation to examine their actions.

2. *The second generic guideline suggests that early evidence of what might be accomplished by working together be provided.* In the situation of the complaining tenants, workers must express verbally and nonverbally their understanding of the frustration engendered by poor services. If the tenants can be helped to see the potential of their

own strength, perhaps they can move to the next stage of acting in their own behalf.

3. *Set specific goals at any one point in time.* If the child's unruly behavior is the presenting problem, action should be targeted to accomplish change in this area. Only if and when the parents arrive at some agreement that the tensions in their own marriage contribute to the child's behavior should contracting focus on the relief of these tensions be considered.

When people who have cared for an emotionally ill person at home come asking for help in managing that person, they may or may not be considering the possibility of institutionalization. Their request should be taken at face value. They may need supportive services (e.g., day care or homemaker services) and the opportunity to ventilate. An early suggestion to institutionalize may well prove a barrier to further help. Should the situation continue to prove difficult after a trusting relationship with the worker has been developed, a family may consider the possibility of alternative care, including institutionalization.

In summary, the generic principles of contracting involve an ongoing effort to tune in to the dynamic, shifting situation, and making of joint plans to attain specific, manageable goals. A mutual effort, consonant with clients' perceptions of the problem, is projected. Recontracting may be necessary as the situation changes.

Adaptation to the ethnic reality. We defined the contract as "a consensus between the concerned persons about why they are working together, how they will work together, and what they hope to achieve."

The discussion on timing and contracting has focused on the need to remain tuned in to client perceptions of problems, and the effort to come to agreement on action.

The work of Good Tracks (1973) and others strongly suggests that speedy contracting as defined here may need to be suspended for some American Indians unless initiated by clients. Similarly, highly focused efforts to suggest behavioral changes or introspection are likely to be viewed as interference. The process of building a relationship, and of showing sensitivity to the culture and problem, in the hope that trust will be developed, is ongoing. The deference to authority, and the fear of shame and self-disclosure shared by many Asian Americans, suggests time might need to be viewed somewhat differently for this group. According to Ho (1976), many Asian Americans who adhere to traditional beliefs are not used to "functioning with ambiguity." Agency functioning should be clearly spelled out in the first contacts; the respect for the deference to authority suggests that clients should be politely informed of what is expected of them. If this is not done, clients may fear that they are imposing on someone in authority by returning. By contrast, contracting for expression of feeling may need to be deferred. This varies with degree of clients' adherence to traditional beliefs (Mokuau and Matsuoka 1986). Just being in therapy may generate such extensive anxiety that the process of verbalization may bring no relief (Toupin 1980). Again, people of the same group differ depending on age and degree of acculturation.

The situation is not dramatically different for many "blue-collar ethnics." Giordano (1977) suggests that many avoid seeking help, particularly in the mental health arena, until problems have reached crisis proportions. The role of client is viewed as stigmatizing. Emphasis should not be on pathology but on "problems in living," "active, practical, and down to earth" (Mondykowski 1982).

Many techniques for contracting have been proposed. These include written agreements specifying the workers' and clients' obligations, written suggestions for avoidance or carrying out of specific behaviors, and time limits by which certain goals are to be accomplished (Fischer 1978; Reid 1978, 1986). These are undoubtedly useful under some circumstances.

WORKING ON THE PROBLEM

Recently one of the authors visited an agency to review a student's progress. From the student's process recording it seemed that any number of times the student deflected a client's attention from the problem at hand. As soon as her clients seemed ready to discuss an emotionally sensitive matter, the student changed the subject. When this was pointed out, this insightful student said, "I know, but if they really tell me I might have to do something about it. And I don't really know how. Those people have terrible troubles, and they won't go away. I can't really change anything for them." This is a common dilemma, not only for the student but also for the more seasoned practitioner.

Some of the dilemma arises from the seeming intractability of the problems for which help is sought, some is related to lack of skill of the worker, and some to the inherent difficulty entailed in forging ahead, on a sustained basis, with efforts to help. These sustained efforts call for extensive commitment, skill, and continuing attention to the diverse helping roles that can be played and to the destructive environments that generate problems.

Much of the "bulk" of the work is a continuation of the processes set in motion in the course of problem identification and contracting. And yet, there is a distinction between the preparatory phase and the ongoing work. Once the work has begun, workers and clients truly become involved in problem solving. The phases of this process can be identified. With some variation, these phases occur whether work is focused on problems of interpersonal relationships with individuals or groups, on planned community or other systems change efforts, or on a variety of planning endeavors. The phases include: (1) ongoing reassessment of the problem, (2) partializing the problem into manageable parts, (3) identifying obstacles, (4) obtaining and sharing additional information, (5) reviewing progress or setbacks, and (6) termination. Environmental work is critical.

No single summary can possibly do justice to the various strategies and skills involved in the problem-solving process. We approach the matter by suggesting, for a number of select areas, how the *work* of problem solving may differ from the beginning phases.

Ongoing Reassessment of the Problem

The process of ongoing reassessment calls attention to many facets of the situation. External changes may take place that can dramatically alter the course of events. For example, life can be measurably altered if a job is lost or obtained, if the child of a couple experiencing marital difficulty becomes seriously ill, if the neighborhood that is organizing for better services is scheduled for demolition. All that need be said is that the worker must be sure to listen and to review. Too often, workers become so caught up in the preparatory work that during visits with the clients they forget to review. Setting aside some time to learn what happened this week, yesterday, or an hour ago is an essential component of interaction. Reid (1986), Lum (1986), and others stress this important component.

Partializing the Problem

In the discussion of contracting, several illustrations were given of how workers begin to help people to identify problems that might be considered. The reader will recall the situation of the Polish man soon to be released from prison. In contracting with him the suggestion was made that he consider his future living and working plans. Mrs. White, the woman who was considering separation from her husband, agreed to review the positives and negatives of the marriage; she also asked for a joint session with herself, the worker, and her husband to see whether such discussion would alter his perspective on her wish to find a job. In these, and many other types of situations, multiple problems present themselves. In the contract phase, it is possible to delineate these and to propose some priorities. As the work proceeds, the initial contract must be reviewed. Is it possible for the soon-to-be-parolee to consider what type of work he might do until he decides whether he can return home to live with his family? Opportunity and financial need may vary considerably, depending on where he goes. He may seem most troubled about how his family might receive him. Earlier it may appear as if discussion of job possibilities is a first-order priority. But as the work progresses he may continually bring up his fear about how his family will act when he is released. If so, the earlier plan will need revision, and discussion will have to be refocused.

Mrs. White may be unable to "see" any positives in her marriage unless there is some indication that her husband will take a positive attitude toward her taking a job. The joint interview with her husband may have priority. If he is adamant about his refusal to "let her" find a job, the discussions may focus on what she needs to do to terminate the marriage. Will she move out right away? Can she afford to do so? What will the financial settlement be? This is a generic phase of the process applicable to all people.

Identifying Obstacles

Obstacles come in the form of emotions, entrenched behavior patterns, discrimination, language barriers, environmental deficits, and so on. Despite this, understanding of barriers or obstacles can help to over-come or minimize them. The tenants and workers who agreed jointly to plan a strategy for the meeting with the landlord to discuss provision of more heat and services may find that the landlord is "not available." This may be an absentee landlord off to places unknown. Does that mean that the plan must be abandoned, or is there a legal recourse? Is it possible to subpoena the landlord? Are there public agencies respon-sible for doing this?

If Mrs. White cannot afford to leave home until she has enough income, what might she do? Is she sufficiently determined to go ahead with the separation to tolerate living with her husband while she pursues a job and tries to save some money?

Adaptation to the ethnic reality. Plans made in the privacy of the worker's office, or in locales in other ways removed from the network of church, community, and kin may flounder when others become aware of what is going on. A Catholic woman planning a divorce may talk to her priest, who suggests she reconsider. The members of a Black neighborhood improvement group may encounter explicit and implicit racism as they meet with the mayor and other city officials. A Chicano woman who has obtained employment encounters the wrath of her husband who may feel his very being threatened by her action.

These and like obstacles derive from deeply ingrained attitudes. Where cultural dispositions serve as obstacles to moving ahead, the following principles are suggested: (1) explore the source and nature of the difficulty carefully and gently, and (2) consider whether the obstacles are of an individual or a collective nature. For example, is the Catholic woman devout enough to stay in any marriage, or is she simply reporting the question raised by the priest? Were the racist slurs encountered by the neighborhood improvement group of such a nature as to warrant investigation and action by the agency? Is the Chicano woman the only one in her community to have taken a job? If not, have other women encountered similar problems? Is it possible to organize a Chicano women's support group? Such support groups have helped others. Outreach can help the elderly to overcome obstacles to service use. Starrett, Mindel, and Wright (1983) found that involvement in informal support systems increased information about and use of social services by the Hispanic elderly.

Obtaining and Sharing Additional Facts and Feelings

Throughout the worker-client encounter, both give each other factual and emotional feedback. If Mrs. White reports happily that she has a job, the worker gets a clue as to whether this is something she really wanted. If, on the other hand, she finds a job and seems depressed, the worker gets a different kind of message. The worker may share her own feeling: "I'm pleased that you seem so happy. It seems as if this really is something you've been wanting for a long time." If Mrs. White is depressed, a feminist worker may find it difficult to hide her disappointment. Perhaps this woman is not a "free spirit" after all. How does the worker "use" her feeling of disappointment? It is here that the process of tuning in must again come into play. For Mrs. White, employment outside the home constitutes "defying convention." Has Mrs. White really changed her mind? Or does she need more support to get her through a difficult transition? Where is she in the life cycle?

Adaptation to the ethnic reality. It is quite possible that ethnicity or culturally sensitive matters may not have surfaced early in the helping process. This may be related to (1) the worker's lack of knowledge,

(2) the client's reluctance to trust at an earlier stage, (3) different ethnic backgrounds of worker and client, and (4) lack of awareness by both that ethnic factors have bearing on the problem.

> Mr. Capella, an Italian group worker, has been working with a group of young, underclass men who were enrolled in a training program to upgrade their job skills. The group's objectives are to share experiences and feelings about the program, and to anticipate problems they might have as they try to get jobs. The men, all in their late teens and early twenties, come from varied backgrounds, including Hispanic, Black, and Italian.
>
> They have readily shared common experiences and have talked about the particular problems of discrimination the Black and Hispanic men might encounter.
>
> During the fourth session, one of the young Black men started the discussion by saying he wanted to thank Mr. Capella, and make a confession. He said he's had his doubts about what a "white dude" would know about how he felt. He almost wasn't going to come, but he thought he'd give it a try. Mr. Capella, though, he really had a "feel for where it's at."

There are other situations in which the basis for lack of progress may be ethnicity. Only when the matter is shared and aired does the work progress. A young Slavic woman was assigned a Black worker to help her think through her job problems. The young woman was working at a semiskilled clerical job and was quite dissatisfied. The worker's efforts to try to find out what the problem was yielded a very fuzzy picture. One day the young client blurted out in a rather embarrassed manner: "You know what's really bothering me on the job is my supervisor. But I never told you about that because she's Black like you, and I thought you'd get mad at me." Only when the worker accepted her feeling and told her it was acceptable to dislike any particular Black person were they able to move on to realistically consider the young woman's situation.

Ethnicity as a variable in the problem being considered may become evident during a later phase of contact.

> Mrs. Miller, a twenty-five-year-old college graduate, had crossed out all sections related to background on the form requesting service for marital counseling. The worker, respectful of her right to privacy, did not ask. The conflict as originally presented revolved around the couple's differences about having children. Mrs. Miller wanted to have children; Mr. Miller did not.
>
> One day Mrs. Miller came in particularly distraught, and said: "I thought we had it all worked out before we got married. But yesterday he told me he doesn't want children because I'm not Jewish. He'll have children if I convert. I told him before we were married I couldn't do that."

Sometimes people are not aware of the importance of their ethnic background until such basic issues as childbearing arise. This client shared a bit of information heretofore unknown even to herself.

The Phasing Out of the Worker-client Encounter

Strean (1978) suggests that the termination of any meaningful worker-client relationship will induce strong and ambivalent feelings. Others (Compton and Galaway 1979; Fox, Nelson, and Bolman 1969; Shulman 1984) variously address the dynamic generated by the separation process, the sense of loss or support that can be experienced in transfer or referral, and the heightened affect sensed by both worker and client as the end of the relationship approaches.

Shulman (1984) suggests a number of principles to be considered in the termination phase: (1) identifying major learning, (2) identifying what is to be done in the future, (3) synthesizing the ending process, and (4) considering sources of support alternative to those obtained from the worker. For the ethnic-sensitive worker the latter has particular significance. The alternative sources of support are often lodged in kinship and neighborhood networks, in the church, or in a newly heightened sense of ethnic identity. These and others are major considerations, requiring particular sensitivity to the possibility that clients may view termination as rejection or that they may be fearful about going on alone.

Most of the skills reviewed—stage setting, attending, tuning in, and identifying areas of concern—continue here. The stage is now set for departure, and all need to articulate what that means.

Will Mr. and Mrs. Jones sustain their efforts to minimize their fighting?

Has the community action group acquired the skills to work alone on new projects as need arises?

In tuning in to these kinds of concerns, workers again need to pay attention to the three levels of understanding, the broad area of concern within which the functioning takes place (e.g., the strains on marriages in general, the way people feel who have experienced marital counseling, and the kinds of strains *any* Mr. and Mrs. Jones are likely to experience). Workers need to think through their own concerns about the termination. Suppose contact was abrupt, and no progress was made. What went wrong? What did they learn? If the encounter appeared successful, are they also losing a valued relationship? In either case, when possible workers should share their satisfaction, their appreciation of the people involved, or their regrets.

"I'm going to miss talking with you every week. I like you a lot, and I've learned a lot."

"I'm sorry it didn't work out. Perhaps someone else will be able to help you more."

The fears and joys surrounding termination are universal. They will be variously expressed. Some clients will bring gifts, others will say their polite farewells, others will want to embrace the worker as a friend. Within the limitations of that which is possible, the worker must respond with grace and sensibility, in this as in all other phases of the work. Relating termination to issues of ethnicity and minority status is important. Lum (1986) has considered some of these. He asks that the following be considered: (1) was effort made to connect people to the positive elements of minority community support, and (2) did gaining a sense of self related to "ethnic selfhood" provide motivation for coping efforts?

We would add to these the continuing importance of attending to the macro issues—especially those related to racism and denigration of group culture and low socioeconomic status—that have triggered or intensified the problems of many clients.

SUMMARY

The practice skills presented represent a composite of many identified in the social work literature. Ethnic-sensitive practice requires adaptation or modifications in keeping with knowledge about prevailing group dispositions to issues such as privacy, using formally organized helping institutions, self-disclosure, discussion of intimate matters outside of the family, and the context in which service is or should be offered. Flexibility is necessary in determining where service is to be rendered and the speed with which workers seek to engage clients in contracting. Simultaneous attention to interpersonal and institutional issues is always crucial.

REFERENCES

Aguilar, Ignacio. 1972. Initial contacts with Mexican-American families. *Social Work* 17:66–70.
Atkinson, Donald R.; Mervin, Maryann; and Matsui, Sandi. 1978. Effects of counselor race and counseling approach on Asian Americans' perceptions of counselor credibility and utility. *Journal of Counseling Psychology* 25:76–83.
Benjamin, Alfred. 1974. *The helping interview.* 2d ed. Boston: Houghton-Mifflin Co.
Brown, Luna Bowdoin. 1950. Race as a factor in establishing a casework relationship. *Social Casework* 31:91–97.

Byler, William. 1977. The destruction of American Indian families. In *The destruction of American Indian families*, edited by Steven Unger. New York: Association on American Indian Affairs.

Chen, Pei-Ngor. 1970. The Chinese community in Los Angeles. *Social Casework* 51:591–598.

Compton, Beulah Roberts, and Galaway, Burt. 1979. *Social work processes*. Homewood, IL: The Dorsey Press.

Compton, Beulah Roberts, and Galaway, Burt. 1984. *Social work processes*. 3d ed. Homewood, IL: The Dorsey Press.

Curry, Andrew. 1964. The Negro worker and the white client: a commentary on the treatment relationship. *Social Casework* 45:131–136.

Dominick, Joan R., and Stotsky, Bernard. 1969. Mental patients in nursing homes, part IV. Ethnic influence. *Journal of the American Geriatric Society* 17:63–85.

Egan, Gerard. 1975. *The skilled helper: a mode for systematic helping and interpersonal relating*. Monterey, CA: Brooks/Cole Publishing Co.

Fischer, Joel. 1978. *Effective casework practice: an eclectic approach*. New York: McGraw-Hill Book Co.

Fox, Evelyn F.; Nelson, Marion A.; and Bolman, William M. 1969. The termination process: a neglected dimension in social work. *Social Work* 14(4):53–63.

Gambino, Richard. 1974. *Blood of my blood—the dilemma of the Italian-Americans*. Garden City, NY: Anchor Press/Doubleday.

Gary, Lawrence E. 1985. Depressive symptoms and Black men. *Social Work Research and Abstracts* 21:21–29.

Ghali, Sonia Badillo. 1977. Culture sensitivity and the Puerto Rican client. *Social Casework* 58(8):459–468.

Giordano, Joseph. 1977. *Ethnicity and mental health: research and recommendations*. New York: American Jewish Committee.

Giordano, Joseph, and Giordano, Grace Pineirio. 1977. *The ethno-cultural factor in mental health—a literature review and bibliography*. New York: American Jewish Committee.

Gitterman, Alex, and Schaeffer, Alice. 1972. The white professional and Black client. *Social Casework* 53:280–291.

Gomez, Ernesto; Zurcher, Louis A.; Farris, Buford E.; and Becker, R. E. 1985. A study of psychosocial casework with Chicanos. *Social Work* 30: 477–482.

Good Tracks, Jimm G. 1973. Native American noninterference. *Social Work* 18:30–35.

Green, James W. 1982. *Cultural awareness in the human services*. Englewood Cliffs, NJ: Prentice-Hall, Inc.

Hepworth, Dean H., and Larsen, Jo Ann. 1986. *Direct social work practice: theory and skills*. 2d ed. Chicago: The Dorsey Press.

Ho, Man Keung. 1976. Social work with Asian Americans. *Social Casework* 57(3):195–201.

Jones, Enrico E. 1978. Effects of race on psychotherapy process and outcome: An exploratory investigation. *Psychotherapy: Theory, Research, and Practice* 15:226–236.

Kadushin, Alfred. 1972. *The social work interview*. New York: Columbia University Press.

Leashore, Bogart R. 1981. Social services and Black men. In *Black men*, edited by Lawrence E. Gary. Beverly Hills: Sage Publications.

Lewis, Ronald G., and Ho, Man Keung. 1975. Social work with Native Americans. *Social Work* 20:379–382.

Lopata, Helen Znaniecki. 1976. *Polish-Americans: status competition in an ethnic community*. Englewood Cliffs, NJ: Prentice-Hall, Inc.

Lum, Doman. 1986. *Social work practice and people of color: a process stage approach*. Monterey, CA: Brooks/Cole Publishing Co.

Maluccio, Anthony N., and Marlow, Wilma D. 1974. The case for contract. *Social Work* 19:28–37.

Mercer, Jane R. 1972. Career patterns of persons labeled as mentally retarded. In *Medical men and their work—a sociological reader*, edited by Eliot Freidson and Judith Lorber. Chicago: Aldine-Atherton.

Middleman, Ruth, and Goldberg, Gale. 1974. *Social service delivery: a structural approach to social work practice*. New York: Columbia University Press.

Mokuau, Noreen, and Matsuoka, Jon. 1986. "The appropriateness of practice theories for working with Asian and Pacific Islanders." Paper presented at the Annual Program Meeting, Council on Social Work Education, Miami, Florida, March.

Mondykowski, Sandra M. 1982. Polish Families. In *Ethnicity and family therapy*, edited by M. McGoldrick, J. K. Pearce, and J. Giordano. New York: The Guilford Press.

Pincus, Allen, and Minahan, Anne. 1973. *Social work practice: model and method*. Itasca, IL: F.E. Peacock Publishers, Inc.

Reid, William J. 1978. *The task-centered system*. New York: Columbia University Press.

Reid, William J. 1986. Task-centered social work. In *Social work treatment*, 3d ed., edited by Francis J. Turner. New York: Columbia.

Reid, William J., and Epstein, Laura. 1977. *Task-centered practice*. New York: Columbia University Press.

Seabury, Brett A. 1976. The contract: uses, abuses, and limitations. *Social Work* 21:16–21.

Shulman, Laurence. 1978. A study of practice skill. *Social Work* 23:274–281.

Shulman, Laurence. 1979. *The skills of helping individuals and groups*. Itasca, IL: F.E. Peacock Publishers, Inc.

Shulman, Laurence. 1984. *The skills of helping*. 2d ed. Itasca, IL: F.E. Peacock Publishers, Inc.

Stack, Carol B. 1974. *All our kin—strategies for survival in a Black community*. New York: Harper & Row.

Starrett, Richard A.; Mindel, Charles H.; and Wright, Roosevelt. 1983. Influence of support systems on the use of social services by the Hispanic elderly. *Social Work Research and Abstracts* 19:35–40.

Strean, Herbert. 1978. *Clinical social work practice*. New York: The Free Press.

Toupin, Elizabeth Sook Wha Ahn. 1980. Counseling Asians: Psychotherapy in the context of racism and Asian American history. *American Journal of Orthopsychiatry* 50:76–86.

Truax, Charles B., and Mitchell, Kevin M. 1971. Research on interpersonal skills in relation to process and outcome. In *Handbook of psychotherapy and behavior change: an empirical analysis*, edited by Allen E. Bergin and Sol L. Garfield. New York: John Wiley and Sons, Inc.

Turner, Sylvester, and Armstrong, Stephen. 1981. Cross-racial psychotherapy: what the therapists say. *Psychotherapy: Theory, Research, and Practice* 18:375–378.
Zborowski, Mark. 1952. Cultural components in response to pain. *Journal of Social Issues* 8:16–30.

CHAPTER
7

Ethnic-Sensitive Practice
With Families

While social work is practiced in many different settings, most practice involves work with families, no matter where the work is carried out: in the voluntary family service agency, the juvenile justice system, the schools, or the health care system. Whether a marriage is tottering, a child is ill, or a child is in trouble at school or with the law, the family as a system is or should be involved. Problems are frequently traced to the family at the same time as the family is sought as a source of support and solution. It is within the family that many life cycle tasks are carried out.

Understanding of family dynamics, of intergenerational struggles, and of how the ethnic reality impinges on the family's capacity to play its varying roles is crucial for the ethnic-sensitive social worker.

In this chapter, a variety of views on family functioning are reviewed. These are related to the assumptions and principles of ethnic-sensitive practice presented in chapter five. Case examples serve to illustrate how the perspectives of ethnic-sensitive practice are brought to bear on work with troubled families.

THE EVOLVING FAMILY

In an early consideration of practice with the family group Mary Richmond (1917) defined the family as "all who share a common table," identifying the parents and children as "the most important members of the group." In the present we still hold the parents and children as most important but have come to recognize a variety of combinations of parents and children.

There is the intact nuclear family, a married couple and their children who live independently from either spouse's parents. While we hold this to be the traditional family, we are aware of emerging variations, including single parents and their children. Most often the parent is a mother, widowed, divorced, separated, or never married. There are fathers who care for their children alone but their numbers are smaller.

There are an increasing number of remarried families in which at least one partner has been married previously. They bring with them children of other marriages and often add their own. The resulting family constellations are extensive. As initial or subsequent marriages end in divorce new relationships are established that lead to new marriages, suggesting a continuing commitment to the value of the family.

We limit our view of family when we hold to the narrow parent-child definition, for there are childless families, couples who chose not to have children. There are middle-aged and elderly couples who have fulfilled their responsibilities as parents and now take on the less responsible grandparent role. Still other couples choose to postpone parenthood while they explore the world of work.

Each family, no matter what the composition, is influenced to some degree by its ethnic history and the dispositions that flow from it. The Irish family is known for hospitality and politeness derived from a genuine selflessness in relationships (McGoldrick 1982). Jewish families place emphasis on the centrality of the family, sharing suffering, intellectual achievement, financial success, and the verbal expression of feelings (Herz and Rosen 1982). The extended family plays a central role in many aspects of the life of an Italian family, in which roles are clearly assigned in relation to age and gender (Rotunno and McGoldrick 1982). In each instance families respond in ways that either accept or abandon the tradition.

FAMILY FUNCTIONS

No matter what the family composition or ethnic disposition, the family continues to have major economic and affectional functions, generally know as instrumental and expressive. The primary instrumental task is accomplished as shelter, food, clothing, and health care are provided. Social class position will dictate the neighborhood and quality of shelter, the quantity and quality of the food, the supply of clothing to respond to various weather conditions, as well as access to adequate health services and facilities. Expressive tasks are accomplished as families socialize their members to accept more mature roles as they pass through their individual life cycles. This socialization prepares the members, particularly the young, for association with various institutions in the community such as the church or the school. There is also the need to establish patterns of communication that allow for a wide range of emotions from aggression to affection.

ETHNIC VALUES AND THE FAMILY

In presenting the assumptions of ethnic-sensitive practice, attention was called to the importance of relating the past history of ethnic groups to the contemporary situations they confront. The exploration of that history will reveal that the values held by various groups are a product of that history, and that these cannot easily be separated from sociopolitical events. For example, the interrelatedness between the "Polish character" and Poland's past history is clarified by this statement made by Edmund Muskie, a prominent Polish-American (1966): "There is much of glory in Poland's past—glory which was the product of the love of liberty, fierce independence, intense patriotism, and courage so characteristic of the Polish people." The past to which Muskie referred included guarantees of religious freedom laid down in 1573, and the development of a constitution in 1791 that considered individual freedom essential to the well-being of the nation. The Polish family of the present is a product of that history and may be expected to hold many of the values that Muskie identifies. Fiery independence continues to characterize many Poles. As we have noted repeatedly, such values seep into individual dispositions toward work, child rearing, and the roles of women. As Polish and other ethnic families encounter mainstream America, struggles may ensue as values begin to shift or take on a different shape. Social workers must be aware of the delicate balance that may result between old values and new. The third-generation Italian father is less distrusting of the outsider than was his grandfather and may allow his daughter to date outside of the immediate ethnic circle; but, at the same time, he may maintain a traditional view on premarital sex (Kephart 1977). This shift accommodates the realities of present-day society but maintains a position in which women are held in high regard and effort is made to protect them from the outside world, which is "not to be trusted." The consequence of this evolution of values is often intergenerational conflict. Daughters in Italian families cannot appreciate the effort it may have taken for their fathers to permit them to date non-Italian men; their fathers cannot understand a changing code of sexual morality that does not condemn a bride who is not a virgin.

Each ethnic family is influenced by various aspects of the larger society. These influences serve to throw into question values that have long been treasured and have sustained the family for several generations in America. The resulting tension between resistance and accommodation may cause family turmoil, some of which may eventually come to the attention of a social worker.

These are but some of the kinds of family issues of which the ethnic-sensitive social worker must be particularly aware. The assumptions and principles for ethnic-sensitive practice presented in chapter five serve as a basis for attention to these aspects of family life.

In order to highlight how the various assumptions and principles may influence practice, a variety of cases are presented here. Each case is distinctive in relation to the ethnic reality and its influences on ways in which families and workers respond to the problems presented. In all cases, social workers are expected to draw on the various layers of understanding and to adapt the various strategies and procedures used to response to the ethnic reality.

SELF-AWARENESS

To achieve the goal of ethnic-sensitive practice, social workers must be continually aware of the fourth layer of understanding that relates to awareness of their own ethnicity, recognizing that such awareness is incorporated as part of the "professional self." Social workers are not immune to feelings of ambivalence about ethnic diversity and their own location in the ethnic geography. Greeley (1974) suggests that we are all torn between pride in our heritage and resentment at being trapped in that heritage. He speculates that the ambivalence is probably the result of the immigrant experience of shame and defensive pride in an unappreciative society. No matter what the origin or nature, social workers must be aware of their own feelings about their ethnic identities.

The Case of Clyde Turner

When Clyde Turner saw the social worker at the Mental Health Unit of the hospital, he said that he had come because he needed "a rest to get himself together." He was self-referred, but had been in mental health treatment centers before. The diagnosis made was depression. The tension and anxiety he felt were evident in his behavior. Problems seemed to be generated by internal and external stresses.

Clyde is Black; he is twenty years old and a sophomore at a university near his home. His father Roland is on the faculty of another university in the area;

he is working on his doctoral dissertation. Eleanor, his mother, is not employed outside of their home. His sister Jeanette, age seventeen, is a high school student who earns excellent grades.

Clyde said that family pressure is a part of his problem. He feels he has not had a chance to become an independent person. The family upsets him and he becomes very argumentative.

His father has urged him to take five "profitable" courses in the next semester. Clyde had planned to take three such courses and two in the humanities, which would lessen his academic burden.

In an effort to "move away" from his family, Clyde joined a fraternity but when the "Brothers" learned of his problems they began to ridicule him and became patronizing.

School, family, friends all became "hassles" and Clyde sought refuge in the mental health unit for a rest.

Clyde's tensions and anxieties are in the present. The diagnosis of depression is not in question. There is sufficient evidence from previous admissions to other mental health centers to confirm the assessment. Relief of his tension and anxiety are of primary concern.

As the perspectives of ethnic-sensitive practice are applied, consideration must be given to the first layer of understanding, knowledge of human behavior. This knowledge provides the data that begin to explain Clyde's illness. His natural struggle for independence at the emerging adult stage is hampered by the acute nature of his depression. The symptoms confound him and his parents, who at middle age have begun to look forward to a life without child care responsibilities. One of their children, however, continues to need care, which they seem unable to provide.

The Turners are a middle-class Black family; these characteristics identify their ethnic reality. Mr. Turner's thrust for advanced education for himself and his son are among the dispositions that often flow from that position. Unlike many Black middle-class families, that status has been achieved with the employment of only one adult. Mr. Turner's salary as an educator provides sufficient income to maintain their middle-class position with appropriate style.

The Turners are members of a continually evolving Black middle class that is moving away from the more traditional professions of teaching and preaching. Instead, increasing numbers may be found in engineering, business management, science, and technology. They find themselves in national banks, insurance companies, retail firms, industries, universities, and government (Kilson 1983). Their children no longer feel limited to enrollment in Black colleges and universities and move in increasing numbers to major American universities.

Roland Turner is among those identified by Kilson who have found employment in a university. He holds a junior faculty position while he completes his doctoral studies. Completion will give him greater assurance of continued employment.

Mrs. Turner has no employment other than the management of their small home. Their suburban experience has been a relatively calm one in relation to the experience of other middle-class Black families who have sought homes away from urban centers (Rubin 1982). Theirs is an integrated neighborhood in which many adults pursue graduate degrees. Despite the appearance of calm, Clyde's social worker must be alert to the potential stress in this environment where there are few Black friends for adolescents and emerging adults. Nor are there Black adult role models in any significant number. The Turners and other Black families often look back to their Black urban communities for support.

As Clyde and his father disagree about his selection of courses for the coming term, they respond to an unconscious, unspoken value of the Black middle class. Education will enable Black people to change their positions in society; it will move them upward. There is no discussion about whether Clyde will return to school. The discussion is about what he will study when he returns.

In the struggle for independence Clyde sought out peers and became a member of a Black fraternity. It is in peer groups such as this, whose membership is comprised of one ethnic group, that one often finds comfort. These groups affirm identity through special social projects and recreational activities. For Clyde, however, they intensified stress because of their inability to respond in comforting ways to his distress. But, like Clyde, they too are emerging young Black men seeking a place for themselves in the larger society. They may be enlisted by the social worker to serve as a support group for Clyde. Efforts to provide them with a clearer picture of Clyde's difficulties may well enable them to refrain from ridicule and include Clyde more completely in the group activities.

Although there is no mention of extended family, further inquiry may uncover a kinship network that is available to give emotional support to the entire family. Martin and Martin (1978) define the Black extended family as a multigenerational, interdependent kinship system welded together by a sense of obligation to relatives. They contend that extended families have been responsible for providing many Blacks with basic economic and emotional security. Given this perspective it would be wise for the social worker to explore this valuable resource as support or refuge for Clyde.

As a young college student, Clyde is subject to the rigors of academic life even without the stress of his illness. How many other students at the university suffer? What resources in counseling are available? How adequate are those that exist? How may the services of the mental health unit be expanded or adapted to meet the needs of students from any college who reside in this suburban community? How does the stress of Clyde's illness disrupt the family as they struggle to maintain middle-class status?

These are among the questions that may be raised by social workers as they work with college students of any ethnic or social class group. Practice should move from dealing with individual client need to modifying those larger systems that influence, positively or negatively, the client's day-to-day activities.

It is not the intention of this discussion to suggest a specific course of action Clyde's social worker might take. That would depend on many aspects of this case not presented. The activity would, however, be related to the route Clyde took to the social worker. It was totally voluntary and based on previous successful experiences in mental health settings. The mental health unit is one of the services provided in a suburban general hospital. A majority of patients of all ethnic groups hold middle-class status. In such a setting there is often little involvement with larger systems. Yet, evidence of systemic failure as it relates to the Turner family may be seen in the pervasiveness of institutional racism. The energy invested in overcoming the obstacles required to attain a middle-class position in this suburban environment may have some relationship to Clyde's problems; the specifics have to be determined by the worker and family.

The social worker, having considered the assumptions and principles for ethnic-sensitive practice, now has more data available that will give a wider view of the Turner family as they struggle to cope with their depressed son.

The Case of Michael Bobrowski

Jean Bobrowski persuaded her husband Michael to accompany her to the Family Counseling Association. It seemed the only way to help him. After he lost his job he sat around the house or wandered aimlessly. She was very worried and went to see Father Paul, who suggested that she take her husband to the association. The priest encouraged Michael's cooperation.

Mr. and Mrs. Bobrowski are Polish. When he was employed, Mr. Bobrowski was a truck driver. His work record was poor. When he backed a truck over a gasoline pump and failed to report it to his employers, he was fired. Because he was a member of the union, Mr. Bobrowski had expected that the union would help him find other employment, but this did not materialize. He is ineligible for unemployment due to the circumstances of his dismissal.

Mrs. Bobrowski now takes care of other people's children; Michael's job had been the sole source of their income. They have lost their home due to nonpayment of the mortgage.

The Bobrowskis have been married for thirty years. He is presently fifty-five, she is fifty. Their son Michael, Jr. is twenty-eight and lives in California with his wife and young son. Debbie, their daughter, is twenty-four, married and lives nearby. She has two children.

Both of the Bobrowskis are members of the Polish American Home, a social club, and the American Legion. They get a great deal of pleasure from the activities of each group, but are less active since Mr. Bobrowski lost his job.

A major problem for this family is financial insecurity; the strain is becoming evident in this couple's relationship. While difficult for most people, the lack of employment is particularly devastating to this Polish working-class family. To the Slavic work is the reason for living; if one cannot work, then one is useless.

The work of Stein (1976, 1978) suggests that this attitude cuts across all social classes. In addition, essential goals of life are to own one's home and to amass cash wealth as a cushion for security. Mr. Bobrowski has failed each area. His behavior has deprived him of work and, although he wishes to work, his union has not supplied employment as he expected. He has lost his home due to his failure to pay the mortgage. There are no cash reserves set aside. His application for unemployment insurance has been denied. The independence of character referred to by Muskie cannot be exemplified when there is no work, no home, no reserve. He is unable to protect his wife who must now take care of other people's children in order to support the family. In their later adulthood, when there is the universal expectation of less responsibility because the children are independent the Bobrowskis find themselves dependent and may need to seek resources from public agencies. The task of coping with a diminishing work role, usually executed at old age, must be accomplished earlier than expected. Although Mr. Bobrowski resists, it is unlikely that he will ever have steady employment again due to his poor work history.

Despite the emphasis on hard work and building up a cash reserve, the chances of attaining the security envisioned are fairly slim for Polish and other working-class families. Their income may appear to be substantial; the hard work they do pays well. But they, like many working-class families, have attempted to find the "good life" through the acquisition of consumer items. Many of these items are purchased "on time". So, the family income that appears to be "good" is spread out to make payments on the car, appliances, mortgage, or perhaps a truck, camper, or small boat before the purchase of food or medical care. Rubin (1976) has identified this precarious position on the edge of financial disaster as one contributor to the "worlds of pain" of the white working class.

An understanding of the realities of Michael Bobrowski's ethclass position, in which he suffers from the pain of a working-class position and failure to meet ethnic group expectations, enable the ethnic-sensitive worker to go beyond the problems of finance and depression.

An awareness of community resources will provide a direction as the worker seeks to help the family. Other resources must be enlisted by the ethnic-sensitive worker committed to simultaneous activity at micro and macro levels.

The couple is active in two secondary groups: the American Legion and the Polish American Home. Both are sources of strength in their lives. In each there is a sense of patriotism, which has been identified as a distinctive Polish characteristic. They are able to affirm their "Polish-ness" among other Poles at Polish American Home gatherings. Their present problems in living have caused them to become less active. They feel the stigma of unemployment and the depression that followed. Yet, this group may be able to help diminish the sense of stigma. Mr. Bobrowski is not the only member who has problems leading to tensions and anxieties. Others may have marital conflict and problems with their children or parents. The nature of interpersonal relationships is such that similar problems may surface in many families.

When marital problems do exist the general attitude appears to be one that accepts suffering rather than seeking professional help. Women may see marriage as "a cross to be borne," while men may believe that an unpleasant marriage must be endured, "come hell or high water" (Wrobel 1979). Is it possible for the Polish American Home, a familiar community institution, to become an outreach center for the Family Counseling Association?

The Polish association could, with joint effort by the social worker and community leaders, become a part of the effort to minimize the stigma attached to mental health problems and to seeking service, which often plagues white ethnic communities (Giordano 1973). Programs and services may be encouraged that span the life cycle from day care services to senior citizens' activities, centered about the home and located in community-based institutions.

Mr. Bobrowski's route to the social worker was highly voluntary. He followed the suggestion of his priest, a significant person in his life. At the family association he may expect to be active in the plans for the solution of his problems. If he chooses not to continue services, he may be encouraged to continue until the work is completed, but he will not be "punished" for this decision.

A Khmer Family

Lai Heng arrived in this country two years ago with five of her eight children. One daughter had arrived several years earlier. Another was still in a refugee camp, and a third was still in Vietnam. Her husband was killed in action in Lon Nol's army in Cambodia.

Lai's adjustment to the small American town was made with relative ease due to the presence of her daughter and an excellent group of sponsors. About two years after the family's arrival, Mrs. Heng felt that she was having problems with Neari, her sixteen-year-old daughter. From Mrs. Heng's point of view, Neari was a problem because she was talking to American boys, wearing American clothes, and taking on too many American ways. This was ironic, because from the public school's point of view Neari had adjusted very well. Her academic work was superior. Neari felt that she was having a problem because of the pressure she felt from constant scolding from her mother and older sister.

The most serious incident in the life of this family occurred when Neari did not come home one night. She walked around the apartment complex and took shelter in the laundry room. Her mother had scolded her severely that afternoon, hit her, and thrown her clothes all over the bedroom. This was in response to Neari's late arrival after school. She was suspected of going to the store with Calvin, an American boy who liked her (Wolff 1986).

This family's route to the social worker is somewhat coercive in that the social worker is linked to the English As A Second Language (ESL) faculty of the school system, and the family is "encouraged" to see the social worker following name calling problems with American children and this new problem in the parent-child relationship. The community has an increasing number of Asian refugees who have confounded the school system. The response has been the ESL program and a social worker to respond to problems as they are identified.

The social worker who meets with the family and other Khmer (Cambodian) refugee families must be aware of the turmoil that has been a part of their lives in the recent past. Cambodian history, however, goes back at least two thousand years to a magnificent civilization with cities of grandeur. In the 1800s they were subjected by Thailand and Vietnam; then the country became a French protectorate. The early 1900s were years of struggle for independence. But the later years have been such that refugees have been called "survivors of an

Asian Holocaust" (Knoll 1982). Mr. Heng had been a member of the army of General Lon Nol in the time of civil war.

His family left in 1975 when the country fell to the Khmer Rouge (the Communists). Like thousands of other families, they were placed in a prison camp. They escaped, walking several days to the Thailand border where they found a refugee camp. After four years in a variety of these camps they arrived in this country.

The social worker must be aware of the universal characteristics of the refugee experience being uprooted, facing possible annihilation. They often know depression and suffering, experience family loss and alienation (Borman 1984). Mr. Heng was killed in the war. One daughter remains in a refugee camp, another is still in Vietnam; there are significant losses. This family has been dramatically affected by recent history. Their two years in this county are not long enough to wipe out that history and its horror.

Lai Heng is a middle-aged single parent, a widow, alone in a strange country without the support of a husband. She is further hampered because she does not speak the language. Others speak in her behalf. Unlike earlier immigrant groups that contained a majority of males, recent Asian refugees admitted under the Refugee Act of 1980 have been primarily women. These women struggle to care for their families and to establish new communities (Rynearson and DeVoe 1984). Mrs. Heng's son-in-law, Suror, serves as head of the family. But he is a young man with a family of his own and needs to find his way in this new country.

As Neari goes through the universal problems of physical growth and hormonal changes, she is also beset with the critical problem of growing up in a country where experiences are unlike any she has known. She, like other Khmer adolescents, finds herself better off than her mother who has not learned the English language and the American way of life. Children like Neari are sometimes ashamed and reject their ethnicity and their parents. On the other hand, others may reject everything that is American (Wolff 1985).

Neari wants the same privileges as American girls. Her mother expects that she will follow the Khmer way whereby girls do not talk to boys or go out with them before marriage. The social worker's task is to mediate the difficulty, enabling each to see the other's position. Neari does not know the Khmer way; she left Cambodia at such an early age that she was not aware of the expectations her family might have had of her. Mrs. Heng needs to understand that American customs related to boy-girl relationships are very different from those with which she is familiar.

Through all of this, the social worker must be aware of personal feelings and attitudes related to the politics of southeast Asia. However, Glassman and Skolnik (1984) call for a connectedness to the client's pain and anguish rather than the politics of the situation.

A greater sense of ethnic identity and cohesion may be found as Neari and other family members become involved in organizations that foster ethnic pride. They must also risk association with the larger community, despite language difficulties.

As the school and other community agencies offer services, the ethnic-sensitive worker helps them to understand that Buddhism, the religion of the Khmers, accepts suffering as a part of life. Followers believe that problems should be kept within the family. Like other ethnic groups who hold similar beliefs, they are reluctant to come forward to seek help. If they do, it is in an indirect way, usually with concrete problems.

Refugee Assistance Programs must be used as a base from which a variety of services may be offered in addition to cash, Medicaid, or food stamps. Such programs include counseling and concrete services as well as education, support, and community enpowerment (Kerpen 1983; Glassman and Skolnik 1984).

Perhaps the most difficult task the ethnic-sensitive worker will have with the Hengs and other Asian families is the adaptation of strategies and procedures in response to the ethnic reality. Probing questions may be rebuffed with "Why do you want so much information?" Private and personal concerns will not be immediately forthcoming. Given this resistance, problem-solving techniques have been shown to be more useful than therapeutic approaches (Kerpen 1983).

Of particular importance is consideration of the use of multilingual workers who function as interpreters. Children, other relatives, or friends may take on this role as well. Some programs have found that multilingual workers will steer clients away from workers they feel to be undesirable. Shama Ahmed (1982) comments on the issue of interpreters and cautions against the use of family members, suggesting that their use serves only to magnify the potential for bias or side-taking. The ethnic-sensitive worker recognizes the need for help in interpretation with Neari and her family. Suror is a valuable resource but he is a member of the family; the worker must be aware of possible bias. Ahmed cautions against the assumption that every bilingual or multilingual person is suitable or competent to all situations. Choosing a competent interpreter is a skill that ethnic-sensitive workers must develop as they work with refugee families as well as those who have resided in America for some time.

SUMMARY

Each of the families presented in this chapter, the Turners, the Bobrowskis, and the Hengs, is attempting to carry out expressive and instrumental functions. Their ability for success will be influenced by the life cycle position of each of the family members.

The potential for successful solutions to the problems they present will be in some measure related to their ethnic reality, their ethnicity and social class positions. An understanding of institutional discrimination has intensified Mr. Turner's efforts to gain more education in order to maintain and enhance the family's middle-class position. Mrs. Heng and her children have been the victims of insult and emotional injury as insensitive Americans call them names. They have few personal resources, having lost their home and possessions in another war-torn country. Perhaps, in time, their social class position will be more secure; at present, they are very dependent upon others. The Bobrowskis' expectations of working-class prosperity are denied, as income is used to "pay the bills" for minor luxuries.

In each family, however, there are the joys of ethnicity that come from associations with others who are like them. This is a source of comfort and power. These ethnic groups and the family will continue to survive as collections of individuals, as groups, as major units of the social system, and as agencies for the transmission of cultural values (Papajohn and Spiegel 1975). It is in the family that the stresses and strains of daily life are played out; children are born and reach adulthood; men and women love and hate; interpersonal and intrapersonal conflicts develop and subside as men, women and children struggle with the demands of the larger society and with their own needs for sexual and emotional fulfillment. This is the base from which the ethnic-sensitive worker involved with families begins. The particular approaches to practice may vary.

Some may choose a broad psychosocial approach with the Turners, Bobrowskis and others like them. Others may find task-centered, structural approaches useful as a way of helping them to struggle with the problems presented. Others may help them to focus primarily on the external, structurally induced sources of their problems. Whichever approach they choose, ethnic-sensitive workers will be aware of how the route to the social worker constrains problem definitions and work values. Essential, also, is simultaneous attention to how micro and macro systems impinge on family functioning, and attention to those macro tasks that will enhance such functioning. Always crucial is awareness of the layers of understanding and a recognition that techniques and skills may need to be adapted in order to respond to the family's ethnic reality.

REFERENCES

Ahmed, Shama. 1982. Translation is at best an echo. *Community Care* pp. 19–21.

Borman, Leonard D. 1984. Self-help/mutual aid in changing communities. *Social Thought* 10:49–61.

Giordano, Joseph. 1973. *Ethnicity and mental health—research and recommendations.* New York: American Jewish Committee.

Gite, Lloyd. 1986. The young tycoons. *Black Enterprise* 16:44–47.

Glassman, Lurania, and Skolnik, Louise. 1984. The role of social group work in refugee resettlement. *Social Work with Groups* 7:45–61.

Gordon, Milton M. 1964. *Assimilation in American life: the role of race, religion, and national origins.* New York: Oxford University Press.

Greeley, Andrew M. 1974. *Ethnicity in the United States: a preliminary reconnaissance.* New York: John Wiley and Sons, Inc.

Herz, Fredda M., and Rosen, Elliott J. 1982. Jewish families. In *Ethnicity and Family Therapy,* edited by Monica McGoldrick, John K. Pearce, and Joseph Giordano. New York: The Guilford Press.

Johnson, Colleen Leahey. 1985. *Growing up and growing old in Italian-American families.* Brunswick, NJ: Rutgers University Press.

Kephart, William M. 1977. *The family, society, and the individual.* 4th ed. Boston: Houghton-Mifflin Co.

Kerpen, Karen S. 1983. Working with refugees. *Public Welfare* 41:18–22.

Kilson, Martin. 1983. The Black bourgeoisie revisited. *Dissent* 30:85–96.

Knoll, Tricia. 1982. *Becoming American, Asian sojourners, immigrants, and refugees in the western United States.* Portland, OR: Coast to Coast Books.

Ladner, Joyce, and Gourdine, Ruby Norton. 1984. Intergenerational teenage motherhood: some preliminary findings. *Sage: A Scholarly Journal on Black Women* 1:22–24.

Lemann, Nicholas. 1986. The origins of the underclass. *The Atlantic Monthly* 257:31–55.

McGoldrick, Monica. 1982. Irish families. In *Ethnicity and family therapy,* edited by Monica McGoldrick, John K. Pearce, and Joseph Giordano. New York: The Guilford Press.

Martin, Elmer P., and Martin, Joanne Mitchell. 1978. *The Black extended family.* Chicago: The University of Chicago Press.

Muskie, Edmund. 1966. This is our heritage. In *The Poles in America 1608–1972: a chronology and fact book,* edited by Frank Renkiewicz. Dobbs Ferry, NJ: Oceana Publications, Inc.

Papajohn, John, and Spiegel, John. 1975. *Transactions in families.* San Francisco: Jossey-Bass.

Paz, Octavio. 1961. Quoted in Queen, Stuart A., and Haberstein, Robert W. eds. 1970. *The family in various cultures.* New York: J. B. Lippincott Co.

Richmond, Mary E. 1917. *Social diagnosis.* New York: Russell Sage Foundation.

Rubin, Lillian Breslow. 1976. *Worlds of pain: life in the working-class family.* New York: Basic Books, Inc.

Rubin, Nancy. 1982. *The new suburban woman.* New York: Coward, McCann, and Geoghegan.

Rotunno, Marie, and McGoldrick, Monica. 1982. Italian families. In *Ethnicity and Family Therapy*, edited by Monica McGoldrick, John K. Pearce, and Joseph Giordano. New York: The Guilford Press.

Rynearson, Ann M. and DeVoe, Pamela. 1984. Refugee women in a vertical village: lowland Laotians in St. Louis. *Social Thought* 10:33–47.

Stein, Howard F. 1976. A dialectical model of health and illness—attitudes and behavior among Slovak-Americans. *International Journal of Mental Health* 5 (3).

Stein, Howard F. 1978. The Slovak-American 'swaddling ethos': homeostat for family dynamics and cultural continuity. *Family Process* 17:31–46.

Wolff, Ida O. 1985. "A cross cultural encounter, personal problems and public issues." Submitted in partial fulfillment of requirements of courses in Masters program. School of Social Work, Syracuse University, Fall.

Wolff, Ida O. 1986. "A Khmer family." Case study submitted in partial fulfillment of course requirements for Social Work Practice with Individuals, Families, and Groups, Syracuse University School of Social Work, Spring.

Wrobel, Paul. 1979. *Our way: family, parish, and neighborhood in a Polish-American community*. Notre Dame, IN: University of Notre Dame Press.

CHAPTER
8

Ethnic-Sensitive Practice With Recipients of Aid to Families With Dependent Children

The Other America—Poverty in the United States was published in 1962. Its author, Michael Harrington, discusses the poor as "invisible people" who are to be found off the beaten track in "valleys of Pennsylvania," along rutted roads in cities and towns, or on farms. He describes them as undereducated, underprivileged, lacking medical care, and in the process of being forced from the land into life in cities where they are misfits. This poverty, he declares, "twists and deforms the spirit." The move to the city has often proved Harrington's prediction to be correct; many are misfits, without skills for jobs above the most menial level. Many have looked to public agencies for financial support. For others the poverty was transitory; they were able to overcome with education, ambition, or the sheer refusal to remain suppressed (*Time Magazine* 1977; Lemann 1986). The remainder have become the core of the present American underclass, a population of some poor Blacks, some Hispanics, some whites, and some American Indians concentrated primarily in large urban centers.

The groups who fell readily into the "invisible poor" population were those most often the victims of racism, discrimination, and prejudice. The physical appearance of Blacks, Hispanics, and American Indians immediately set them apart. For many, language was an additional burden. Mainstream institutions denied them access to adequate education or housing and offered few opportunities for employment in positions with dignity.

Twenty years later in a discussion of *The New American Poverty* Harrington (1984) begins by claiming that, "the poor are still there." The war on poverty continues to exist and we must contend "with a new poverty much more tenacious than the old." This new poverty is influenced from the outside by the growth of foreign industry and from within by a technological revolution.

Poverty statistics in 1983 showed "that there were as many poor Americans in 1982 as in 1965." Joblessness continues as industry combats the foreign markets. Housing for the poor remains inadequate, as do educational opportunities. Some have made significant strides. Many of the working poor have fought their way out of poverty; the aging have made gains through Medicare and increased social security. Blacks, Chicanos, and Filipinos have benefited from the eradication of Jim Crow and a labor union in the fields (Harrington 1984).

The poor are less invisible in the 1980s as various news media publicize the residual effects of layoffs, poor housing, inadequate education, and homelessness. The poor are more visible as immigrants take on the unskilled, low-paying jobs refused by Americans who are more wary of exploitation. Poverty continues as a political issue.

The poor and responses to their needs continue as a part of our sociopolitical history at all governmental levels, federal, state, and local. The result is a vast, pervasive network of social services designed to provide financial help and a variety of services to enable people to obtain the essentials for living: food, clothing, and shelter. These services now range from day care centers for children to nutrition programs for older Americans. The largest of the many governmental programs is for dependent children. Known as Aid to Families with Dependent Children (AFDC), this program is supported by federal and state funds. Its vastness has become a concern for those who would reform the welfare system. At the time of this writing the report of a presidential commission appointed to review the current potential for welfare reform is awaited.

The ethnic-sensitive worker must be aware of this historical perspective, aware of the continued struggle of the poor for visibility and appropriate responses that will encourage and support their independence.

THE WORK ETHIC

The call for reform is based on the American ethic that requires able-bodied adults to work for their own subsistence rather than rely on the public for support. This was not the case, however, when the Social Security Act of 1935 was introduced. This act enabled mothers to remain home with their children to rear them without the need to seek employment. But, as the numbers of mothers in the work force grew, a thrust for reform arose to induce welfare mothers to seek work (Rein 1972). The mothers and fathers were subject to value judgments that questioned their worthiness for public support. Many of the children of poor families were born out of wedlock; fathers abandoned their children, legitimate and illegitimate, leaving them to bear the stigma of being "on welfare."

In a society that adheres to the residual conception of social welfare, which expects the individual to look to institutional supports only after the "normal structures of supply, the family, and the market" have broken down, those who look to welfare programs are less valuable (Wilensky and Lebeaux 1958). The poor in ethnic minority groups continue to look to government for assistance; the needed response is not readily provided. A reason may be found in the following observation: "The laziness and immorality of the lower classes were constantly referred to and alleged to account for their inferior standard of living. At no stage were the lower classes considered full members of society with rights in any way comparable to other classes" (Mencher 1967). Although this reflects seventeenth-century British attitudes, twentieth-century American mainstream attitudes are similar as they label the poor lazy, immoral, unappreciative, unable to manage their lives, and generally a blight on the nation.

The ethnic-sensitive worker must be aware of these attitudes that demand work instead of granting "relief." At the same time, the worker must recognize that the needs of the poor must be met. Their lives are continually judged by others. Although some ethnic groups are judged more harshly than others, all are judged.

The "feeling" of being a poor child is expressed in this poem:

> It's not so bad being poor,
> If you don't mind
> That you can't really help the way you are
> 'Cause you haven't had the proper socio-
> Economic upbringing.
> Your skin's too dark, your hair is too curly
> And your father never married your mother
> (Sermabeikian 1975).

The child who speaks in this poem recognizes the barriers of ethnicity and social class and the powerlessness of an underclass status.

Poor men who attempt to provide the essentials for their wives and children are often frustrated in that effort by unemployment. There are a variety of solutions that will provide the needed income. They may abandon their families in order to make them eligible for AFDC, or remain and apply for assistance as unemployed fathers. In either instance, they can expect to be judged, particularly if they belong to a poor ethnic minority group. Feelings of frustration and the resulting questions are expressed in this excerpt from a long poem about white urban poverty:

> The Black
> Welfare woman says,
> "Don't you know that you're
> White and
> Blond and
> Blue-eyed?
> Don't you know that you can
> Get a job easily?
> You can't get on welfare.
> No way!"
> So,
> How come I can't get work?
> So,
> How come I can't get work?
> So,
> How come I have no money for
> Bread and mustard
> Sandwiches?
> For milk and baby food for
> The babies?
> How come? I'm white . . . but I'm poor.
>   (Brown 1974).

SELF-AWARENESS IN THE PUBLIC WELFARE SETTING

The poet feels the attack of the social worker, who makes assumptions that in his position as a white male he should have no problem finding the employment he sorely needs. This worker and others who find themselves in similar positions must look closely at attitudes and assumptions they hold that may interfere with the helping process.

In chapter three the layers of understanding were introduced; they call for an understanding of human behavior and of the ethnicity of others and of oneself. The examination of self and others in this setting involves many questions; among them is the pervasive welfare question, "Why can't *they* get jobs?" Why are there so many unemployed Blacks when there are so many more opportunities than there were in the past? When are *they* going to learn to speak English and stop using their children and friends to interpret? With all the birth control available, why do *they* keep having babies? Some of them are only babies themselves. I'm like them (Black, Puerto Rican, Asian, American Indian) and I'm working; why aren't *they*? Why are there grandmothers, mothers, and daughters all without husbands?

As these questions are considered again and again, the social worker must recognize the individual recipient's responsibility for his or her own behavior and, at the same time, understand that there are indeed systemic failures that perpetuate the welfare system. Engaging in coercive activities that attempt to force adults to go to work in many ways blames the victim. The answers are to be found as each social worker develops a skillful use of each level of understanding. The final question becomes "How do I help to make a difference?"

ORGANIZATION OF THE WELFARE SYSTEM

Making a difference in a large complex system is not an easy task. A developing self-awareness must confront the realities of the welfare system. Although applicants and recipients are viewed as persons with particular needs and desires, the conditions for their eligibility for assistance are established outside of the local welfare agency where applicants and social workers meet. The rules and procedures are determined by a state division of public welfare. All assistance allowances are made in accordance with federal law and regulation, which permit a wide variation in assistance payments throughout the United States. Welfare is not limited to AFDC; it includes related services such as the food stamp program, administered by the U.S. Department of Agriculture. Cities maintain general assistance programs; some states have medical assistance for the aged, most have Medicaid. The latter is a benefit that provides payment for medical care for all financially eligible individuals and families. Special programs have addressed the needs of recent immigrants conforming to the mandates of the Refugee Act of 1980. This act provides for financial assistance to individuals and families from Cuba, Vietnam, Cambodia, Laos, and other countries.

Payments of grants and the provision of social services are administered at the state and local level. The organizational structure, however, begins at the federal level in the office of the Secretary of Health and Human Services. Such elaborate and large systems always face potential problems in coordination of the individual components and effective communication (Federico 1980). The smallest component of this system, the client, seems to be powerless in the face of such complexity. A welfare recipient who receives assistance for two sons comments upon her feelings of powerlessness:

I had no other choice but to apply for assistance. My family was no help when my husband took off. I was five months pregnant. If I ask my Income Maintenance Worker for help with a personal problem I get referred to my case worker. Sometimes I don't know who my case worker is. I had an IM worker who I never met at all.[1]

Another comments:

The system is not set up to help you. It's set up to pull you down and keep you down. They tell you they are there to help you help yourself; . . . it's not true. They are out there to keep your face in the dirt (Mauch 1972).

The social worker caught up in the vastness may have a sense of powerlessness that begins to equal that of the clients. One begins to question the real purpose of the welfare system and the ability of any one social worker to make changes. The frustration of work in a seemingly noncaring organization is expressed by a social worker in a large urban welfare agency: "No one would work if they knew what the policy is; if it was explicitly stated that we are here to pacify people so that they won't cause trouble, to let some people barely subsist so that other people can live the good life" (March 1972). This realization is often hard to take, as is the grueling work load. The result in many agencies is a constant turnover of professional staff.

The ethnic-sensitive worker who remains must understand the complexities of the organization and seek to enforce the values of the profession, which recognize the worth and dignity of all people and their capacities to change, their responsibility for themselves and others, and their need to "belong" (Morales and Sheafor 1980). The importance of these values may seem lost in the maze of the public assistance structure, but they must be remembered. Persons who apply for or receive assistance are among our most vulnerable citizens. Their worthiness is questioned continually by the mainstream society as well as by other agency staff members. "Why don't you have a job?" is repeated again and again.

In our explorations we have found no ethnic group whose members refuse to work; indeed, the perspectives on work may be different, but people do work. In the American Indian tradition work is not a good

---

[1]Conversation with an AFDC mother

thing in itself, and so many Indians work only as much as they need to (Peretti 1973). The Mexican-American may also view work as necessary for survival, but not as a value in itself (Murillo 1970), while the Japanese have a reverence for hard work and achievement (Kitano 1976). The work ethic takes on different forms in relation to ethnicity. Each form must be respected for its own uniqueness in a setting that provides help when a person is without work.

WORKFARE —AN EFFORT TOWARD
WELFARE REFORM

Continued efforts to promote workfare as a response to the welfare dilemma rest upon adherence to the work ethic. Four general propositions can be identified:

Welfare recipients should work for the benefits they receive.

Work experience will improve job skills and work habits of participants.

Requirements will discourage malingerers from applying for, or staying on, welfare.

Welfare rolls and costs will decline as malingerers drop out of welfare and employable recipients gain experience needed to obtain a job (Goodwin 1981).

A national workfare policy enacted in 1981 permits states to require recipients to work at designated jobs for their benefits. In 1984 the U.S. General Accounting Office reported that sixteen state programs had begun by early 1983. The objectives of these programs are similar to the propositions presented by Goodwin; they are intended to reduce welfare dependency, deter new applications, reduce welfare costs by requiring participants "to work off" AFDC benefits for no extra pay, and to increase clients' employability (Dickinson 1986).

As in the AFDC programs, there are variations from state to state. There are states such as Delaware, Idaho, and West Virginia in which participants are required to work off their AFDC grants fully at unpaid jobs (Dickinson 1986). The Maine WEET (Welfare, Employment, Education, and Training) program requires registration for recipients of AFDC with children over five who live in areas accessible to WEET offices. Here case managers make assessments, plan for employment, provide job search assistance, and job development and placement services (Petit and Wilcox 1986).

The goal of the California GAIN program is to improve work skills through sharpening of job-seeking skills, building self-confidence, providing on-the-job training, or the use of any other means that meets the specific needs of an individual (Swoap 1986).

Advocates for the Massachusetts ET (Employment/Training) program claim that: "this innovative welfare employment program has disproved the popular myth that welfare recipients do not want to work" (Atkins 1986). The innovative characteristic appears to be choice among the various elements present in the program. Rather than forcing recipients into "job clubs" the ET program recognizes that many persons are not ready or qualified to hold down a full-time job. Recipients may choose what they need to get a job that pays enough to support their families. The choices may range from basic education to on-the-job training to supported work (Atkins, 1986).

No matter what the plan, the ultimate goal is greater independence, a life free from the welfare system, which takes its toll upon recipients. The burden of the stigma causes embarrassment about getting food stamps. There is a sense of entrapment without any ability to break out of the system. In addition, there is the potential for guilt and shame because, no matter how hard they try to succeed, they maintain the societal stigma that devalues the poor who look to welfare for support (Goodban 1985).

Successful workfare programs report that participants are able, through education and training, to become self-sufficient and no longer in need of AFDC (Petit and Wilcox 1986). The most successful workfare programs provide skill training and academic remediation in a work-type program with supportive services. Recipients in such programs experience significant levels of improvement in employability and earnings (Sklar 1986).

The controversy over workfare began as early as 1625 when Cardinal Richelieu called for the creation of institutions in which "able-bodied poor could be employed in public works" (Goodwin 1981). It continued in Europe as the poor were required to work off the public assistance they received, and was evident in the United States as early as 1789 when Alexander Hamilton established a manufacturing society for the purpose of having persons work in exchange for public assistance (Goodwin 1981). It continues in the present as some question the actual savings in cost of public assistance or the ability of such programs to enhance the employability of welfare recipients. Civil service employees challenge the concept as workfare participants are assigned to perform the same types of tasks covered by civil service job descriptions. The labor union of state, county, and municipal employees (AFSCME) opposes workfare on displacement grounds, claiming that workfare assignments tend to displace established workers (Sklar 1986). At present it is not clear that workfare is the best road to take toward welfare reform.

The ethnic-sensitive public welfare worker must be attuned to the reality that a significant number of welfare recipients are women and families who are members of ethnic minority groups. They are often required by state workfare programs to enroll in work programs. This is coercive activity. As social workers respond to this requirement of their employment they must continually hold the values of the profession that view each client as unique and able to make responsible choices in planning for the future. When there is demand for workfare involvement, the worker must respond to the client as a person of dignity who, for the most part, shares the goal of independence intrinsic to the workfare philosophy.

ETHNIC-SENSITIVE RESPONSES

It might seem that, in this massive system burdened by rules, regulations, and procedures, ethic-sensitive practice would not be possible; not only is it possible, it is urgent. The large number of ethnic minority recipients has been recognized. At times when these recipients are most vulnerable, without power to control events about them, a social worker who is attuned to the impact of the ethnic reality and its various dispositions is important.

The Route to the Social Worker

To be a recipient of AFDC suggests failure in a society that expects self-sufficiency. Eligibility for assistance requires an absent parent or, if both are present, then one must be disabled or unemployed. In each instance there is deficiency, an inability to provide for children in the expected way. Given this requirement, who wants to be on public welfare? The route may be called voluntary, yet the circumstances suggest pain from illness or failure. Husbands and lovers walk away, leaving women to ask, "Why?" Death comes to a young father, leaving his wife and children alone. An unfortunate automobile accident leaves a mother physically handicapped. Each of these events may create eligibility for AFDC, but who would invite such pain? The trip to the agency is a response to the need to provide food, clothing, shelter, and medical care for the children. Applicants do not choose a relationship with a social worker; it is part of the procedure. Social workers must recognize this as a possibility when recipients seem to be "uncooperative." Unnecessary coercive activity must be avoided if the rights of recipients are to be respected. The directive that insists on pushing adults to work makes this difficult to achieve. In the following cases there is an undercurrent of coercive activity that appears to be unavoidable due to agency policy. Nevertheless, social workers must be aware of the values, assumptions, and principles for ethnic-sensitive practice as well as the layers of understanding. Whenever possible, attempts must be made to work simultaneously for individual and systemic change.

The Case of Marie and Hector Padilla

Marie and Hector Padilla are a young Puerto Rican couple with a six-week-old baby girl. They are eligible for Aid to Families with Dependent Children (AFDC) because Mr. Padilla has been on strike. They do not want any services offered by the agency, only the grant.

Although they are polite, friendly, and straightforward in their answers to questions, they do not respond to any attempts to discuss any problem areas such as child care, particularly because the baby is so young, nor do they have any interest in training programs. Mr. Padilla insists that they have no problem other than the fact that he is not working.

After the company went on strike Mr. Padilla asked his family, friends, neighbors, and *compadres* for help before he applied for public assistance (Ghali 1977). The welfare department was his last resort. He needs to maintain his machismo, his role of authority, as husband and father; unemployment has put a strain on those relationships (Papajohn and Spiegel 1975). However, if he does not present this potential stress as a problem, it is inappropriate for the social worker to assume that it must exist, or that they are unable to care for their child. To insist that they "accept" counseling would be viewed as coercive. Lack of cooperation may threaten eligibility. A large family network is available for support in child care; in fact, as their daughter grows she will be disciplined, when misbehaving, by any number of relatives, with her parents' approval (Papajohn and Spiegel 1975.) The strength of this ethnic family system is available to Marie and Hector. The assumptions of ethnic-sensitive practice suggest that this strength be recognized and counted as an available resource. No further direct efforts are called for, except for the continual payment of the monthly allowance of $336.[2] Considering the inadequacy of this allowance, it is suggested that the social worker give considerable thought to entering into alliance with other social work professionals, community service agencies, the Urban League, Puerto Rican action groups, and any others who may choose to join. These professionals, along with the recipients, may organize to

---

[2]AFDC grant, July 1986, New York Department of Public Welfare.

work toward legislation that would increase grants to a level that allows for a standard of living with some dignity.

One of the tasks assigned to welfare social workers is to assist clients in the management of their finances; often recipients are accused of irresponsibility because the money never lasts a whole month. One AFDC mother explains how she budgets each month:

> I get $336 each month. First I pay the rent. I never keep the money from the landlord. Then I buy food with the food stamps, and I pay the phone bill and the electric. Last month my son needed sneakers. . . . No sneakers. . . . I take anyone's leftover furniture and even curtains. If they don't fit my window I may give them away or keep them in case I move to another apartment. We eat good at the first of the month, but by the end it's really bad. Sometimes I have to borrow money from a friend.

The Case of Sally Jackson

Ms. Jackson is a burden to her social worker. No matter how she tries, Ms. Jackson is never able to learn how to manage her money. She is always running out. She is always on the brink of disaster. Like other recipients she receives her grant of $467 for her family of four, plus food stamps and Medicaid, but she still cannot seem to manage.

Sally Jackson is Black and a recipient of Aid to Families with Dependent Children. Her eligibility is based on the fact that she has three minor children. She was married at one time, but her husband deserted the family after the birth of their first child. Soon after, she established a relationship with Ray Evans, and they began to live together. They had two children. He was employed in a local factory. Unfortunately, he was abusive and Sally left him, taking her children with her.

She is thirty-two years old. Her children are twelve, ten, and eight years old. On occasion Ms. Jackson works in housekeeping in a hospital. When she works her grant is reduced in relation to her income. The procedure is very complicated, but in the end she seldom has more than $467; so, she does not pursue work heartily, although she enjoys being away from the house and with other people during the day. Work, the desired activity, is not financially worthwhile.

If Ms. Jackson were to work full time her income would be marginal, and she might lose her food stamp privileges as well as Medicaid benefits, so important when there are growing children subject to colds, contagious diseases, and broken limbs. As Ms. Jackson attempts to change her life, she finds her efforts fruitless. She feels powerless and impotent.[3] This feeling of powerlessness may be found in Blacks at all

---

[3]The preceding discussion of workfare suggests that where progressive programs are being implemented there may be a reduction of these self-defeating cycles.

social class levels, as society places all Blacks in the same single category regardless of attainment or income. The fruits of the impotence Ms. Jackson feels are a "loss of autonomy, a diminished sense of self-worth, and low self-esteem" (Chestang 1972), which are even more debilitating at her underclass level. Leon Chestang, in a discussion of "character development in a hostile environment," adds that the emotional effects originating from impotence are feelings of fear, inadequacy, and insecurity (1972). Again and again the literature alludes to the history of Blacks in this country as involving the experience of degradation and humiliation. This affects present attitudes of society and the availability of educational and occupational opportunities.

The assumptions for ethnic-sensitive practice call for attention to Ms. Jackson's problem in the present, recognizing the effects of the history of Blacks upon her situation. But, like Mr. and Mrs. Padilla, Ms. Jackson's problem is financial. As she looks to her siblings for support, as is often the custom in the Black underclass, she finds that they too are struggling with barely enough to cover their own needs. Her tenth-grade education limits her job opportunities (Willie 1974); she is "stuck" in the welfare system.

It is primarily through systemic change that Ms. Jackson's life will become less oppressive. The change must provide a reasonable income, employment with dignity, and training programs that do not carry a coercive overtone. These changes come about slowly and Ms. Jackson's problems with money are overwhelming today. But, the problem is not hers alone. The monthly allowance is not budgetable, yet families seem able to survive; how do they do it?

A group of AFDC mothers who meet together regularly may be able to share their "survival techniques" with Ms. Jackson; indeed, she may have some to contribute herself. Such a gathering recognizes the strengths in families and provides an opportunity to visit and be among friends. Ms. Jackson's attempts at employment were largely motivated by a desire to be among other adults. While efforts are made toward systemic change, Ms. Jackson's need for immediate help in making the money last as long as possible can be found among other AFDC recipients.

The grants Ms. Jackson and others receive are provided to give support to dependent children, a powerless, helpless group. They remain powerless and helpless as the program responds continually to the problems of adults (Federico 1980). Social workers must not forget that the assistance is for children and must begin to organize for change that affects their lives more directly. This effort may be as small as negotiating with the neighborhood school administration to open the gymnasium for a few hours on weekday evenings and on Saturday mornings, thereby providing a recreational resource previously unavailable for Ms. Jackson's sons and the other children in the neighborhood.

The Case of Marie Santangelo

Marie Santangelo is thirty-seven years old. She receives Aid for Families with Dependent Children for the support of her son Mike, who is seventeen years old. He is a high school senior and will graduate in a few months.

They have lived with Jerry Rossi for most of Mike's life. Jerry is unemployed but receives social security disability benefits due to a work injury. He is forty years old.

Their life together has been one of striving to make ends meet. Mr. Rossi says that he would marry Miss Santangelo but it would be too expensive; the grant from AFDC would be decreased. In a few months, however, Mike will be eighteen and no longer eligible for assistance. When it is suggested that Miss Santangelo begin to consider employment, Mr. Rossi becomes very agitated, claiming that it is not right for her to work away from home. Both Miss Santangelo and Mr. Rossi are Italian.

The reality of lost income is a threat to the Santangelo-Rossi family. But, the eligibility criteria are clear. Children are eligible for AFDC from "birth to eighteen or to twenty-one if in school, college, vocational, or technical training."[4] Mike's eighteenth birthday and graduation from high school are only a few months apart. He expects to find employment in one of the small industries in the area. His earnings will no doubt exceed the $275 that his mother receives for their support, but neither will any longer be eligible for food stamps or Medicaid.

Adherence to the assumptions and layers of understanding for ethnic-sensitive practice will alert the social worker to the possibility that Mr. Rossi's agitation when employment is suggested for Miss Santangelo may be the response to an ethnic disposition. The family has continued to be the central focus in Italian interpersonal relations. Women are expected to "take care" of their men. A majority of Italian women in Krause's study (1978) believed that women do best as wives and mothers and that true women are happiest with their husbands and children. If this is the feeling of Miss Santangelo as well, then resistance to employment is not as irrational as it seems in a system that is beginning to consider the employment of women to be a major determinant of their worthiness.

The dilemma may be compounded. Miss Santangelo, like the respondents in Krause's study, may feel that women are too emotional for some jobs and that they perform differently from men in the workplace. If this is so, then social work efforts to steer Miss Santangelo

---

[4]New Jersey Department of Human Services, Department of Public Welfare, July, 1978.

toward training and/or employment may meet with minimal success.

Miss Santangelo does have two resources immediately available: her son and Mr. Rossi. It is possible that they are willing to assume the responsibility for the support of their "wife" and mother. Since Mr. Rossi insists that work is not appropriate for his friend, then he must recognize the consequence of his position. He has been a part of this family for most of Mike's life; his discussion of marriage suggests a commitment to Miss Santangelo. A worker's insistence that she enter training or find employment is coercive activity that does not take into account the wishes of this AFDC family.

A study of community resources may reveal social service agencies, churches, or women's groups that will be able to assist the Santangelo-Rossi family when the AFDC grant has been discontinued.

In our present society it does not seem unreasonable to expect high school graduates to seek employment if they do not intend to continue their education. Mike, in fact, looks forward to the independence that will come with a job. As an Italian male adolescent moving toward emerging adulthood, he has become more involved with friends at school and in the community. He has done without many of the "extras" that are important as children grow, but he now looks forward to independence.

Solutions that please the system are not always forthcoming. The social worker must respect Miss Santangelo's decision not to work and provide her with knowledge about community resources that may be helpful to her in the future.

In each of the instances described in this chapter families are unable to carry out the instrumental functions assigned to them by society without assistance from public welfare through the Aid to Families with Dependent Children program. Ethnic-sensitive responses have been delineated. Workers must be continually sensitive to the impact of the ethnic reality on families in the underclass as they confront the continuing stigma of poverty and welfare dependency.

THE REFUGEE ACT OF 1980

With the enactment of the Refugee Act of 1980 Congress continued "the historic policy of the United States to respond to the urgent needs of persons subjected to persecution in their homelands." The objectives of the act are to provide a permanent and systematic procedure for the admission of refugees of special humanitarian concern . . . and to provide comprehensive and uniform provisions for effective resettlement and absorption of those refugees who are admitted.

Among the most recent refugees to the United States are individuals and families from countries that did not participate in the earlier streams of migration. Among these new groups are Vietnamese, Cambodians, Cubans, Haitians, Afghans, Laotians, Angolans, or Ethiopians (Kerpen 1983). Their needs are similar to the earliest arrivals: to become accustomed to the United States and to find ways by which they may be "absorbed," as the Refugee Act proposes.

In order to hasten this process the act calls for the Office of Refugee Resettlement within the Department of Health and Human Services to provide a variety of programs for resettlement and assistance. These include employment training and placement in order for refugees to achieve economic self-sufficiency as quickly as possible, opportunities to acquire English language training to encourage efficient resettlement, and cash assistance in a manner that encourages self-sufficiency. A final mandate ensures that women will have the same opportunity as men for training and instruction (Refugee Act of 1980).

Cash assistance and medical benefits are provided through established state public assistance programs. This provision makes many families eligible for Aid to Families with Dependent Children (AFDC). In order to respond to the call for assistance in learning English, job training, and placement, special centers have been established, particularly in areas of dense refugee settlement. Such centers may extend themselves to take on the roles of advocate and broker to assist refugees in encounters with social security offices, schools, and hospitals. Counseling and a variety of concrete services may be offered as well (Kerpen 1983).

The Case of Mr. and Mrs. Dinh Nguyen

Mr. and Mr. Dinh Nguyen are Vietnamese. They have a four-month-old child. Mrs. Nguyen's brother Pao lives with them. They are all quite young. Mr. Nguyen is twenty-four. His education in Vietnam was extensive and he holds what could be called a baccalaureate degree. At present, however, he is not employed, but attends the county vocational school to learn new skills. In the evening he attends an adult program for refugees.

Pao is nineteen. He is employed as a maintenance person in a local supermarket. In the evening he too attends school to learn English. Some evenings he goes to the vocational institute to learn a new trade. In Vietnam he was a factory worker.

Mrs. Nguyen is twenty-five. Her primary task is to take care of the baby. The family was sponsored by a local church. The congregation assumed responsibility for locating housing when they arrived. The house was furnished with secondhand and new items supplied by the congregation. Members have assisted with shopping for household supplies and food.

They were most helpful when the baby was born, providing the necessary clothing and furniture.

The family receives cash assistance through the state public welfare program. Their grant of $469 is based on AFDC allowance. Months before the Nguyens arrived, a local church began its efforts to sponsor a Vietnamese family. Contacts with the denomination headquarters and Church World Service led to the assignment of the Nguyen family. The congregation agreed to help in the ways described and have continued to do so. This initial institutional response to need is supported by the legislation that gives financial support to the Nguyens and Pao.

As social workers apply the assumptions for ethnic-sensitive practice in work with the Nguyen family they realize that history has had an immediate impact upon their lives. Past and present history of oppression, war, and their aftermath have caused their migration to a new country. Their ethnicity causes immediate strain as they confront an entirely new environment in which they are dependent upon the church and the welfare system for support. Strength and support may be found in relationships formed with members of the church, but the most comforting are found among other participants in the refugee assistance program. The bilingual and bicultural counselors understand the tensions that are present as the Nguyens and Pao find their way.

In the public agency workers must be aware that Asian recipients are most responsive if, at initial contact, agency functions, services, and the kinds of assistance available are made very clear (Ho 1976). Ho suggests that short-term service with concrete goals is usually needed.

Ryan (1985) supports this perspective as she discusses the needs of immigrant Chinese families. This initial concrete support along with active referral and outreach is valuable as it promotes engaging in discussion of other individual or family issues that might be withheld in response to ethnic dispositions concerning the use of social services.

The ethnic-sensitive worker will consider the life cycle position of the client, degree of acculturation, educational background, and social class—the ethnic reality (Ryan 1985).

There are those whose experience with Asian refugees reflects Ho's observations concerning short-term use of public assistance. Kerpen (1985) voices concern for the continued dependency that was not expected when Congress enacted the law in 1980. The goal was rapid economic independence or self-sufficiency for each refugee. Rather, there is evidence of continued dependency on public assistance. The call is for the reduction of welfare dependency, a call similar to that for other families who receive AFDC. Indeed, as new arrivals learn English, many leave the welfare rolls. Others are less successful in their search for jobs and training, finding inadequate resources in counseling or in the programs such as those available for Dinh Nguyen and Pao.

The Refugee Act of 1980 provides for special programs to meet the needs of particular groups of Asians; however, there are countless Asian Americans who are without the many resources available to new arrivals. Elderly Japanese, Chinese, and Koreans are hidden in many "Chinatowns" of our urban centers. Japanese families have problems with alcoholism, mental illness, and retarded children, as do other American families; yet there is a negative attitude toward mental illness in the Japanese community (Mass 1976). Chinese youth are faced with the tensions common to adolescence as well as cultural value conflicts that may arise with their Chinese-born parents (Ryan 1985). At each stage of the life cycle some Asian families are in need of various services, including public assistance. The need for systemic support is evident but this support is lacking. The tendency of Asians to hide problems because of their sense of shame and pride makes work difficult, but efforts must be pursued. Chen (1970) has presented steps that need to be taken in working toward change in the Chinese community. They are useful in other Asian communities as well: (1) inform the general public and the Chinese community of problems and the need for changes, (2) develop community resources to cope with the existing problems by initiating social programs, (3) promote social action, (4) initiate constructive legislation, (5) develop leadership, (6) educate bilingual social workers, and (7) conduct research and surveys into the changing Chinese-American family structure. These steps enable the ethnic-sensitive worker to move in an organized fashion toward change in neglected Asian communities; the effort may well begin with an Asian recipient of public assistance.

SUMMARY

This chapter has considered the assumptions and principles for ethnic-sensitive practice in the public welfare setting. We recognize that recipients for the most part do not wish to be a part of this system. They are continually negatively viewed for behavior that is acceptable at other social class levels. There is continual coercive activity, which provokes a sense of powerlessness, and a budget allowance that barely meets minimal requirements for survival. Many recipients are women and their children; often they are members of ethnic minority groups and are judged more harshly than other recipients. The ethnic-sensitive worker must recognize these factors and work continually for systemic change that will support voluntary employment training programs and provide grants to enable parents to provide their children with nutritious meals all month, appropriate clothing as the seasons change, and a few of the extras that make childhood a joyful experience.

REFERENCES

Atkins, Charles M. 1986. 20,000 choose paycheck over welfare check. *Public Welfare* 44:20–22.

Brown, Sam Ervin. 1974. From "Poetic expressions of a white urban family." Submitted in partial fulfillment of course requirements for The Urban Family, Rutgers University, School of Social Work, Fall.

Chen, Pei-Ngor. 1970. The Chinese community in Los Angeles. *Social Casework* 51:591–598.

Chestang, Leon. 1972. *Character development in a hostile environment*. Chicago: The School of Social Service Administration, The University of Chicago.

Dickinson, Nancy S. 1986. Which welfare strategies work? *Social Work* 31:266–272.

Federico, Ronald C. 1980. *The social welfare institution—an introduction*. Lexington, MA: D.C. Heath and Co.

Ghali, Sonia Badillo. 1977. Cultural sensitivity and the Puerto Rican client. *Social Casework* 58:459–468.

Goodban, Nancy. 1985. *The psychological impact of being on welfare*. Social Service Review 59:403–422.

Goodwin, Leonard. 1981. Can workfare work? *Public Welfare* 39:19–25.

Harrington, Michael. 1962. *The other America—poverty in the United States*. Baltimore: Penguin Books.

Harrington, Michael. 1984. *The new American poverty*. New York: Holt, Rinehart, and Winston.

Ho, Man Keung. 1976. Social work with Asian Americans. *Social Casework* 57:195–201.

Kerpen, Karen S. 1983. Working with Refugees. *Public Welfare* 41:18–22.

Kerpen, Karen S. 1985. Refugees on welfare—is the dependency rate really a problem? *Public Welfare* 43:21–25.

Kitano, Harry H. L. 1976. *Japanese American*. 2d ed. Englewood Cliffs, NJ: Prentice-Hall, Inc.

Krause, Corinne Azen. 1978. *Grandmothers, mothers, and daughters: an oral history study of ethnicity, mental health, and continuity of three generations of Jewish, Italian, and Slavic-American women*. New York: American Jewish Committee.

Lemann, Nicholas. 1986. The origins of the underclass. *The Atlantic Monthly* 257:31–56, and 258:54–68.

Mass, Amy Iwasaki. 1976. Asians as individuals: the Japanese community. *Social Casework* 57:160–164.

Mauch, Joan. 1972. Voices never heard, faces seldom seen. *Public Welfare* 30(3), Summer.

Mencher, Samuel. 1967. *Poor law to poverty—economic security policy in Britain and the United States*. Pittsburgh: University of Pittsburgh Press.

Morales, Armando, and Sheafor, Bradford. 1980. *Social work—a profession of many faces*. 2d ed. Boston: Allyn and Bacon, Inc.

Murillo, Nathan. 1970. The Mexican-American family. In *Chicano—social and psychological perspectives*, edited by Carrol Hernandez, Marsha J. Haug, and Nathaniel N. Wagner. St. Louis: The C. V. Mosby Co.

Papajohn, John, and Spiegel, John. 1975. *Transactions in families*. San Francisco: Jossey-Bass, Inc.

Peretti, Peter O. 1973. Enforced acculturation and Indian-White relations. *The Indian Historian* 6 (1), Winter.

Petit, Michael R., and Wilcox, Linda A. 1986. Inestimable—but tangible—results in Maine. *Public Welfare* 44:13–15.

Rein, Martin. 1972. Work incentives and welfare reform. *Urban and Social Change Review* 5:54–58.

Ryan, Angela Shen. 1985. Cultural factors in casework with Chinese-Americans. *Social Casework* 66:333–340.

Sermabeikian, Patricia. 1975. "What's so bad about being poor?" In *A little piece of the world*. Submitted in partial fulfillment of course requirements for The Urban Family, Rutgers University, School of Social Work, Fall.

Sklar, Morton H. 1986. Workfare: is the honeymoon over—or yet to come? *Public Welfare* 44:30–32.

Swoap, David B. 1986. Broad support buoys California's GAIN. *Public Welfare* 44:24–27.

Time Magazine. The American underclass. August 29, 1977.

Wilensky, Harold L., and Lebeaux, Charles N. 1958. *Industrial society and social welfare*. New York: Russell Sage Foundation.

Willie, Charles V. 1974. The Black family and social class. *American Journal of Orthopsychiatry* 44:50–60.

CHAPTER
9

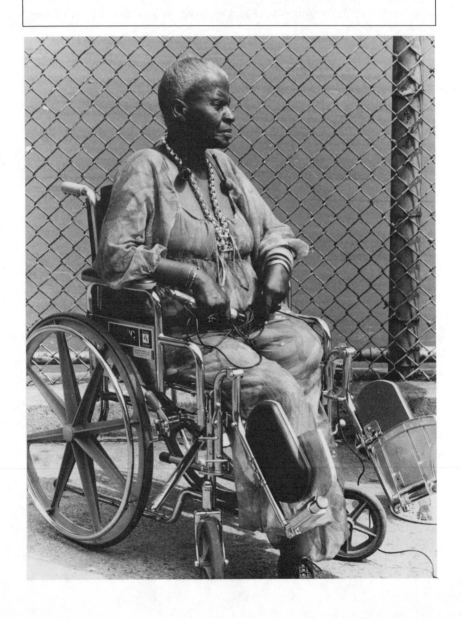

Ethnic-Sensitive Practice in Health Care

Social work's involvement in health care has a long and honorable history. Indeed, it has been suggested that the roots of social medicine, medicine that looks beyond the diseased body to the social antecedents and consequences of illness, are to be found in social work in health care (Rosen 1974).

"Medical social work," a term more commonly used in the past than in the present, was introduced at Massachusetts General Hospital by Dr. Richard Cabot, a physician of vision who suggested that: "The average practitioner is used to seeing his patients flash by him like shooting stars—out of darkness into darkness. He has been trained to focus upon a single suspected organ till he thinks of his patients almost like disembodied diseases" (Cabot 1915, p. 33).

Cabot looked to social work to help identify and intervene in those social factors behind "individual suffering." He recognized that work pressures, political organization, and inadequate income are factors that affect health and illness. His vision was far-reaching. He understood early what has become more evident and intensified since the days when he invited Ida Cannon to begin a social work department at Massachusetts General Hospital. Since then health care has become more complex, more specialized, and more fragmented. Unprecedented advances in technology continue to hold out hopes for cure and relief of distress. At the same time, specialization intensifies the likelihood that health care practitioners will focus on the diseased organ, having limited training and time to look beyond that organ at the person suffering from the disease.

Social work in health care is fast-paced and most often crisis oriented. Intervention involves work with people who may be experiencing acute pain and undergoing traumatic procedures about which they have limited understanding. Both client and practitioner are struggling with the ever-present threat of loss of life. Psychosocial problems inevitably precede, accompany, or follow illness. Health care social work is focused on these concerns. Psychologically and culturally induced responses to pain and illness are often evident. Social work is committed to functioning as a professional, humane link between patients, families, health care providers, and the political and social system that shapes how care is rendered and what care is available. Included is attention to prevention and intervention.

> Physicians care for ailing organs. Hospitals provide facilities for diagnosis and for acute care. A variety of rehabilitation specialists assist in the development of occupational or physical or other faculties. No one seems to be able to deal with the whole person and all of that person's complex needs. . . . These tasks should be carried out by social workers (Dinerman, Schlesinger, and Wood 1980, p. 14).

The assumptions of ethnic-sensitive practice presented in chapter five, and the layers of understanding delineated in chapter three provide important perspectives for practice in this area. In this chapter the components of ethnic-sensitive practice are integrated with some key concepts that aid in understanding the problems and experiences of sick people and their encounters with the health care delivery system. These include: (1) self-awareness including insight into one's own ethnicity,(2) health and illness behavior, (3) the view of illness as deviance, (4) the sick role, (5) the cultural roots of illness behavior, (6) prevailing patterns in the organization and financing of health care, (7) the relationship between socioeconomic status and illness, (8) the role of social and community networks in curing and caring, and (9) populations at risk as a framework for practice.

SELF-AWARENESS

Chapter two stressed that the disciplined and aware worker remains one of the profession's major tools. The ability to be nonjudgmental, to reach out, and to make use of self-awareness to help others to cope is essential. In health care, self-awareness is focused on understanding one's own feelings about physical disability, pain, emotional turmoil, disfigurement, the changes in quality of life engendered by much illness, and death itself. Also important is a sense of professional identity. For health care social work is an interdisciplinary endeavor that inevitably challenges the social worker's competence and "reason for being" on the health care scene.

The accelerating rate of technological change in health care has brought about heretofore unimagined changes in life saving procedures. Renal dialysis, kidney transplants, some surgical procedures, and chemotherapy all have the potential of prolonging life while dramatically altering the quality of that life. Concern about the ethical and moral implications of using machines to sustain the life of comatose people are daily topics in the media. These and related issues were the subject of a major commission appointed by the President (1983). Religious and ethnic precepts provide no clear direction, as churches and other religious institutions have taken stands on both sides of related issues.

Whether a woman has the right to make decisions concerning her own body, as implied in the legalization of abortion, has become a social issue with heated proponents on both sides.

Social workers inevitably become involved with people who must make decisions on these matters, and must be ever on guard against imposing their own feelings. For example, Holden (1980) points out that the staff in renal dialysis units often do not offer patients a real choice. Social workers need to advocate for patient choice. Eloquent, meaningful advocacy can only be carried out by workers who are keenly aware of their own feelings on these matters.

The views of some other cultures on the preservation of life are different from those often espoused by Western medicine. For example, American Indians do not always seek to prolong life (Coulehan 1980). The distinction between life and death is viewed differently in different cultures. Social workers must continually examine their own experiences and recognize that their own deeply ingrained dispositions readily come to the fore as they attempt to help their clients to struggle with these issues.

The legalization of abortion has created a moral dilemma for those workers whose own belief systems are at variance with the view that women have the ultimate right to make decisions affecting their own bodies. Social workers who view abortion as sinful need to be on guard against imposing their values on those who seek their help in making decisions. Some workers who do not believe in the right to abortion ask to be excused from working with women having abortions. This reflects appropriate self-awareness. Workers who feel strongly that to give birth to an unwanted child is a grave error are similarly obliged to be sure that they do not impose their own bias on clients who are in the throes of making excruciatingly painful decisions.

Changing life-styles in regard to sexuality sometimes offend social workers whose own background has not exposed them to sexually active teenagers, lesbians, gay men, or people living together without benefit of wedlock. We have seen many students struggle in the effort to present a nonjudgmental stance when working with poor teenagers who are having their second or third out-of-wedlock babies. The clash between their own value system and view of what's "best" for children, and the lives of these teenagers is extensive, calling for profound self-examination and skill in working with the client in terms of the way the client has identified the problem.

It is not uncommon for social work students, particularly those of middle-class background, to describe their first exposure to ghetto clients as involving culture shock. On closer questioning, we find that the reaction of shock is often triggered by adolescent sexuality and out-of-wedlock pregnancy.

For those workers who in their own lives do not call on God or other supernatural beings for help the type of faith expressed by those who do can be unsettling. Such workers need to think and feel through how faith might sustain others through trauma.

Social work in health care is intrinsically an interdisciplinary endeavor. Those working in hospitals, clinics, and other health settings often resent their relative lack of authority and autonomy, and the degree of control accorded physicians. These feelings may be accompanied by confusion about their sphere of expertise. At the same time they need the confidence that goes with assumption of the advocacy, broker, and mediator roles. This is not easy to achieve when working with physicians or hospital administrators.

Advocating for the poor, for those who do not speak English, and for those who have greater faith in the spirits than in modern medicine requires a high degree of self-awareness and comfort with the identity "social worker."

Members of minority groups have a special struggle as they try to acquire a comfortable sense of autonomy and competence vis-a-vis dominant professionals who may well represent the dominant majority groups. Lister (1982) has identified how related factors can interfere with interdisciplinary work.

CONCEPTUAL FORMULATIONS FOR
HEALTH CARE AND THE ETHNIC REALITY

We begin this discussion by presenting two case examples. The context in which care is rendered, the health problems presented, and the class and ethnic group membership of the involved people vary considerably. Despite this divergence, it shall become evident that some common themes emerge.

> Mr. Mangione, a fifty-five-year-old Italian man, is referred to the hospital social work department by the department of physical medicine. He is said to be "resisting" rehabilitation efforts. The social work department is asked to explore the basis for his reluctance and to help in eliciting his cooperation in the treatment plan.
>
> Victim of a stroke, Mr. Mangione has undergone considerable rehabilitation therapy. His speech, though still slightly slurred, is readily understood. He walks quite well, though he still has a slight limp.
>
> He thinks he is ready to return to his job as a clerk in a local hardware store. He is refusing to undergo any more rehabilitation therapy, feeling he has had enough.
>
> In exploring the situation the worker discovers that Mr. Mangione's employer agrees that Mr. Mangione is now capable of working in the store. However, he has let Mr. Mangione know that he does wish that he "would speak just a little better so that the customers don't know there's anything wrong with him."
>
> The staff in physical medicine is frustrated. They know that with just a bit more effort he could improve considerably. "We've put in so much time, we don't want him to let us down now."

Coulehan (1980) cites the case of Tommie Chee, a thirty-eight-year-old Navajo man who lives on a 25,000-square-mile reservation.

> Mr. Chee, a married man, employed at a boarding school dormitory, left his job, feeling too sick to work. He had chronic low back pain and insomnia. His appearance deteriorated, and he would often not return home for several days at a time. At one point he was found wandering aimlessly in the desert, near the family camp.
>
> On hospitalization, a diagnosis of endogenous depression was made. Antidepressant medication was prescribed, and he was referred to a mental health clinic in a town sixty-five miles away from home. He did not keep clinic appointments or take his medication. Over the next period of time he got worse.
>
> Following this the family engaged a shaker. He thought Mr. Chee had married into the wrong clan, was possessed by the ghost of his mother's brother, and thought too much, thus lowering his resistance and allowing the

ghost to gain possession. After a Nine Day Sing, Chee was cured of possession. Following this he returned to work and was relieved of symptoms.

These examples illustrate the diverse expectations and prescriptions related to illness. Mr. Mangione considers himself "cured" when he feels able to function. This is at odds with the view of others close to him. Mr. Chee does not get better until traditional healers help him. In both situations, social workers are obliged to be aware of these divergencies. Illness behavior varies in other respects.

In some groups people are expected to be stoic when experiencing pain (Zborowski 1952). In others, distress is vigorously expressed. A set of symptoms consisting of tearing off one's clothing in public, screaming, and falling into a semiconscious state while twitching is considered a culturally recognized cry for help when people are experiencing a lot of strain. This set of symptoms, described as an *ataque*, is not uncommon among Puerto Ricans on the mainland (Garrison 1977; Kumabe, Nishida, and Hepworth 1985). Mechanic (1978) suggests that: "Illness, illness behavior, and reaction to the ill are aspects of an adaptive social process in which participants are often actively striving to meet their social roles and responsibilities, to control their environment, and to make their everyday circumstances less uncertain and, therefore, more tolerable and predictable."

Mr. Mangione, Mr. Chee, and people who experience *ataques* are responding to personal stress. They are all seeking means to relieve stress in ways that are consonant with their personal histories and with how the ethnic and class group in which they are enmeshed tend to deal with that stress.

Italians are said to be particularly concerned with the immediate relief of discomfort (Zborowski 1952). Many American Indians attribute disease to a variety of extrahuman forces which must be dealt with if the causes of the illness are to be removed (Coulehan 1980). Analogous beliefs are held by many Hispanics (Garrison 1977; Samora 1978; Stenger-Castro 1978).

The problems of all of the people described can be diagnosed and understood in varying terms. *Ataques* are variously diagnosed as schizophrenia, as the state of being possessed, and as hysteria (Garrison 1977).

The examples cited suggest that they must be viewed within the cultural contexts of the people's lives. Understanding of the interplay between ethnically derived attitudes toward health and illness and biopsychosocial factors are critical to accurate assessment and intervention (Kumabe, Nishida, and Hepworth 1985). How these conceptions aid in assessing and developing intervention strategies will be considered in various sections of this chapter.

Illness as Deviance, Sick Role, and Illness Behavior

With few exceptions, almost all groups and societies view illness as a negative phenomenon. Whether illness is perceived in purely physical terms—as pain and injury—or at an emotional level—as in the case of extreme anxiety, depression, or disorientation—illness involves discomfort and disruption. When people are sick, they are usually totally or partially unable to go about their daily business.

For these reasons, illness has been characterized as "legitimated deviance." Because of its disruptive effects all societies and social groups define the rights and obligations associated with being ill, and develop mechanisms to control illness and its social consequences.

Closely related to the concept of illness as deviance is the concept of the sick role. Parsons's (1951) initial formulation, though considerably extended and critiqued, is incisive. There are four key elements: (1) since people do not choose to be ill, they are usually not held responsible for their illness, but curative processes independent of their desire to get well are essential for recovery (e.g., penicillin, not motivation, will "cure pneumonia," and only an appendectomy will serve to prevent the negative consequences of appendicitis), (2) while ill, people are excused from carrying out their obligations, (3) this exemption is contingent on the "sufferer's recognition that illness is an undesirable state not to be maintained," and (4) the sick person is obliged to seek competent help.

Some of the criticism and extensions of these formulations are particularly relevant for social workers in the health arena. Freidson (1970) suggests that the view is limited to Western conceptions of the doctor-patient relationship and that not all groups share the view that all sick people are to be exempt from carrying out their ordinary responsibilities. He suggests that Parsons's perspective focuses on acute illness, assumes the availability of cure, and does not allow for analysis of what happens to those who are chronically ill. Important is the notion of stigma (a spoiled identity) (Goffman 1963). Those with visible physical handicaps, with incurable illness, or with illness for which they are held accountable (e.g., venereal disease) develop a negative sense of self and are often treated negatively.

Rehabilitation efforts are frequently targeted to minimize the discomforts of the nonafflicted, who want the disabled person to conform to their vision of normality. An example is having blind people face the persons whom they are addressing. Rehabilitation agencies are in the business of defining what is proper recovery (Freidson 1972).

Ethnicity, the Sick Role, and Health and Illness Behavior

Illness behavior has been defined as the ". . . varying perceptions, thoughts, feelings, and acts affecting the personal and social meaning of symptoms, illness, disabilities, and their consequences" (Mechanic 1977, p. 79).

The relevance of these conceptions for social work practice in health care are illustrated by the cases presented. The situation in which Mr. Mangione finds himself points to differing views on what it means to be "well" and what "competent help" means. He considers himself sufficiently well to sell hardware. But, in the view of his employer, a slight limp or slurring of speech may be discomforting to customers. The staff of the Department of Physical Medicine wants to do "their thing." When he refuses further treatment, Mr. Mangione is preventing them from showing what they can do. Perhaps much more improvement could be effected.

What is the social worker's obligation? First and foremost, workers must assess the basis of the client's wish. Is Mr. Mangione fearful he will lose his wife's respect as head of the household if he continues to be dependent? This holds considerable importance for Italians of their generation. Is the worker aware that the medical opinion is only one among many? Can the staff be helped to recognize that Mr. Mangione has fulfilled many of the obligations of the patient role? Keeping in mind these kinds of considerations is likely to facilitate the effort to help Mr. Mangione arrive at a decision congruent with his sense of himself, his need to continue work, and the way in which his disability is perceived by his own ethnic and class group. It is most likely that, economically, he cannot afford to continue treatment. As a fifty-five-year-old, semi-skilled, working-class man, he has little chance of finding another job. A number of factors, previously discussed, determine whether intervention will be effective.

First, social workers need to be aware of how their own ethnic and class dispositions affect their positions concerning the degree of rehabilitation efforts considered appropriate. If they have internalized the view that "total rehabilitation" or recovery is a desired goal, they may characterize Mr. Mangione's reaction as "pathological;" or "resistant." Perhaps in their view he is really trying to get out of working, hoping he'll be fired and eligible for long-term disability payments. Or how do they really feel about incorporating the handicapped into the work force? How have they felt about and dealt with handicapped people in their own work settings? Is there a way they can sensitize other staff members and other patients with problems similar to those Mr. Mangione is experiencing? Is the staff aware of different ethnic and class dispositions toward the process of physical rehabilitation? The "stoicism" of some older Americans and the volatility of some Italians and Jews may well have a bearing on their views toward this issue. Can efforts to enhance such understanding be built into staff seminars? Would patients of varying ethnic and class groups benefit from group counseling?

Is there a way in which the social worker can reach employers to explore the problems they experience when the handicapped return to work? Perhaps Mr. Mangione would be too embarrassed to have the social worker contact his employer. But the ethnic-sensitive social worker might think about joining with physiotherapists, other rehabilitation specialists, and representatives of such groups as the Chamber of Commerce in organizing educational and discussion sessions to interpret and share issues.

In the case of Mr. Chee, both Western physicians and native healers viewed his illness as disruptive. Marked differences prevailed as to "who the appropriate healers are." The fact that mental health clinics, removed from the center of the community, are perceived as alien has been frequently documented, as has the positive role played by folk healers. Social workers who view folk ministrations as "mumbo jumbo" or, even worse, fail to be informed of their existence, will not gain the trust required for work with people who hold strong adherence to such belief systems.

The discussion to this point has stressed that many health beliefs and behaviors—both those congruent with Western medicine and other systems—have ethnic, class, and cultural roots.

It has been suggested that: "Culture exerts its most fundamental and far-reaching influence through the categories we employ to understand and respond to sickness" (Kleinman 1978). Considerable evidence exists to support this assertion. Differences between Western and traditional precepts may be profound.

The Nature of the American Health Care Delivery System

The American system is in large measure an outgrowth of our reverence for science and technology and the conviction that nature can be mastered. It is secular and rational and future oriented (Parsons 1951). The belief systems of many middle-class people representing various ethnic groups are reasonably congruent with this view (Greenblum 1974; Zborowski 1952). This is particularly true of Jews, who have a long history of extensive concern with matters of health, a concern attributed to "the sense of precariousness" and fear for survival related to centuries of dispersal and persecution (Howe 1975).

Zborowski (1952) and others (e.g., Greenblum 1974) have suggested that these cultural themes manifest themselves in a volatile, emotional response to pain accompanied by a concern about how the illness will affect the future. Medical specialists of all sorts are highly valued and their advice sought frequently.

Consider the following example as a case in point.

The Case of the Jewish Adolescent

A fifteen-year-old Jewish boy had been diabetic since early childhood. The son of parents who are both professionals, he was a good student who knew that he was expected to go to college.

His parents were solicitous and highly attuned to every nuance of the disease. His mother was particularly solicitous, fussing a lot about the diet as well as the mildest symptoms. He was seen by the "best" internists and frequent consultation was sought. His good adaptation to the illness was noted by doctors, relatives, and friends alike. He was a good athlete, affable and outgoing. While admiring this, his parents let him know that he should not "overdo;" at the same time visiting grandparents were admonished not to remind him of his illness or suggest that he restrict his activity.

During his sophomore year in high school he began to neglect his school work and found many excuses to not go to school. He seemed somewhat distracted and anxious, despite the fact that symptoms had considerably abated and the disease was well controlled. When anxiety increased to the point at which he virtually stopped going to school, psychiatric care was sought. The evaluation revealed that the young man was extremely worried about how he would be able to function in a year or two, when he would be expected to go off to school and care for himself.

A number of factors have converged to generate a crisis. The adolescent boy, long dependent because of his illness, became fearful at a point in life when increasing independence is expected. The family's handling of the illness with extensive concern and some degree of overprotectiveness is in part related to ethnic dispositions to health, illness, and the parenting role.

Could an ethnic-sensitive perspective on the part of health care professionals have helped to avert a crisis? Perphaps the parents could have been helped to minimize the "shopping" for specialist care, thus reducing the ongoing attention to the illness. And how about their expectations for achievement? Could they have been helped to reduce the mixed messages? "You're so sick, my dear, but we expect you to excel anyway!"

There are other views of illness. Illness is variously viewed as a punishment for sin (Samora 1978; Stenger-Castro 1978), as a function of supernatural forces, as "disharmony" (Coulehan 1980), as a force to be mastered, or as a fact to be passively accepted. Many tribal cultures make no distinction between religion and medicine. Healing experiences are an integral part of community life. Harmony—of people with nature, with each other, and with gods—is the desired state. Symptoms or disease states are viewed as reflections of underlying disharmony. This disharmony may be caused by witchcraft, spirits, storms, or animal contamination (Coulehan 1980).

Analogous beliefs and related health practices are found among Puerto Ricans and Chicanos and many Vietnamese, Cambodians, and Laotians. These groups also use non-Western healers. In fact, among many members of these groups, there is a marked tendency to use both folk and Western healers simultaneously (Fuchs and Bashur 1975; Garrison 1977; Lazarow 1979; Schultz 1982).

Puerto Ricans use healers known as espiritistas, who claim to have supernatural inspiration they bring to bear on health and illness. "There is a strong belief that any individual jealous of the achievements or abilities of another, in love, business, or politics can arrange to have an evil spell cast on the adversary (Wintrob 1973). Spiritist treatment procedures focus on exorcising harmful spiritual influences and strengthening benign spiritual influences.

Many Mexican-American beliefs about health relate to the view that God, the Creator of the universe, is omnipotent. Personal destiny is subject to God's judgment, and suffering is a consequence of having sinned and a punishment (*castigo*) for disobeying God's law. Witchcraft also plays a part in this belief system. The practice of *curanderismo* invokes the belief that the natural folk illnesses that commonly afflict people within the Mexican-American culture can be cured by a *curandero* (folk healer), who has been chosen for this mission by God (Stenger-Castro 1978).

Schultz (1982) reviews the medical belief systems of the Vietnamese, Laotians, and Cambodians. Each embodies three categories of healers including traditional and Western. Magic as a source of illness and cure is a common theme. Ancestral spirits are thought to play protective as well as malevolent roles.

As Vietnamese, Laotian, and Cambodian refugees settle in this country they experience conflict and misunderstanding. Some seek links to traditional healers, even if these are at some distance from their homes. Others, though using Western systems, experience conflict and fear, especially in respect to some procedures. For example, laboratory tests involving taking blood are feared. For, to some members of this culture, blood is thought to be replenished slowly and doctors are expected to be competent without the benefit of laboratory work.

The extent to which these types of belief systems are held by those who also use Western health care systems, and the social worker's role is of major concern here.

Interviews with Anglo social workers in a Colorado hospital suggested how frequently these traditional belief systems appear. The following type of situation is illustrative.

> A Chicano woman who uses the services of a neighborhood health center for routine care for herself and her children one day voiced the opinion that a lizard had entered her stomach. The social worker, though attentive, did not assume that extensive pathology was present, though she did not rule this out. On subsequent visits, she talked some more with the woman. She seemed well and no further mention was made of the lizard.[1]

In explaining this situation to one of us,the social worker noted her awareness of Chicano health belief systems, and the fact that many clinic patients used *curanderos* to rid themselves of the visits of the spirits. She also knew that, by and large, Anglos were not privy to the information she obtained, and so she "stayed out of that area." Mexican-American patients fear ridicule when they express such beliefs. Further, in some areas *curanderos* are subject to prosecution for practicing medicine illegally, despite the fact that in many places folk healers have been invited to join the health care team of the "official" health care delivery system.

The ethnic-sensitive social worker has many options when working with such populations. Our informant respected the client's belief system and did not impose a definition of pathology. The "joining" of traditional and Western healers has been proposed in many contexts. Some have suggested a role for the *culture specialist* in crisis intervention (Campos and Podell 1979). They describe such a specialist as someone who is trained to recognize cultural universals and variations. This knowledge enables the worker to discover the relevant cultural factors as the psychiatric institution interfaces with patients from many diverse cultures, and to communicate these to the clinical staff responsible for the patient's treatment. They point out that social workers have traditionally interpreted cultural factors in team deliberations. Ethnic-

---

[1]Conversation with Jane Collins, director, and staff of the Department of Clinical Social Work, Denver General Hospital, 1978.

sensitive social workers, attuned to the cultural roots of illness behavior, will continue to play such a role and attempt to effect administrative and attitudinal changes that facilitate attention to these matters. In chapter five we presented the case of a Chicano woman who fled the delivery room, fearing alien surroundings. We suggested how some alteration in delivery room practices could accommodate the needs of this woman and others who are likely to have similar fears. This kind of structural intervention is critical as is attention to ethnic based illness behavior.

Other examples of intervention at the systemic level can be presented. Cultural sensitivity training can alert emergency room personnel who see Hispanics suffering from *ataques*. Mental health staffs who serve American Indians must be alert to the high risk of noncompliance when recommending treatment modalities that do not include the family and community networks in intervention. Psychiatrists who may interpret the behavior of the Jewish diabetic boy (referred to earlier) as a manifestation of pathological, infantile dependency needs should be educated about the ethnic roots of Jewish health behavior. While excessive dependency may be a part of the picture, its origin in the disease itself, which does require more than the usual dependence on others, must be understood. The ambivalence about dependence and independence, spurred by the Jews' particular fear that illness will affect survival and achievement, must also be understood. These considerations all require extensive knowledge of human behavior and values, understanding of how the culture shapes behavior toward illness, and the social context in which care is rendered.

Health Care Organization: Providers and Financing

The social worker is obliged to understand the social policies governing health behavior. This has been presented as the third "layer of understanding" (see chapter three). Volumes have been written on each of these topics (e.g., Freeman, Levine, and Reeder 1979; Fuchs 1974; Mechanic 1978, Schlesinger 1985). The following case situations, though by no means illustrative of all of the complexity of our delivery system, exemplify some of the issues and dilemmas faced by many Americans.

The Case of the Jankowitch Family

The Jankowitches are a Polish working-class family. Mr. Jankowitch is employed as a semiskilled laborer in a small factory. Mrs. Jankowitch is a housewife. They have three children, ages three, six, and nine, and live in a suburban community about fifty miles from the nearest big city.

John, the three-year old, developed a high fever, sore throat, and aching limbs. His parents noted that he bruised easily. After a week of persistent symptoms, they took him to see the family doctor, who said John must be hospitalized immediately for a diagnostic workup.

Test results confirmed what the doctor had feared. John had leukemia. Treatment for this condition has progressed considerably. However, he needs extensive ongoing treatment. The nearest hospital equipped to render the care he needs is fifty miles away.

These processes have set into motion a round of trauma. First, there was the confirmation of a dreaded diagnosis. Will the child live, and for how long? The treatments (usually chemotherapy) may produce nausea, hair loss, and other complications.

The horror of the diagnosis is compounded by involvement with a maze of specialists in a distant city. The hospital is a research center, so most of the actual cost of care is covered. There is, however, the cost of travel and babysitters for the other children, and time lost from work when Mr. Jankowitch accompanies his wife and child to the hospital.

The social worker and medical staff at the hospital are kind and caring. But distance precludes their making home visits, or maintaining close ties with the family physician, whom the family has come to trust.

The social worker understands their difficulty. Despite the reluctance of many Poles to share intimate feelings with "formal caretakers," she is able to help them to communicate their fear and hurt. She is aware that the costs not covered are a burden and offers to find sources of help. This proud Polish family, accustomed to taking care of themselves and not asking for help, is burdened with this additional insult to their integrity.

The Case of Mrs. Owens

Mrs. Owens, a Black childless widow in her early seventies, lives with a widowed sister. Her husband and she had been accustomed to a comfortable working-class life-style. She has a small pension and, although she is eligible for health services under Medicare because of her age, her income makes her ineligible for services available to Medicaid recipients.

Mrs. Owens has hypertension, arteriosclerotic heart disease, and mild diabetes. Although able to carry out minor chores, she tires easily and can no longer shop for herself. Her sister, somewhat younger than Mrs. Owens, is also frail but continues to do domestic work several times a week. Some nieces and nephews who live nearby help out by taking the women shopping and to church.

Mrs. Owens's medical condition is not considered acute. This disqualifies her from receiving regular homemaker services under the Medicare program.

On her regular visits to the hospital outpatient clinic she shares with the social worker her concern about needing some help at home. Unable to locate a source of funding for ongoing home health or homemaker services, the social worker asks whether Mrs. Owens would consider going to live in a home for the aged. Mrs. Owens vigorously rejects this suggestion.

Both families suffer because of the organization of the health care system. Health care is provided in a variety of organizations and contexts. Many Americans still receive the bulk of their care from private practitioners, working alone or in small groups, who provide services for a fee. But, other modes of practice are on the increase. These range from health maintenance organizations, to neighborhood health centers, to hospital-based practice. Some, such as neighborhood health centers, are primarily designed to serve the poor.

Hospitals vary in complexity, function, and auspice. They range from the large university-affiliated research centers, like the one to which John Jankowitch was sent, to community hospitals such as the one attended by Mrs. Owens, to those focusing on care in one problem area.

The sources of funding are complex, ranging from voluntary contributions, to such publicly sponsored programs as Medicare and Medicaid, to reimbursement through private insurance carriers (e.g., Blue Cross/Blue Shield Major Medical). Medicare covers approximately 40% of health care costs incurred by those over sixty-five years of age. Medicaid financing is uneven and contingent on state funding matches. There are many programs often termed categorical. These focus on such services as maternal and child health, renal dialysis, and services for the developmentally disabled.

There is no question that the poor and many members of minority groups suffer from comparatively limited availability and accessibility of services. The United States is the only major industrialized nation that does not have some kind of comprehensive system of national health insurance or other ways of assuring access to care to all, regardless of ability to pay.

Medical specialization is extensive. At least twenty-two approved medical specialties have been recognized (Mechanic 1978). In addition there are the nurses, physiotherapists, social workers, technicians, physicians' assistants, and many others. The availability of folk healers in some groups has already been noted.

Negotiation of this complex, fragmented system, in which the availability and quality of care is in no small measure related to residence, social class, and ethnicity, can be highly problematic. The problems faced by the Jankowitch family only begin to illustrate what confronts a family when serious illness strikes.

It is unlikely that any country could make the specialized care needed for an illness such as leukemia available in every community hospital. But a program of national health insurance would ease the burden as would the ready community availability of networks of families with similar problems. The principles of practice presented in chapter five suggest that workers assigned to such families can move beyond the traditional counseling role, though that role is basic and essential.

People who view illness as an "act of God" or as punishment need help in expressing these feelings, or workers may need to help them to utilize their churches and their community networks to deal with grief in culturally syntonic ways.

When older children afflicted with leukemia or other dreaded diseases return to school they may be bald, frightened, and feel ill. Their teachers and their fellow students may need some help in adapting to the youngster experiencing these difficulties. Programs designed to help the schools to deal with these issues are most helpful.[2]

The case of Mrs. Owens illustrates some of the absurdities of present delivery and organizational mechanisms. Because the system is focused on making provisions for acute care, the needs of the chronically ill who could well sustain themselves with some help are overlooked. Mechanic (1978) makes a succinct statement on the issues.

> While aging is experienced as a personal crisis, it is largely socially caused. Since it is unlikely that we have the capacity or will to set back social trends, remedies must lie in developing group solutions that build the resources, coping capacities, supports, and involvement of the aged. While the United States invests vast resources in the medical care of the aged, these are devoted almost exclusively to staving off the infirmities and disabilities of old age or to long-term institutional care. Only meager resources are invested to maintain the social integration of the aged, to protect them from loneliness and inactivity, to insure adequate nutrition, or to assist them in retaining a respectable identity. Quality of life of the aged could be enhanced if some of the resources now wasted on relatively pointless technological efforts were invested in programs to repair old social networks among the aged or to devise entirely new ones. The population of retired people have enormous resources of their own that would be valuable assets once such a program were initiated. What is needed is the construction of a basic model; the aged themselves could then do the rest (1978, p. 308).

Mrs. Owens's rejection of placement in a home for the aged was quite appropriate, given her physical and mental state, the availability of caring relatives, and her participation in her church.

Prevailing emphases, such as those noted by Mechanic, constrain the potential for humane attention to her needs. Aside from offering Mrs. Owens the opportunity to ventilate, what is the social worker's responsibility? The principles of practice presented in this book call attention to the need to pursue, simultaneously or sequentially, individual and

---

[2]Conversation with Judith Ross, MSW.

institutional tasks as they are identified by the client, by professional assessment, and by the client's ethnic reality.

The plight of Mrs. Owens is to some extent shared by many Asian Americans, Chicanos, and other groups. Many elderly Chinese and Japanese live alone and in poverty (Chen 1970; Kitano 1976), as do many more recent Asian immigrants. The old Asian benevolent societies are losing ground as the young move away and become assimilated into the mainstream culture. Yet there is an upsurge of ethnic consciousness. Social workers would do well to take up the challenge of "repair[ing] old social networks," as proposed by Mechanic.

Ongoing efforts are needed via professional associations to effect legislation to bring health care policy in line with the real needs of population groups such as the elderly and the chronically ill. If appropriately revised, such policy would not tie eligibility for home health care to acute medical conditions, but to social need. "Following the demands of the client task" (see chapters four and five) is an ongoing obligation.

Mrs. Owens's ethnic reality suggests additional tasks. In exploring alternative sources of home health care, was the Women's Association of her church contacted? Is it possible that the church or other neighborhood groups, such as other Black senior citizens, could provide such service? This would enable them to play a useful role. Many members of diverse ethnic groups reject institutional care for their elderly. For example, Blacks are underrepresented in nursing homes (Lowy 1979; Wolf 1978). How much of this is caused by the disposition of the Black community and how much a function of discrimination should be further clarified. Whatever the case, these services, when needed, must not be denied because of discrimination. Lowy (1979) suggests that a battle must be waged to prevent this discrimination.

The Relationships Among Socioeconomic Status, Ethnicity, and Illness

Repeated studies have shown that the highest rates of mental and physical illness are to be found in those groups at the bottom of the socioeconomic strata (Dohrenwend and Dohrenwend 1979; Hollingshead and Redlich 1958; Kosa and Robertson 1975; *United States Health* 1985; *Health Status of Minorities and Low Income Groups*, undated). The disproportionate rate of hypertension in the Black community is well known; while not all agree with the view that this can be partially explained by oppression, this matter warrants ongoing inquiry (Eyer 1975).

The fact that on most indicators of health and mortality, American Indians and nonwhite groups have substantially higher rates of illness and disease than the rest of the population is deplorable, as is the fact that infant mortality rates for the Black community are considerably higher than those for whites (*United States Health*, 1985). Individual efforts aimed at changing health behavior are important. Institutional change efforts intended to effect health legislation to benefit the most disadvantaged minorities is critical.

The Case of Mrs. Green

Mrs. Green, a forty-year-old, friendly, hypertensive, obese Black woman is told she must take her antihypertensive drugs regularly. She's also advised to reduce her salt intake and to lose weight. She feels healthy and is employed at night as a nurse's aide. Her husband takes over with their three children when she goes to work.

Review of her dietary habits indicates that, in her hectic schedule, one of her great pleasures is to stop at the local fast food store for hamburgers, French fries, and soft drinks. She also snacks a lot on the job.

Weekends are happily spent with gatherings of the family, to which all bring food.

As a nurse's aide Mrs. Green sees many sick people; she has little trouble understanding the consequences of her disease and takes her medication regularly. But she fears losing weight and reducing salt intake will take a lot of the pleasure out of her life. "What am I going to do?" she asks the social worker, in a half-joking, half-dejected manner.

Together she and the social worker arrive at an idea. A lot of people in this community eat at the fast food store. How about asking them to reduce the salt used in cooking their food? And what about a family discussion concerning the weekend get-togethers? For, Mrs. Green has discovered that many friends and relatives also have hypertension.

Both efforts were successful and involved family and community cooperation. These have a major bearing on illness and the role the ethnic-sensitive social worker in health care must play.

The Role of Social and Community Networks

Our ongoing review of the literature revealed a persistent theme. Over and over again the importance of family and community as sources of caring and healing was stressed. These sources of help take many forms. The role of the non-Western healers can readily be described as deriving legitimacy and success from understanding of and immersion in community networks, culture, and ritual. Extended family and community-based ethnic networks play caring roles, help to facilitate the use of health care resources, and sometimes serve to buffer stress related to minority status (e.g., Dressler 1985; Mirowsky and Ross 1984; Gary 1985). Cento (1977) describes the use of small group approaches to help

Hispanic women enhance care during labor and delivery. Starrett, Mindel, and Wright (1983) show that informal support systems among the Hispanic elderly positively affect their use of social services by serving as information processing structures. Similarly, immersion in informal social support groups, can positively affect the depression symptoms of Black men (Gary 1985). Dressler (1985) has observed similar effects for men in Southern Black communities. Mirowsky and Ross (1984) note that among Mexican-Americans immersion in culturally based networks reduces anxiety.

Collaboration between natural support networks and healers is crucial and dovetailing services between formal and informal networks requires much thought by ethnic-sensitive social workers.

Culturally appropriate services, based in the community, and avoiding the term mental health services[3] where possible, are consonant with understanding of ethnically based support systems and ethnic-sensitive practice (e.g., Murase, Egawa, and Tashima 1985).

Folk healers. The clients of *espiritistas* receive advice about interpersonal relations, support, encouragement, and physical contact such as stroking or massage; treatment typically takes place at public meetings of spiritist groups. The patient's family is often required to be present in the healing process (Harwood 1977; Lazarow 1979).

The Navajo sing is a public event that draws in the entire community in behalf of the afflicted person:

> Sings are group ceremonials, which involve the patient, the Singer, his assistants, the immediate and extended family of the patients, and many friends. Family members contribute both money and other resources, such as sheep. When the time comes, all drop their ordinary duties and gather together for the event. The patient becomes the center of interest. The support of the whole community is lavished freely. The community recognizes that by restoring harmony to one person the ceremony improves the harmony of the people as a whole. It relates person to environment, past to present, and natural to supernatural. The Sings involve "an interplay between patient, healer, group, and the supernatural, which serves to raise the patient's expectancy of cure, helps him to harmonize his inner conflicts, reintegrates him with the group and spirit world . . . and, in the process, combats his anxiety and strengthens his sense of self worth" (Coulehan 1980).

This vivid description gives powerful credence to the notion that family and community support systems can and do play an integral part in the

---

[3]This is especially important among peoples to whom being designated as having mental health problems is extremely painful.

healing process. This is true not only for groups who share non-Western belief systems. Giordano and Giordano (1977), Fandetti and Gelfand (1978), and Krause (1978) all point to the fact that "extended family is seen as the front-line resource for intensive advice on emotional problems" for many white ethnic groups.

That is not to say that these resources always serve cohesive, caring functions. Old practices are often rejected by the young. There is a risk that folk healers will deal with matters in which they are not expert, or that the "Sing" will delay emergency treatment. Most important, these resources are not always available, particularly as American Indians or other young generations move away from the ethnic communities (Alba 1985; Gans 1962; Krause 1978; Fandetti and Gelfand 1978; and others).

People who are enmeshed in these community networks need and use the full range of prevailing mental and physical health services. But, there is considerable evidence that health facilities, particularly mental health services, are underused. This is true for Mexican-Americans and for many Eastern Europeans (President's Commission on Mental Health 1978; Murase, Egawa, and Tashima 1985; Martinez 1978). This pattern of underuse is attributed to many factors. Included is the system's failure to provide services congruent with the values, belief systems, and support networks available within these people's communities. Language differences also often pose a major barrier.

In addition to the other roles played by social work in health care, the functions of interpreting and serving as a source of cohesion and support are crucial. Most important, workers msut use their skills to marshall and organize ethnic and class-based sources of support. Effective medical care cannot be rendered—particularly to people who mistrust or do not understand the system—without such interventions.

Populations at Risk and Ethnic-Sensitive Practice

The concept of "population at risk" and related epidemiological perspectives basic to public health concerns provide a useful frame of reference for the practice principles proposed here (see chapter five), particularly as they pertain to the incorporation of ethnically based networks. Emphasis is on identifying those aspects of group life that generate health and those that generate illness.

Public health principles specify and clarify the objectives of ethnic-sensitive practice in health care. Some of these principles are listed by the Task Panel on Special Populations in their reports to The President's Commission on Mental Health (1978). The reports focused on Asian Americans, American Indians, and Alaskan Natives. Without exception, the various reports stressed the need (1) to train personnel who clearly understand and are sensitive to the needs, values, beliefs, and attitudes of these special population groups, and (2) to increase the number of mental health professionals who themselves are members of these groups.

Preventive components are stressed throughout, including the provision of day care and recreational facilities. The provision of services in the context of the group's own definition of their community, with funding made directly available to service settings that are part of the community's natural support system, is stressed by the report on Americans of European origins. The subpanel on American Indians points to the need for developing Family Resource Centers on the reservations. Mechanisms designed to assure the preservation of the cultural heritage and the protection it offers are emphasized by all the reports.

Yet the ethnic sensitive social worker cannot wait for enactment of legislation designed to enhance ethnic diversity and minimize the effects of oppression. There is much that workers can do from the vantage points of their assignments to a home health agency, the neighborhood health center, and many others.

The underutilization of mental health services by the Asian American community is frequently noted. Among the reasons are the Asians' "notion that one's capability to control expression of personal problems or troubled feelings is a measure of maturity" (President's Commission on Mental Health 1978). Because of this, mental health services emphasizing self-revelation are anathema to some members of this population group. This is not universally true (Mokuau and Matsuoka 1986). Generational differences and degree of immersion in the host culture are important factors determing the receptivity to various types of health services. Culturally relevant mental health services are essential. Benevolent societies and churches might well help; young Asian students who have a renewed sense of ethnic identity could be called upon to help develop culturally relevant mental health programs. These may involve inclusion of folk healers (e.g., acupuncturists and herb healers) and services based in and organized by the community (see especially good discussion by Murase, Egawa, and Tashima, 1985). The Asian American community is highly protective of its own; many Asians do not come to the attention of public facilities until mental health problems have reached the stage of psychosis (President's Commission on Mental Health 1978).

In many of the case examples cited, there was a need to move from micro to macro tasks, and to consider how community networks could be drawn in. Mrs. Green was helped to control her diet by calling on the family to cooperate in a common concern about hypertension. Mr. Mangione, the Italian man recovering from a stroke, may need the support of the Italian American Club; his employer may need positive sanction from fellow employers before he can feel comfortable about having Mr. Mangione work in the hardware store again. Mrs. Owens needs her church, and the Jankowitches may derive some strength and sustenance if they meet with parents of other children who have leukemia. None of these people, or for that matter most others who have contact with the health care social worker, are voluntary clients.

Throughout this chapter, reference has been made to the fact that minority groups are at particular risk for many health problems, that the very nature of our health system is fragmented and pays too little attention to ethnically derived health beliefs, and that supporting, caring networks are an essential component of health care practice. For all these reaons, simultaneous attention to micro and macro issues is critical.

People who face the prospect of nursing home placement may be experiencing the major crisis in their lives. Those who are diagnosed as having cancer or severe heart disease must make major changes in the way they live and love. Diabetes and hypertension are insidious diseases. Constant care is required, often in the absence of symptoms. People with these and similar problems often do not quite know whether to view themselves as ill or well. They fear that others will withdraw their love, or that they will lose their jobs.

Those who by cultural disposition are prone to reject the sick role will experience illness as a particular threat to their integrity. Those who have always worried about illness may have their worst, perhaps nonconscious, fears realized.

The illustrations given so far have all focused on chronic illness. While there are many other health problems, chronic illness is on the increase. Medical treatment can provide some relief from distress, but there are few cures. Social work involvement is essential if the caring, linking function is to be expanded.

THE ROUTE TO THE SOCIAL WORKER

With few exceptions, people do not choose to be ill, whether physically or emotionally, to go to the doctor, or to be hospitalized. When they do require health services, they usually do not choose to see the social worker. They come because of injury or pain, to deliver babies, or to obtain relief from depression, frightening hallucinations, or overwhelming anxiety. While social workers are increasingly perceived as professionals who have the skill to intervene and be helpful, involvement with the social worker is often somewhat coercive.

The Case of Mrs. Slopata

Mrs. Slopata, a thirty-five-year-old Slavic woman, is in the hospital because of severe abdominal cramps, vomiting, and diarrhea.

Although very weak, this Slavic woman insists she can go home and take care of her children. The doctors have advised her that unless she has help at home and stays in bed for a few weeks, these episodes will recur.

The social worker goes to talk with her to help her make a decision and tell her about available services. Grimacing with pain the whole time she speaks, Mrs. Slopata nevertheless insists she needs no help.

Understanding the Slavic need to prove stamina and independence, the worker supported Mrs. Slopata for her past and future efforts in caring for her home and family (Stein 1976). Mrs. Slopata did agree to have her sister-in-law come in to help her out; a paid homemaker would be too difficult to accept.

Coercion is illustrated by the highly progressive practice known as *high-risk screening* or open access. On the assumption that early social work intervention can forestall some of the psychosocial problems related to illness, social workers assess patient records and see those patients and families who, in their view, might benefit from social services. This practice permits social workers to use their own expert judgments about who might need service, rather than wait for physician referral or patient request. While patients are free to reject social work services thus offered, it is important to remember that the hospitalized patient is in a vulnerable and dependent state (Wolock and Schlesinger 1986). Many such patients are members of populations at risk for psychosocial crisis, for example, the young underclass married and unmarried mothers who are at the beginning of a critical life cycle stage. Members of these high-risk groups require extensive social care, consisting of the availability of counseling services, resources to provide adequate nutrition, home health services, and humane administrative practices.

In characterizing these services as falling on the coercive end of the "route to the social worker," we do not imply that negative factors are involved, but that problem definition is affected by the social context of the problem, and social workers may be the first to recognize a need for their services. Elderly, chronically ill people may prefer to stay in the hospital rather than be transferred to nursing homes or to their own homes where they have no one to care for them. The hospital, constrained by high costs, cannot allow them to remain there longer than absolutely necessary for treatment of acute symptoms.

Given this, social workers have a particular obligation to help patients frame the problems they perceive in terms they understand. The patient who does not want to leave the hospital, and is simply put in an ambulance, is somewhat like the mother whose child is being taken from her because of her abusive behavior. The social worker who participates in such actions without intervention on the patient's behalf is carrying out a social control function. How much better to anticipate and attempt to forestall such a tragedy! While this example is extreme, there are many poor, chronically ill, minority people who face these kinds of dilemmas. Fearing the fate that might await them in nursing homes, they also do not want to go home. If they are alone, with insufficient resources, their eligibility for publicly financed home health services will vary with age and eligibility for Medicaid and/or Medicare.

Teenage mothers about to take their newborn babies home from the hospital may not define their problems in psychosocial terms. Outreach is needed to help them anticipate and plan for the day-to-day vicissitudes of caring for the demanding newborn.

These are but a few examples to illustrate the importance of outreach, using our skills in helping people to articulate their concerns; at the same time it must be recognized that institutional constraints have an effect on how these problems are perceived and articulated.

In the process of *high-risk screening*, those population groups at particular risk for the social consequences of illness are seen without their request. They are often the poor, minorities, the elderly, and those bereft of community networks. Ethnic-sensitive social workers would not be carrying out their responsibilities if they ignored these tasks.

SUMMARY

This chapter has considered the application of the principles of ethnic-sensitive practice to social work practice in health care. People who encounter health care social workers are, for the most part, involuntary clients. Their problems are pressing, usually involving serious illness, the fear of death, disability, or discomfort, and the need to change life-styles because of their illnesses. The social worker serves as a link between troubled people and the complex, fragmented health care system.

People's responses to illness are in large measure governed by cherished ethnic and cultural dispositions. These affect the way people experience pain and the kinds of healers to whom they turn when physical or mental illness strikes.

Caring as well as curing functions are essential. Effective care requires simultaneous attention to micro and macro tasks. The ethnic-sensitive social worker must be knowledgeable about the diverse responses to illness, and call upon community-based caring networks in the effort to generate a more humane health care environment. Public health principles specify and clarify the objectives and concerns of ethnic-sensitive practice in health care.

REFERENCES

Cabot, Richard. 1915. *Social service and the art of healing.* New York: Moffat, Yard and Company—NASW Classic Series.

Campos, Daniel, and Podell, Judith. 1979. "The role of the culture specialist in crisis intervention." Prepared for Annual Meeting of the Society for Applied Anthropology, Philadelphia.

Cento, Margarita H. 1977. Group and the Hispanic prenatal patient. *American Journal of Orthopsychiatry* 47:689–700.

Chen, Pei-Ngor. 1970. The Chinese community in Los Angeles. *Social Casework* 51:591–598.

Coulehan, John L. 1980. Navajo Indian medicine: implications for healing. Family Practice 10:

Dinerman, Miriam; Schlesinger, Elfriede G.; and Wood, Katherine. 1980. Social work roles in health care: An educational framework. *Health and Social Work* 5(4):13–20.

Dohrenwend, Bruce P., and Dohrenwend, Barbara Snell. 1974. Social and cultural influences on psychopathology. *Annual Review of Psychology* 25:417–452.

Dressler, William W. 1985. Extended family relationships, social support, and mental health in a southern Black community. *Journal of Health and Social Behavior* 26:39–40.

Eyer, Joseph. 1975. Hypertension as a disease of modern society. *International Journal of Health Services* 5:539–558.

Fandetti, Donald U., and Gelfand, Donald E. 1978. Attitudes towards symptoms and services in the ethnic family neighborhood. *American Journal of Orthopsychiatry* 48:477–486.

Freeman, Howard E.; Levine, Sol; and Reeder, Leo G. 1979. *Handbook of medical sociology.* Englewood Cliffs, NJ: Prentice-Hall, Inc.

Freidson, Eliot. 1970. *Profession of Medicine.* New York: Dodd, Mead, and Co.

Freidson, Eliot. 1972. Disability as social deviance. In *Medical men and their work,* edited by Eliot Freidson and Judith Lorber. Chicago: Aldine-Atherton.

Fuchs, Michael, and Bashur, Rashid. 1975. Use of traditional Indian medicine among urban Native Americans. *Medical Care* 13:915–927.

Fuchs, Victor R. 1974. *Who shall live? Health economics and social change.* New York: Basic Books, Inc.

Gans, Herbert J. 1962. *The urban villagers.* New York: The Free Press of Glencoe.

Garrison, Vivian. 1977. The Puerto Rican syndrome in psychiatry and *Espiritismo.* In *Case studies in spirit possession,* edited by Vincent Crapanzano and Vivian Garrison. New York: John Wiley and Sons, Inc.

Gary, Lawrence E. 1985. Depressive symptoms and Black men. *Social Work Research and Abstracts* 21:21–29.

Giordano, Joseph. 1973. *Ethnicity and mental health: research and recommendations.* New York: American Jewish Committee.

Giordano, Joseph, and Giordano, Grace Pirreiro. 1977. *The ethnocultural factor in mental health: a literature review and bibliography.* New York: American Jewish Committee.

Goffman, Erving. 1963. *Stigma.* Englewood Cliffs, NJ: Prentice-Hall, Inc.

Greenblum, Joseph. 1974. Medical and health orientations of American Jews: a case of diminishing distinctiveness. *Social Science Medicine* 8:127–134.

Harwood, Alan. 1977. Puerto Rican spiritism, Part II: an institution with preventive and therapeutic functions in community psychiatry. *Culture, Medicine, and Psychiatry* 1:135–153.

Health Status of Minorities and Low-Income Groups. 2d ed. (Undated). DHHS Pub. No. (HRSA) HRS-P-DV 85–1. Washington, DC: U.S. Government Printing Office.

Health, United States. 1985. DHHS Pub. No. (PHS) 86–1232. Washington, DC: Government Printing Office.

Health-United States. 1976–1977. Pub. No. (HRA) 77–1232. Hyattsville, MD: U.S. Department of Health, Education, and Welfare, Public Health Service, Health Resources Administration, National Center for Health Statistics and Health Services Research.

Holden, Mary O. 1980. Dialysis or death: the ethical alternatives. *Health and Social Work* 5:18–21.

Hollingshead, A.B., and Redlich, F.D. 1958. *Social class and mental illness.* New York: John Wiley and Sons.

Howe, Irving. 1975. Immigrant Jewish families in New York: the end of the world of our fathers. *New York* 8:51–54; 61–64; and 66–77.

Kitano, Harry H.L. 1976. *Japanese Americans.* 2d ed. Englewood Cliffs, NJ: Prentice-Hall, Inc.

Kleinman, Arthur. 1978. Clinical relevance of anthropological and cross-cultural research: concepts and strategies. *American Journal of Psychiatry* 135:427–431.

Kosa, John, and Robertson, Leon S. 1975. The social aspects of health and illness. In *Poverty and health: a sociological analysis,* edited by John Kosa and Irving K. Zola. Cambridge: Harvard University Press.

Krause, Corinne Azen. 1978. *Grandmothers, mothers, and daughters: an oral history study of ethnicity, mental health, and continuity of three generations of Jewish, Italian, and Slavic-American women.* New York: American Jewish Committee.

Kumabe, Kazyue, Nishida, Chi Kae, and Hepworth, Dean H. 1985. *Bridging Ethnocultural Diversity in Social Work and Health.* Honolulu: Hawaii, University of Hawaii, School of Social Work.

Lazarow, Cynthia. 1979. "Puerto Rican spiritism: implications for health care professionals." Submitted in partial fulfillment of course requirements for Survey of Health Care, Rutgers University School of Social Work.

Lister, L. 1982. Role training for interdisciplinary health teams. *Health and social work* 7:19–23.

Lowy, Louis. 1979. *Social work with the aging.* New York: Harper and Row.

Martinez, Ricardo-Arguigo. 1978. *Hispanic culture and health care.* St. Louis: The C. V. Mosby Co.

Mechanic, David. 1977. Illness behavior, social adaptation, and the management of illness. *The Journal of Nervous and Mental Disease* 165:79–87.

Mechanic, David. 1978. *Medical sociology.* 2d ed. New York: The Free Press.

Mirowsky, John, and Ross, Catherine E. 1984. Mexican culture and its emotional contradictions. *Journal of Health and Social Behavior* 25:2–13.

Mokuau, Noreen, and Matsuoka, Jon. 1986. "The appropriateness of practice theories for working with Asian and Pacific Islanders." A paper presented at the Annual Program Meeting, Council on Social Work Education, Miami, March.

Murase, Kenji; Egawa, Janey; and Tashima, Nathaniel. 1985. Alternative mental health services models in Asian/Pacific communities. In *Southeast Asian mental health treatment prevention services training and research*, edited by T.C. Owan. Washington, DC: National Institute of Mental Health.

Parsons, Talcott. 1951. *The social system.* New York: The Free Press.

Parsons, Talcott. 1972. Definitions of health and illness in light of American values and social structures. In *Patients, physicians, and illness: a sourcebook in behavioral science in health*, edited by E. Gartley Jaco. New York: The Free Press.

President's Commission on Mental Health. 1978. *Task Panel Reports* 3, Appendix.

President's Commission for the Study of Ethical Problems in Medicine and Biomedical and Behavioral Research. 1983. Library of Congress, 83–600501. Washington, DC: U.S. Government Printing Office.

Rosen, George. 1974. *Medical police to social medicine.* New York: Science History Publications.

Samora, Julian. 1978. Conceptions of health and disease among Spanish-Americans. In *Hispanic culture and health care*, edited by Ricardo Arguido Martinez. St. Louis: The C.V. Mosby Co.

Schlesinger, Elfriede G. 1985. *Health Care Social Work Practice: Concepts and Strategies.* Columbus, OH: Merrill.

Schultz, Sandra S. 1982. How Southeast Asian refugees in California adapt to unfamiliar health care practices. *Health and Social Work* 7:148–156.

Starrett, Richard A.; Mindel, Charles H.; and Wright, Roosevelt. 1983. Influence of support systems on the use of social services by the Hispanic elderly. *Social Work Research and Abstracts* 19:35–40.

Stein, Howard F. 1976. A dialectical model of health and illness attitudes and behavior among Slovak Americans. *International Journal of Mental Health* 5.

Stenger-Castro, Earl M. 1978. The Mexican-American: how his culture affects his mental health. In *Hispanic culture and health care*, edited by Ricardo Arguido Martinez. St. Louis: The C.V. Mosby Co.

Wintrob, Ronald M. 1973. The influence of others: witchcraft and rootwork as explanations of behavior disturbances. *Journal of Nervous and Mental Diseases* 156:318–326.

Wolf, Rosalie S. 1978. A social systems model of nursing home use. *Educational Trust*, Summer.

Wolock, Isabel, and Schlesinger, Elfriede G. 1986. Social work screening in New Jersey hospitals: progress, problems, and implications. *Health and Social Work* 11:15–25.

Zborowski, Mark. 1952. Cultural components in response to pain. *Journal of Social Issues* 8:16–30.

APPENDIX
Community Profile

This outline for a community profile is intended to help the individual worker or agency to develop a detailed picture of the community within which services are located. The profile should serve to highlight the basic population distribution of the community, and the relationship between its location and access to major transportation routes; these in turn may affect access to places of employment, health and welfare services, and recreational facilities.

Also important is a picture of existing health and welfare resources, as well as gaps in these resources. Resources are defined to include the formally organized helping institutions such as those developed by the public sector, trade unions, and churches, as well as those more informal resources such as identifiable helping networks, folk healers, and the like.

Of importance is the political structure, the representation of ethnic minority groups on the staffs of community institutions such as the schools and social agencies, and the attention to the special language, cultural disposition, and needs of groups represented in the community.

Such a profile can be developed by use of census data, publications developed by local organizations (e.g., League of Women Voters, County Planning Boards, Health and Welfare Councils), interviews with community leaders, and data available in the agency's files.

Identification
1. Name of community (e.g., "The North Ward," "Watts," etc.)
2. City (or township, borough, etc.)
3. County
4. State
5. Traditions and values

Local History
1. When settled
2. Changes in population
3. Major historical incidents leading to present-day development
4. Principal events in the life of the community, etc.
5. Traditions and values

Geography and Transportation
1. Location—is it located near any of the following?
    a. Principal highways
    b. Bus routes
    c. Truck routes
    d. Railroad routes
    e. Airports/air routes
    f. Rivers, oceans, lakes
2. Do any of the above facilitate/hamper residents' ability to get to work, major recreational centers, community services?

Population Characteristics
1. Total size of population
2. Breakdown by
    a. Age
    b. Sex
    c. Minority groups
    d. Other ethnic groups
    e. Religious affiliations
3. Educational level
    a. Median educational level for total adult population
    b. Median educational level for women
    c. Median educational level for each of the major ethnic and minority groups
4. Have there been major shifts in the population composition over the past five to ten years (e.g., in migration of minority groups, departure of sizable numbers of people in any one population group)?
    a. Are there any major urban renewal or other redevelopment efforts?

Employment and Income Characteristics
1. Employment status
   a. Major sources and types of employment for total adult population
   b. Major sources of employment for women
   c. Major sources of employment for each of the major ethnic and minority groups
2. Median income
3. Income characteristics below poverty level
4. Type of public welfare system (e.g., state, county jurisdictions; state involved in Medicaid program?)

Housing Characteristics
1. Prevailing housing type (apartments, private homes, mix)
2. Percentage of population owning, renting homes
3. Housing conditions (e.g., percentage characterized as "dilapidated" by the census)

Educational Facilities and Level
1. Types of schools available
2. Do the schools have bilingual programs?
3. Are minority and ethnic group members found in the members of staffs, school boards?
4. Are the schools aware of the particular problems and strengths of minority and ethnic group members?
5. Do the schools promote cultural awareness and sensitivity programs?

Health and Welfare Resources
1. Important resources available
   a. Health and medical (hospital, clinics, public health facilities, "folk healers")
   b. Recreational and leisure time facilities
   c. Social agencies
2. Are staff members bilingual where appropriate?
3. Is there adequate representation of minority/ethnic group members on the staffs of hospitals and social agencies?
4. Do these facilities develop cultural awareness and sensitivity programs?
5. What are the prevailing formal and informal community networks?
   a. "Swapping networks"
   b. Church-supported health and welfare groups
   c. Ethnic-based lodges, fraternities, benevolent societies
   d. Union-sponsored health and welfare facilities

   e. Self-help groups of people with special problems (e.g.,
      alcoholics, the physically handicapped)

Special Problems and Strengths
1. What are the major social problems (e.g., prevalent health problems, housing, schools)?
2. Is there a particular concern with crime, delinquency, underemployment?
3. Are there particular intergroup tensions, efforts at intergroup coalition?

Evaluation
1. What do you consider are some of the major problems of this community?
2. Does this community have a positive identity, loyalty? Describe.
3. What are the major strengths and weaknesses of the health and welfare community?
4. What are the major gaps in services?

Index